D0845739

The End of Modernity

The End of Modernity

*What the Financial and Environmental Crisis
Is Really Telling Us*

STUART SIM

EDINBURGH UNIVERSITY PRESS

Edinburgh University Press Ltd
22 George Square, Edinburgh

www.euppublishing.com

Typeset in 10.5/13 pt Palatino
by Servis Filmsetting Ltd, Stockport, Cheshire, and
printed and bound in Great Britain by
CPI Antony Rowe, Chippenham and Eastbourne

A CIP record for this book is available from the British Library

ISBN 978 0 7486 4035 5 (hardback)

Contents

Acknowledgements

This book marks twenty years of publishing ventures with my editor, Jackie Jones, and I would like to express my very deepest gratitude for all her help and guidance over that time. Dr Helene Brandon was her usual supportive self throughout the writing process, and provided many helpful suggestions on draft material. My thanks also go to Peter Andrews for the copy-editing.

Preface

Financial crisis, environmental crisis: what is the combination of credit crunch and global warming telling us about the way we live? I would contend that such events signal modernity has reached its limit as a cultural form. In consequence, we have to face up to the prospect of life 'after modernity' where a very different kind of mental set than the one we have been indoctrinated with will be required. Modernity, my argument will go, has collapsed under the weight of its internal contradictions; the modern world's insatiable need for technologically driven economic progress has finally been revealed as unsustainable and, even more importantly, potentially destructive of both the planet and the socio-economic systems so painstakingly developed over the past few centuries. We have been encouraged to believe that those systems would roll on into the indefinite future, yielding ever better returns as they went; now, we shall have to think again. In 1989 Francis Fukuyama had proclaimed that the Western system had emerged triumphant from a period of sustained ideological conflict, and that history therefore had 'ended'.[1] It has, but not in the way he envisaged it: less than two decades later, we can recognise it is modernity as a historical phenomenon that has ground to a halt rather than its competitors. Some commentators are even beginning to speak of 'the end of the Western world', warning us that we shall have to plan soon for a very different sort of future than we had been expecting, with a completely new set of geopolitical priorities based on the rapid rise of nations like China and India.[2]

Modernity's reputation has been founded on its ability to deliver continual economic growth (small blips in this being discounted in terms of the overall upward trajectory), which in its turn has led to an increasingly high standard of living, in the material sense anyway, across the globe. Even if the fruits of this growth have been unequally distributed between the developed and developing world, they have nevertheless been measurably real, as metrics such as the Gross Domestic Product (GDP) have revealed. The credit crisis, however, has made us realise just how flimsy, and in some cases downright illogical, the structures of our financial system actually are. In order to achieve the high levels of growth that have marked out the last couple of decades in particular, underpinned by the spread of the globalisation ethic, there has to be as unregulated a market in operation as possible, with governments adopting a 'light touch' approach to the business world in general. But, as we have now found out to our cost, this kind of market encourages excessive greed in those running the financial sector, to the extent of destroying almost all their sense of social responsibility and with that the stability of the financial system itself: in one commentator's emotive words, 'an unleashed and unhinged financial industry is wreaking havoc with the economy'.[3] This is not how the twenty-first century was supposed to develop, and it has left most of us floundering.

The fact that the Western financial system is currently being propped up by government money, with all taxpayers as unwitting guarantors, is testament to how the most highly touted model of economic modernity has failed – and failed in such a spectacular fashion that it is unclear when, if ever, it will recover in anything like its previous form. More to the point, we have to wonder whether such a recovery would be desirable: unregulated free market capitalism may still have its defenders, but their credibility outside their own circle of true believers is at present very low. We have seen the damage done to the economy and are understandably wary of those who caused it.

Hand in hand with this economic collapse has come the

unmistakable beginnings of the collapse of the planet's environmental systems, in the wake of the onslaught of decades of accelerated global economic growth.[4] The more that national economies
expand (and, as Neal Lawson has put it, we are now locked into a
lifestyle of 'turbo-consumerism'),[5] then the more fossil fuels they
use to meet their energy requirements; the more fossil fuels they
use, then the more carbon emissions are released into the atmosphere. While there is widespread recognition among the world's
governments that this cannot go on, there is as yet no binding international agreement to prevent it from happening – Kyoto is a dead
letter, its protocols largely ignored. Neither is there any collective
political will to campaign strongly against economic growth, even
with the increasingly alarming projections that scientists are giving
us of what the consequences of steadily rising carbon levels in the
atmosphere are likely to be, even in the short term of a few decades
(although efforts are being made to inspire that will).[6] Economic
downturn will at best slow this process somewhat, whereas any
economic upturn will only succeed in driving it forward ever
more relentlessly. The real underlying problem, that our current
cultural paradigm, modernity, has exhausted itself, goes largely
unexamined.

Neither is this just another argument on behalf of the proponents
of postmodernism and postmodernity. Postmodernism has been
an abiding concern of mine for quite some time now, and I have
generally regarded it as a positive phenomenon with a thought-
provoking agenda about how to correct the many abuses committed in the name of established authority in the modern world order,
while also noting that in recent years its claims about how much
our culture had changed were looking overly optimistic (an issue
I pursued in particular in *Fundamentalist World*).[7] Postmodernism
has been an essentially intellectual challenge to modernity, criticising its power relations rather than its overall objectives (although
one might just absolve the Greens, especially in their more radical
manifestations, from that charge to some degree).[8] What we have to
prepare ourselves for now is the *real* postmodern; that is, the situation after modernity implodes and cannot be reconstructed as it

was. What lessons must we learn from this? What adjustments need to be made to our ideological outlook to cope with the aftermath of the collapse? The difference between postmodernity as an intellectual response to modernity (an anti-modernity, in effect), and *real* postmodernity as an actual state of affairs requiring a concerted socio-political response from all of us, regardless of our political orientation, will be outlined, indicating that we need to move well past the critique that the former offered. What postmodernists were fighting against may no longer exist: the grand narrative of modernity no longer rules, having sustained arguably irreparable damage. In that sense, we have transcended postmodernity as the term has been understood, just as much as we have modernity.

The new landscape that has been created – socially, politically, economically, intellectually – will be explored here from a consciously interdisciplinary approach designed to give as wide-ranging an assessment of the developing situation as is currently possible, while making various suggestions as to how we might set about coping with life after modernity. In Part I I shall be identifying the various aspects that go to make up the cultural dimension of the crisis, then in Part II those of the economic dimension, concluding in Part III with consideration of the kind of world that is now looming up beyond modernity. While it cannot be predicted with accuracy exactly how life past modernity's breakdown will shape up – the twists and turns the crisis has taken to date have already been bewildering enough, and that in a very short period – we should be giving some concentrated thought nevertheless as to what courses of action will help or hinder the situation. It has to be emphasised that it is not just an economic challenge we face, but also an intellectual one – and the latter is arguably the more important. I think it is time for some polemic to be advanced on behalf of that new intellectual orientation.

Part I

The End of Modernity?
The Cultural Dimension

1
Introduction: The End of Modernity

The architectural theorist Charles Jencks once claimed that modernism ended when a particular inner-city American apartment block was demolished:

> [W]e can date the death of Modern Architecture to a precise moment in time . . . Modern architecture died in St. Louis, Missouri on July 15, 1972 at 3.32 p.m. (or thereabouts) when the infamous Pruitt-Igoe scheme, or rather several of its slab blocks, were given the final *coup de grâce* by dynamite. Previously it had been vandalised, mutilated and defaced by its black inhabitants, and although millions of dollars were pumped back, trying to keep it alive (fixing the broken elevators, repairing smashed windows, repainting), it was finally put out of its misery. Boom, boom, boom.[1]

Tongue in cheek though the claim was (history is rarely that neat), there is no doubt that the event had considerable symbolic significance extending well beyond the architectural profession, as Jencks was keen to make us realise. A typical product of modernist ideology, Pruitt-Igoe had failed to achieve what that ideology said it should – to effect a radical improvement in the lifestyle of its inhabitants by offering them an exciting and attractive new cityscape with up-to-date amenities. Le Corbusier, the doyen of modernist architecture, had firmly believed that such projects would transform people's lives, speaking poetically of 'towers which will shelter the worker, till now stifled in densely packed quarters and congested streets' in 'flats opening on every side to air and light, and looking, not on the puny trees of our boulevards of today, but upon green sward, sports grounds and abundant plantations of trees'.[2] So much for the vision; the reality, as far as most of the inhabitants of Pruitt-Igoe had found it, was instead something soulless and lacking in any sense of community, something to which they could feel no sense of personal commitment. While modernist buildings continued to be constructed after the demise of Pruitt-Igoe, for such as Jencks the writing was now on the wall and postmodernism was to be the future for the architectural profession: modernism's credibility was undermined.

A similar claim has been made for modernity, of which modernism was only a subset (the aesthetic theory that incorporated modernity's values), that its death too could be precisely marked. The critical event this time around was the collapse of the high-profile, and until that point apparently highly successful, American investment bank Lehmann Brothers on 15 September 2008 (presumably we could be precise here too if we wanted, and identify the exact minute of its announcement). Again, this is far too neat historically, but the symbolism remains potent. Lehmann Brothers had prospered on the basis of a huge credit bubble created by a progressively less regulated financial marketplace, in which they were a major player: now that the logical contradictions this involved had come to the surface, Lehmann's business was unsustainable. Judged by its own criteria modernity had failed, and failed on the large scale. To echo Jencks, this was no longer a blip in the market cycle, but 'boom, boom, boom', the demolition of an entire ideology. After this, financial modernity could never be the same – and if financial modernity was in trouble then so was the entire socio-political system that depended upon it.

How should we respond to this predicament? The argument I will be pursuing for the rest of the book is that we have no alternative but to look beyond modernity. The main point to be established in this chapter is that there is currently an ideological vacuum where modernity once held sway, and we need to start considering what we should do in the aftermath of the system's breakdown, how we adapt to such a momentous event. Nor is it just damage limitation we should be concerned with: an ideological vacuum also presents an opportunity to construct a better kind of lifestyle, one more rooted in social justice than of late. Let us see where such speculation leads us, both psychologically and environmentally.

Modernity and the Cult of Progress

Modernity has been founded on a cult of progress, and in some fashion or other this has been embraced by every nation in the world. There is a general expectation globally that living standards will continually improve, and a correspondingly deep faith in the ability of science and technology to provide the means by which this objective can be achieved. Global warming was the first signal that progress was not the unalloyed good it was made out to be and that economic growth could harm the planet's environmental balance, perhaps catastrophically so. The steep rise in the world's population in the last century has exacerbated the problem, driving the use of fossil fuel up to unprecedented levels as all nations have striven to raise the living standards of each successive, and numerically larger, generation. There is a general agreement in the scientific world that our culture is fast approaching a series of critical environmental tipping points and that we just cannot go on as we have been doing in the recent past in terms of our fossil-fuel energy usage level.[3] (Even renewables, originally heralded as our energy saviour, are not without their problems either, varying from unreliability, as in the case of wind or wave power, to being prohibitively expensive.) Apart from anything else, the population is still rising remorselessly.

We seem also to have experienced an economic tipping point which has shattered most people's trust in our financial systems – with Lehmann Brothers a particularly high-profile example of what has gone wrong. Western culture in particular has been the scene of a huge credit bubble, and now that this has burst, taking many well-known and highly respected banks and investment houses in several countries along with it, confidence in the financial sector has largely disappeared. Without readily available credit it is hard to see how economic growth can be sustained, and for the first time in living memory we face the possibility of rapidly declining living standards, with no obvious method of halting the slide. The GDP of the major economies has been dipping sharply, and unemployment is a spectre that is beginning to take shape in many's people's lives already. Fear of the creation of yet another bubble is paralysing the world's financial markets (despite frantic efforts by the political class to ease the blockage by interest rate cuts, putting more money into circulation, etc.), and even if this is overcome in the near future the threat of another crisis will continue to haunt both politicians and the general public. This is not going to be an event which will quickly fade from the collective consciousness: its echoes seem destined to resonate around our culture for a considerable time yet.

Modernity as a cultural ethos gives every impression of having exhausted itself therefore, collapsing under the weight of its internal contradictions: it demands constant progress, but this is simply not possible, neither logically nor materially. Complexity theory has given us a host of examples of how cultures can overreach themselves and then collapse – often quite rapidly.[4] We cannot assume that modernity will never suffer a similar fate; that we will never be guilty of overreaching ourselves to the point of danger. The cult of progress will have to acknowledge that it too has limits that cannot be breached. But how we move away from that cult, and its stubborn hold on our minds, is a more vexed issue requiring an uncompromising investigation into our belief system.

In a provocative study entitled *Life Inc.: How the World Became a Corporation, and How To Take It Back*, Douglas Rushkoff lays the blame for our current troubles squarely on corporatism, whose 'tenets . . . established themselves as the default social principles of our age', destroying 'social capital' and leaving us at the mercy of the corporate sector.[5] In the process, the author argues, '[w]e behaved like corporations ourselves, extracting the asset value of our homes and moving on with our families, going into more debt and assuming we'd have the chance to do it again', thus stoking up the crisis even further.[6] It is an interesting argument, and there is no denying that the public. has little say in what the corporate sector gets up to. I think it goes deeper than that, however, and that corporations are a part of the problem rather than the problem itself: it is the belief system that provides the conditions for things like corporatism to become so entrenched in our culture which has to be held to account.

The Waste Land: Economic Version

T. S. Eliot saw April as the cruellest month in his apocalyptic vision of post-First World War culture in *The Waste Land*, but for economic modernity 2008 turned out to be the cruellest year.[7] It was the year that saw the collapse of several huge financial institutions throughout the West, most significantly in the USA and Britain, and in which the green shoots of economic recovery heralded by various politicians turned out to be false, merely a prelude to the onset of even more serious economic problems than the early days of the credit crunch had promised. The hopes of a short, sharp crisis that would quickly run its course, perhaps leaving a leaner and more efficient business world in its place which would help to generate a new economic boom, gave way to a recognition that we were instead heading into what was to all intents and purposes a new depression. The more that politicians denied that this was what was happening (the 'd' word being treated as largely taboo among that class), the more the situation came to resemble it.

Worse yet, it was a new depression with no end in sight that anyone was prepared to predict with confidence. Rather than taking on the form politicians had hoped for, a U- or better yet V-shaped recession that we climbed out of fairly rapidly (the pattern of recent decades), the economy instead seemed to be at best flatlining. Conventional economic wisdom had been turned on its head, and both economists and politicians were being forced to admit that they had no clear idea of how to address the problem successfully: whatever they did seemed to have very little effect in curing the crisis, and the more this happened then the gloomier the prognosis for our future proceeded to become. Interest rates were pushed down to negligible levels, the lowest in modern history in many cases, but the economy remained stubbornly unimpressed and just refused to recover as the models claimed it should after such action was taken. We were stuck in an economic waste land, and no-one seemed to know quite how to lead us out of it: doom and gloom had become the prevailing mood.

The waste land was characterised by a drastic drying-up of loans and credit from the financial sector – even between banks themselves, who could no longer bring themselves to trust in each others' liquidity, and with genuine reason (such lending being 'the deep, arterial life-source of modern capitalism', as one commentator has aptly described the process);[8] widespread defaulting on mortgages (particularly in the USA); a static housing market despite steadily falling house prices; decreasing consumption (especially of non-essential goods); rapidly growing unemployment; massive government borrowing that was reaching stratospheric levels unheard of outside wartime; and a fear of a slide into deflation. The effect of deflation would be to undermine most economies and severely retard economic recovery, not just in the short but quite possibly in the much longer term (as had already happened in Japan from the 1990s onwards, meaning it had not experienced the full benefits of the global economic boom during the intervening period).[9] Inflation, generally regarded as the enemy by economists and politicians alike, began, ironically, to seem like a desirable condition for a state to find itself in, almost a mark of national economic health (the one exception was Iceland, where inflation soared after the meltdown of the local banking industry, to the further detriment of the beleaguered populace; but we shall be looking at that special case in Chapter 6).

Increased demand for goods would have resolved the situation to some extent, but as usually happens in economic recessions this went down markedly, with the public fearful of using up its savings given the uncertain economic indicators for the future. The more the public held back then the more likely the prospect of deflation became, and since unemployment had the effect of further depressing demand, and of reducing tax revenues into the bargain, this merely exacerbated the problem overall. Threats of cuts to government services (health and education, for example) made personal savings seem even more of a necessity than ever, and it was consumerism that suffered. Generally speaking, the outlook was very bleak, and governments were being faced by a situation of which few of them had any significant experience (certainly not on this scale) or, even more worryingly, seemed to have the necessary expertise to overcome. Every economy was geared for growth after all, not for managing decline.

The cruellest year rolled on into 2009 with no visible improvement to the global economic condition, or even hope of any immediate improvement: instead, projections as to the end of the crisis were being pushed further and further into the indefinite future, with some commentators speaking of years, or even decades, before the system eventually righted itself and growth could begin properly again. Free market capitalism has continued in the interim, but in a somewhat ghostly fashion – more as a reflex than anything else, with confidence in the system badly shaken on a global scale; but no-one has been able to suggest anything better to replace the current system, with governments falling over themselves to prop that up instead. Even governments as ideologically deeply opposed to such intervention as the Bush administration in the USA were forced into de facto nationalisation of key national financial institutions. President Bush may have believed that '[h]istory has shown that the greater threat to economic prosperity is not too little government involvement in the market, it is too much government involvement in the market', yet even he felt compelled to compromise his principles when companies such as the investment bank Bear Sterns and the AIG Insurance Group (the world's largest, significantly enough) appeared to be going under.[10] (It is unlikely that Bush has been all that avid a student of market history; this is, as we shall go on to see in Chapter 6, precisely the kind of of attitude that arises in those inspired by the economic theories of Milton Friedman.) Perhaps the most suggestive sign that we had indeed reached the end of modernity, however, was that none of the traditional remedies for correcting economic disorder seemed to be working any longer: we were in uncharted territory, a situation which was severely testing the skills of politicians and economists alike.

The Ideological Vacuum

Earlier in the twentieth century, socialism would have been put forward by many thinkers as the solution to such a major rupture in the capitalist system, and some version or other of the command economy – either totally administered by the government or planned by them – recommended as the best method of restructuring national economies to protect them from such destabilising crises. Socialism was an immensely powerful force in twentieth-century politics, and its supporters were vocal in its cause, claiming it represented the only way to create a more egalitarian society without the gross exploitation and inequalities that had marked out industrialised capitalism from its very beginnings. Yet socialism in its traditional sense has largely disappeared from the global scene in the new century: China hardly qualifies for that description now with its state capitalist structure, and neither North Korea nor Cuba are significant enough forces on the world stage to act as role models for a socialist renaissance. There is no longer a fully fledged alternative on the horizon, no matter how flawed it may be, to counterpose to the free market economic system that we currently live under. More is the pity, many of us would want to say.

It could be said that we are inhabiting an ideological vacuum at present in the economic sphere, with a discredited laissez-faire market theory inspiring very little confidence – either in investors or the general public. We seem to be stuck with that theory in the absence of any credible competitor, however, which only adds to the pervasive sense of doom and gloom: no-one has a magic formula to make it all come right again. To deploy a well-known literary reference, we are mired in the Slough of Despond, and no-one appears to know how we can escape from its clutches.[11]

Modernity and the Nation State

Part of the reason why we are in an ideological vacuum is that we are still very much influenced by the notion of the nation state – and recent events mean this is now under considerable strain as a viable political concept. While national consciousness and the territorial imperative certainly predate the Enlightenment, it is still fair to say that the concept of the nation state as we know it really took form under the aegis of modernity. The world is now carved up into independent nation states, all of them in some sense in competition with each other for resources and a share of the world trading market. Most of the time this competition is amicable enough, expressed through such things as export drives, although it can on occasion break down, leading to confrontation and even outright war. Periodic attempts have been made to create larger world political forums – the League of Nations after the First World War and and then the United Nations (UN) after the Second, for example – but these have proved to be governed in their actions to a large extent by national considerations. Impressive in size though the UN may be as an organisation, it is still quite limited as to its political impact, with nations feeling free to ignore its resolutions if these are perceived to clash with their national interests – an event which happens on a fairly regular basis. General agreement can be gained for campaigns against poverty and disease, etc., but the more sensitive political issues, such as the spread of nuclear weaponry, remain largely beyond the UN's power to affect.

In recent history the European Union (EU) has constituted a more interesting example of transnational cooperation than the UN, in that it does have a specific political remit over a group of highly developed, and traditionally very assertive, nation states who accept its overall authority – particularly with regard to economic matters. Although there is still some scope for opt-out, and it has by no means eliminated all national differences, the EU may nevertheless point the way forward in a world where national governments seem increasingly unable to exercise effective control over their economic destinies, and need to have more substance behind them to cushion the risks this state of affairs brings in its wake. What the political theorist Ulrich Beck has called 'the national idyll' may now be over, and we have of necessity to start thinking transnationally if we are to survive economically.[12] Beck feels we have at the very least to invest more effort in the EU, otherwise there is a distinct danger at the level of the individual nation state of going under when crisis strikes:

> The crisis cries out to be transformed into a long overdue new founding of the EU. Europe would then stand for a new realpolitik of political action in a world at risk. In the interconnected world, the circular maxim of national realpolitik – that national interests have to be pursued at the national level – must be replaced by the maxim of cosmopolitan realpolitik: the more European, the more cosmopolitan our politics becomes, the more nationally successful it will be.[13]

It is a bold claim, and it has to contend with a significant degree of Euroscepticism throughout the EU, 'the national delusion of its intellectual elites', as Beck witheringly refers to the phenomenon (particularly strong in the UK, as we know).[14] For Beck, the economic crisis has merely magnified that delusion, which is a product of an outdated mindset. It is a mind-set based on the competitive imperative underlying modernity, the assumption that nations are, and should be, motivated almost exclusively by self-interest – that is simply taken to be the natural order of things, the source of the rules by which we must all live. The realpolitik involved is largely market oriented, with each nation striving to improve its share of the market at the expense of its neighbours and thus maximise its power and standing in the world: economic power always garners much respect and admiration from one's peers, and every nation craves it.

The EU is one way of trying to overcome this national delusion, although it still demands a great deal of closely reasoned argument to be brought to bear on public opinion to do so – again, especially in a country like the UK, which leads the way in Euroscepticism. But as we are finding out, the current crisis of modernity requires action on the largest possible scale. The EU itself cannot survive unless it is in close collaboration with the rest of the globe: the interconnected world is a reality, and no area or political grouping can go it alone when it comes to dealing with economic or environmental crisis; everyone gets dragged in whether they deserve that fate or not. It is not just trade that has been globalised, crisis has too, and the full implications of this are only just coming to be widely realised. We have to face up to the fact that the modern nation state probably has outlived its usefulness, and that politics will have to be conducted on a very different footing than hitherto. As Ulrich Beck has put it, politics is now 'glocal' in character;[15] everything that happens at global level becomes a local issue (and, all too frequently, a local problem) and vice-versa, and we have to start acting accordingly.

The Waste Land: Environmental Version

Pruitt-Igoe and Lehmann Brothers give us symbolic events by which to chart modernity's decline as a credible ideology, but in reality it has been heading towards crisis for quite some time now in the form of the phenomenon of global warming. Climate change is an undeniable fact and, although the exact causes are still a matter of some dispute, the scientific evidence for this being fundamentally a man-made crisis is becoming overwhelming.[16] The greater the Earth's population and the greater the increase in global standards of living, then the greater also is the volume of carbon emissions being released into the atmosphere and the subsequent rise in global average temperatures. The rise in temperature this century, amounting to roughly 0.7 °C so far, is relatively modest, but it is already enough to be causing the break-up of the ice shelves in the Arctic and Antarctic – regions which worryingly are warming much faster than the rest of the globe. Current predictions suggest that a 2 °C increase within a few decades is now probably unavoid-able (there is something of a scientific consensus on this), and that would generate significant rises in sea levels as the ice sheets in the polar regions begin to melt as a result. The scenarios from then on are truly describable as catastrophic, with each degree C rise triggering further rises in sea levels which would swamp large parts of the globe, as well as turning much of the Earth's temperate zones into deserts unable to support agriculture – and therefore much in the way of human habitation.[17] Widespread drought and increased storm activity would add to the general misery should we pass through some key tipping points, as many voices in the scientific community, with varying degrees of frustration and desperation to them, insist we are well on our way to doing at present.

It could be claimed that the major cause of this process is modernity, with its cult of progress requiring ever-increasing consumption of fossil fuels which then go on to clog up the atmosphere further with their emissions. The global ideal is now a Western-style quality of life driven by constant technological improvement: hence the desire of so many inabitants of the developing world to emigrate to the West, with the USA a particularly favoured destination. Such improvement involves energy and energy usage equals carbon emissions. A growing world population (which has doubled in the last half-century or so to its current total of 6.7 billion) piles even greater pressure on the environment, and that population is expected to go up by more than a third again by 2050. As things go, that can only mean a progressively worsening predicament with carbon emissions, whereas massive cuts in emissions are required just to prevent us going past the 2 °C increase that currently seems to be the least we can expect to experience in the short term. We are stumbling on without a coordinated plan for the future (as noted before, the Kyoto protocols are being largely ignored), almost as if we were in a collective state of denial about the entire affair. There is certainly a robust attitude of denial among the oil companies, seen in their willingness to fund foundations which are sceptical of the scientific evidence for climate change, as well as to explore potential new deposits no matter how inaccessible their location may be. Oil remains a hugely profitable business, and as such a considerable obstacle to taking serious action against global warming.

Despite the many warning signs as to the consequences, economic expansion has continued to be the major concern of almost all the world's nations, and the system of globalisation has encouraged this to the hilt. The volume of world trade has dramatically increased in recent decades as the market system has been deregulated (leading to extensive outsourcing of production around the developing world), and this serves to drive up carbon emissions just as dramatically. Globalisation is a logical extension of modernity, which requires constant expansion if its goal of progress is to be achieved, and globalisation offers new markets and rising production year by year. It is only now that we are starting to realise the environmental costs that the relentless pursuit of progress brings along with it, although dealing with these is another issue altogether: taking a voluntary step back from economic expansion is not part of contemporary mainstream political discourse. Any politician in government forced to admit either that growth has slowed down or, as is increasingly the case at the moment, that the economy is retracting is invariably desperate to claim that this is only a temporary setback and that growth will resume again shortly (even if there is little hard evidence to support this, rhetoric standing in for it instead). Economic growth remains the primary rationale of politics in the developed world, although we are going to have to be schooled out of it – and soon.

Pandemic Progress?

One of the consequences of the world's increased market and rapidly growing population has been a move into intensive factory farming, and this has not been without its problems. There have been various health scares arising from this practice in recent decades, such as BSE and bird flu spreading out from cattle and chicken farms respectively. With some difficulty – and for the countries involved significant, if temporary, losses of trade – these have been overcome, but sporadic outbreaks have kept cropping up around the world all the same. The latest to emerge is swine flu, which as I write has just been declared a pandemic by the World Health Organisation (2009), after months of careful monitoring. Links have been suggested between the development of the flu in the pig population and the factory farming system (initially in Mexico, where the disease first appeared), thus creating the conditions where the disease can spread rapidly and pandemics become a possibility.[18] Factory farming is designed to make farming more productive, and that of course is a continual concern of modernity: yet another sign for its proponents of progress in exploiting the environment for human gain. Few will question the system and its methods – until something goes wrong. But once the problem clears, then the system resumes in response to the same pressures that created the problem in the first instance: the need for more food and the desire for more profit.

Even if the current pandemic proves to be of a relatively mild form (although it should be noted that, by July 2009, the World Health Organisation was reporting a death total of around 800 worldwide), then there is the clear risk of something similar happening again in the future. Increased risk of pandemic therefore comes to be a side-effect of modernity, yet another example of where it hits limits in its ability to exercise complete control over the environment. Swine flu, as the food policy commentator Felicity Lawrence has put it, is the 'pig's revenge' for yet another market-driven abuse of the natural environment.[19] It seems unlikely that it will be the last we shall have to deal with either; modernity's insatiable desire for increased production, and the profits which flow from this, will not be so easily halted. Then there is the factor that flu viruses have an acknowledged ability to mutate, and very rapidly so (as happened notably in the 'Spanish flu' pandemic that occurred in the closing days and then immediate aftermath of the First World War, which increased markedly in ferocity in its second round).[20] In Lawrence's tart summation: 'If we carry on as before, the pigs may yet have their revenge. And if not the pigs, the chickens.'[21] To which we might add, or the cows, or the lambs, or the turkeys – indeed, any farmed meat you care to name. The ranks of vegetarianism or veganism could well swell considerably under those circumstances.

Aftermaths

There is little doubt that the credit crisis will have a profound effect on both public and private life, and that we do not yet know where this will all end. It is in the nature of such serious crises that both individuals and nations eventually seek to protect themselves as best they can, and although the degree of international cooperation has so far been quite high (G20 summits, etc., even if their decisions as to what requires to be done have been disappointingly anodyne), voices also have been raised in favour of trade protectionism and against immigration – policies which can only increase global political tension if put into play in any really extended fashion. While trade protectionism can be defended to a certain extent as a method of coping with unrestrained globalisation and the unregu-lated market, especially on the part of developing economies with their often uncompetitive home industries, it becomes counter-productive if everyone is using it in an aggressive manner to dis-criminate against exports. Trade can easily seize up under such circumstances, rather in the manner that banks protecting their own assets, and thus not extending credit to consumers (or even each other), has frozen up the economy in recent years. Again, while a certain amount of this could be justified as a response to the climate of uncertainty which overtook the financial sector in the wake of the sub-prime mortgage fiasco in the USA, when carried to extremes, as it subsequently was, then the effect is that the system just ceases to function at all. The end of modernity must not be allowed to signal the end of transnational cooperation – we require that more than ever to counter the pull still being exerted by the 'national idyll'.

Anti-immigration policies by definition affect the most vulner-able, particularly those from the developing world. Economic refugees suffer the most, and that is a category which can only grow substantially in size in a massive downturn of the kind we are experiencing. Developing countries have minimal reserves to fall back on when recession strikes, and their populations often opt for emigration out of sheer desperation when their govern-ment proves powerless to offer any substantial help to them in their distress. There are already worries being expressed about the impact of any large-scale population shift from South to North, East to West, because of global warming's effect on the environment, but the process could begin earlier than expected if the economic downturn is not arrested, if recession really does turn into outright, long-lasting, soul-destroying depression.[22] Sadly, such arguments often trade on prejudice, which traditionally tends to thrive in times of economic distress, immigrants constituting handy scapegoats for problems before which individuals feel helpless. While we can understand the psychology of this response, we must be careful to ensure that the end of modernity does not also come to mean the end of social tolerance.

Another possible outcome of the aftermath of the crisis is a turn towards religion, since that offers a sense of security to believers, directing their attention away from the trials of everyday life to the larger scheme of the spiritual, giving them something in which to believe when their socio-political scheme is signally failing them.[23] Religions are generally quick to capitalise on such situations and the personal distress that inevitably follows in their wake. Understandable though the phenomenon is (and it need not be seen as entirely a cynical exercise on the part of organised religion, which is generally sincere enough in its belief that it can offer solace to the afflicted), it is not a recipe for global harmony either. Monotheistic religions are not exactly noted for their tolerance towards each other, and can easily be used to justify a campaign of expansion to realise their assumed destiny, which all claim to have on behalf of the whole human race. The less the secular ideal appears to be working, then the more attractive other options can come to appear and the secular ideal in the West is heavily implicated in the success of modernity as a cultural formation. Take away economic progress and secularism's appeal is tarnished and can fall away quite dramatically. Arguments against a materialistic society can sound very persuasive in hard economic times when individuals come to feel themselves at the mercy of much larger forces.

The poorer the society is then the more likely it is that religion will manage to exert such an appeal as this too. We have already seen in recent years how Islamism has grown into a substantial global cultural force from just such a situation, the religion giving a sense of purpose to many living under extremely harsh conditions that have been only barely touched by the modern world.[24]

Preventing support for secularism from eroding will constitute yet another critical task to be undertaken in the aftermath of modernity (although criticism of the excesses of the financial world from major religious figures, as is becoming more frequent, is a welcome contribution to the debate over the credit crisis and its causes).

In a sense it is easier to predict what the effects of global warming will be than those of the credit crisis, since the former are more susceptible to computer modelling, which has become a highly developed method in the scientific community in recent years and the basis for most of the debate on climate change. The predictions generally make for depressing reading, with some of them taking on an apocalyptic dimension where the bulk of humanity is wiped out and the remainder confined to those few parts of the globe that have not seen their environment so catastrophically degraded that it cannot support life any more (James Lovelock is the most pessimistic voice in this regard).[25] These are of course just predictions and the very worst-case scenarios may not come to pass (and for all our sake we have to hope not), but it is far easier to plan for dealing with physical phenomena than psychological – which is the problem that the credit crisis is setting us. We may not be doing so very effectively at present, but at least it is fairly clear what we should be doing if we want to arrest the course of global warming before it spirals totally out of our control.

In the case of global warming it is also more apparent what the adverse effects of modernity actually are. We can even see some of them unfolding around us in today's world, as in the rapidly warming climate of the polar regions and the increased incidence of long-term drought in areas like the Sahel and Australia (years long in many instances, with an increasingly savage impact on both the environment and the lives of the local inhabitants). Sceptics may claim that such events either do not add up to a pattern or are the result of changes in solar activity and their effect on the Earth's homeostatic system which cannot be avoided; but such arguments are becoming harder and harder to sustain in the face of the scientific evidence linking these events to carbon concentrations in the atmosphere. Solar activity – as revealed in sunspots and the solar wind, for example – is clearly a major factor in the conduct of the Earth's weather systems, but the effects of humankind in what has been dubbed the 'anthropogenic' era, outstrip it. It is humanity which is driving the Earth's thermostat at present; it is our activities, our collective consumption, that is causing huge polar ice shelves to break up, and which in the worst-case scenario will lead the ice sheets to melt and sea levels to rise catastrophically (75 metres has even been suggested).[26] If that happens we cannot really lay the blame elsewhere.

Another suggestion as to how to reconstruct society in the aftermath of the credit crisis has been to pursue the cause of egalitarianism much more vigorously, on the grounds that it is societies with the greatest economic discrepancies between rich and poor which tend to suffer the most from social problems. In their book *The Spirit Level*, Richard Wilkinson and Kate Pickett mount a strong argument for the benefits of egalitarianism, pointing out how statistics back up their claim that egalitarian societies – such as those found in Scandinavia, for example – are on the whole socially more stable than their counterparts around the world. They point out that, '[p]eople trust each other most in the Scandinavian countries and the Netherlands; Sweden has the highest level of trust, with 66 per cent of people feeling they can trust others'.[27] In Portugal, in contrast, the figure is only 10 per cent. Income disparities tend to be less in Scandinavian countries too, with the richest 20 per cent of the population only around four times richer than the poorest 20 per cent (Japan just slightly edging that bloc of countries to take top place), whereas in the USA it is nearly nine times as much, and in Singapore almost 10.[28] Sweden and the Scandinavian bloc also score very highly on such things as the UNICEF index of child wellbeing.[29]

It could be argued that if egalitarianism was more widespread than it is at present then the incidence of greed would drop and societies would be less likely to get themselves into the kind of economic tangle in which we are now caught up. The implication is that egalitarianism promotes a stronger sense of social responsibility than an unregulated free market culture ever can, tempering one of the more problematical drives to be found in human nature. It would be a case of emphasising a particular aspect of our nature at the expense of the one that has been given priority in recent years in market-driven countries like the USA and the UK – our social side over our individual, our responsibilities over our desires. For Wilkinson and Pickett the evidence for the social benefits of egalitarianism is overwhelming, and we should be acting on it:

> To sustain the necessary political will, we must remember that it falls to our generation to make one of the biggest transformations in human history. We have seen that rich countries have got to the end of the really important contributions which economic growth can make to the quality of life and also that our future lies in improving the quality of the social environment in our societies . . . [G]reater equality is the material foundation on which better social relations are built.[30]

There is no denying that the UK and the USA are far less egalitarian societies now than they have been in the past, and that the range of income levels is far broader than it was even just a few decades ago; no denying either that the general public has become progressively more appalled at such phenomena as the huge bonuses paid out in the financial sector. Bankers' public image is not currently very high, and the scale of the reward they have been routinely receiving in recent years is a major cause of that coming to pass. The fact that such massive remuneration packages have been paid while bankers at the same time have been running their companies into massive debt has, not surprisingly, generated a public outcry and brought the issue of income differentials very much into the public domain. Success may have disguised the unfairness of the bonus culture but failure has created a new cultural climate underpinned to at least some extent by an egalitarian imperative. If there is a shift towards a greater egalitarianism that would be a real social gain in the aftermath of modernity. This need not be taken as an argument against income differentials (they seem endemic to human society), and there would have to be extensive public debate about what would be considered acceptable in this regard in future. One would assume that something closer to the Scandinavian situation than the Singaporean would be more likely to gain general approval. A debate would represent a recognition, however, that, bearing the public good in mind, some parts of our nature are best left unexpressed and that the end of modernity really does require a very significant reorientation of our outlook.

How Much is Enough?

Calls for a simpler lifestyle avoiding the excesses of modernity and conspicuous consumption have come from the religious end of the spectrum frequently before now, and the collection of essays *Simpler Living: Compassionate Life. A Christian Perspective* makes a persuasive case for a theology based on the concept of 'enough'. As the editor, Michael Schut, puts it, '[i]n our culture where at every turn we are encouraged, if not induced, to consume more, more, more . . . the question "how much is enough?" is radical'.[31] Schut and his fellow contributors go on to recommend that the way forward is to opt for a 'voluntary simplicity' in our lives, as part of 'a vision that sees the connections between ecological and social decline; between environmental and social justice, between personal choices and global issues; a vision of the abundant life that emerges as a prophetic, compassionate response to today's world'.[32] Simplicity would mean acknowledging that consumption, especially the conspicuous variety, is a significant barrier to our spiritual development, and that we should therefore strive hard to overcome it. I intend to appropriate that notion of 'enough' for the purposes of this study from now on, arguing that it is in our collective interest to start cultivating a 'politics of enough' and an 'economics of enough', that unless we do so we can only magnify the problems the end of modernity has already set for us. It is a theme which is also followed up in a recent book by John Naish, who argues that we are drowning in an excess of goods, activities and information:

> We have some evolving to do. And quickly. We need to develop a sense of *enough*. Or, if you fancy enoughness. Or even enoughism. We have

created a culture that has one overriding message – we do not yet have all we need to be satisfied. The answer, we are told, is to have, see, be and do even more. Always more.[33]

Naish is not persuaded by that answer, and neither am I.

The perspective will not be religious here, as it plainly is in the Schut collection; but there is common ground between us in thinking that there comes a time when we must acknowledge the necessity of limits to our consumption, a time to start weighing up the benefits of a simpler lifestyle than we have come to expect from our economic system. Or, at the very least, that we should suspend indefinitely our belief that there always has to be material improvement looming up on the horizon and investigate other ways of channelling our energies – and for the public rather than the private good this time around. *Simpler Living* was published in 1999, when most of the world considered itself to be in the midst of an unprecedented economic boom, confident this was the face of the future, the days of 'boom and bust' being declared over by most of the major politicians; but a decade later it no longer seems at all radical to question conspicuous consumption and its impact, not just on our individual psychology but on the environment. Global warming has made us horribly aware of the intimate connection between ecological and social decline, environmental and social justice, and the credit crunch has revealed how a multitude of personal choices – by investors, traders and financial managers – based on an uncritical faith in the market's soundness can lead to economic meltdown at global level.

I will be returning to the virtues of the politics and economics of enough at various points over the course of the book. But before doing so, let us consider in more detail what is involved in the cultural formation which does not believe there ever can be, or should be, enough – modernity.

2
Modernity: Promise and Reality

What did modernity promise, and how successful has it been at delivering on its promises over the last few centuries? Modernity has involved a strong commitment to a free market economic system, and it has tended to advocate democracy as the most efficient way of running that system, although the dramatic rise of China as an economic superpower in recent times has undermined the notion to some degree, given the country's notably authoritarian political structures. Modernity can appear to be an egalitarian movement, the premise being that anyone can join in, and that eventually all who do so and put in the appropriate effort will be rewarded with an improved lifestyle replete with the latest consumer goods. But in reality the West has been quite happy to exploit developing world cultures for their raw materials and cheap labour (a process exacerbated considerably by the spread of globalisation), and we have become increasingly aware in recent years of the disparity in wealth between those cultures and the West. The cheaper the jeans, the tee-shirt, the toys or the computer, for example, then the better for the Western consumer, but all too often the worse for the developing world contract employee.[1]

Even within the West itself the disparity between those in the upper and lower reaches of the socio-economic scale has become progressively more marked in the last few decades (a phenomenon particularly noted in the USA), with the fruits of unregulated free market capitalism being unequally distributed across the class spectrum. The bonus system in the financial sector, still in operation in many cases despite the severity of the crisis and the sector's shameful role in generating it, provides a particularly stark example of this unequal distribution in action. We might also note that when the free market came to Russia in the aftermath of communism's collapse, the state's assets were rapidly snapped up by a small group of entrepreneurs who proceeded to become billionaire oligarchs, creating massive wealth discrepancies in Russian life at a stroke. If nothing else, this constituted a crash course in the ethics of advanced capitalism for the Russian masses.

Modernity has always encouraged self-interest as the best means of generating economic and technological progress for the public good, but of late this has too often manifested itself in the form of acute personal greed with no accompanying conception of the public good to temper it (there is little evidence of that in Russia, for example, with much of the oligarchs' fortunes being invested outside the country, thus bringing little in the way of benefit to the mass of the nation's citizens). The relationship between modernity's promises and the reality which has followed on from these, in both the economic and socio-political domains, needs to be mapped out more fully if we are to understand how we have ended up where we now find ourselves.

The Promise

Modernity is not something that can be dated precisely, being more of an accumulation of attitudes and ideas over time that eventually have come to be taken for granted as the basis of our culture. It is common to regard it as an outgrowth of the Enlightenment movement, and in particular its belief in the improvability of humankind and the human condition, as well as its commitment to reason – and, by extension, to science as a way of applying reason to the business of exerting ever greater control over the environment to humankind's ultimate benefit. The notion of progress certainly put down deep roots in the West and created expectations which

25

are still largely with us today: that science and technology should continue to seek out new discoveries and perfect their techniques such that our lives are made easier and more fulfilling by the products that ensue; that living standards should improve noticeably generation by generation; that the quality of life overall should improve noticeably for each generation, including standards of health and wellbeing; that opportunities for self-development and self-expression should increase and become a cornerstone of our social existence, our society facilitating these as best it can through institutions such as the educational system. Gradually, it has become accepted doctrine that the best way of delivering these objectives is through a system of democratic politics allied to the free market, although these activities can be interpreted with a certain amount of flexibility by individual countries to take account of their particular traditions. This is the grand narrative which has been driving geopolitics for the last century or so, the most powerful of our time in terms of its impact on human behaviour, a narrative accepted and promoted by both left and right across the political spectrum.

The culture that modernity replaced in Europe would have little attraction for most of us nowadays. It was excessively hierarchical, had only a rudimentary concept of human rights and was controlled to a large extent by the dictates of Christian belief – often to the point of theocracy, which is certainly not to the modern taste, secularism having been pushed hard in the interim as the best basis for a civil society. Politics was the preserve of the social elite, with the bulk of the population having no effective input to a system which was founded on the exclusionist principle of heredity: rising in the social scale, although not entirely impossible, was nevertheless a fairly rare phenomenon. Yet the pre-modern world had its virtues too, and we must be careful not to assume an attitude of cultural superiority over the past. Religion, for example, provided a very coherent grand narrative that was psychologically and metaphysically very satisfying to the vast majority of the European population. Restrictive though it undoubtedly was, it did provide an explanation for everything that happened in the world – and, as we know with the growth of religious fundamentalism in our own time, many do crave that kind of comfort, even if they also partake in, and appreciate, the material and political fruits of modernity. Neither was there the same degree of pressure to compete with one's peers in the marketplace (although a marketplace of sorts did exist).

But we must not romanticise pre-modern culture either. Modernity opened up far more opportunities for individuals, and personal autonomy is an accepted, and strongly defended, part of our cultural heritage now. Hierarchy may still exist within modernity, but it is nowhere near as repressive as its pre-modern counterpart and it will bend when put under pressure by determined enough individuals: rising in the social scale is no longer a rare phenomenon. I will go on to consider the extent to which modernity delivered on its promises below, but before that let us briefly look at one of its more problematical legacies, a trait which can be read either negatively or positively – greed.

Greed is Good?

Few supporters of modernity would want to argue that it is founded on greed, which has largely negative associations among the general public, but there is no denying that the desire for more – wealth, property, possessions, etc. – has been a powerful motivational force within modernity's development. The argument of the modern lobby is that this drive has a beneficial outcome for us all, leading to an expansion of production and trade which improves living standards across the board: admittedly, some may gain more than others, but everyone recognisably gains. The more entrepreneurial activity there is then the better as far as this constituency is concerned, and whatever inspires it has to be accepted as being in the public interest. Not everyone displays this characteristic as a central motivating factor of their life, but in theory anyone could develop it if they chose to: it is there in our nature waiting to be accessed if wanted (and there are lots of books on the market these days claiming to offer the appropriate advice).[2] Entrepreneurialism is a highly respected activity in our culture, therefore, and one that

27

most Western governments are very keen to promote: part of our strong commitment to personal autonomy and individualism.

Belief in the social value of the 'trickle-down' effect is still quite common among the political class, who are generally willing to give entrepreneurs the benefit of the doubt when it comes to justifying their business practices as long as they visibly generate wealth and employment – or at any rate appear to have the potential to do so at some future date. Without entrepreneurialism, it is argued, we would all be the poorer materially. The communist system of the twentieth century largely frowned on the entrepreneurial spirit (on the part of individuals anyway – some scope for initiative was there at the ministry level), while the West has consistently encouraged it, and there is no mistaking the greater effectiveness of the latter in delivering economic progress. At least in part it was failure on this score that finally undermined communism as a political system: the discrepancy with the West became just too large to keep disguised. As far as the entrepreneurial community and its defenders go, greed is in the public interest and demands constant cultivation (although they would rather call it by some other, less aggressive-sounding, name, such as enterprise – a topic now widely taught in British schools and universities, by the way).

Whether individual or corporate greed is the only way of delivering and sustaining economic progress or whether it has to involve such a rejection of social responsibility as we have seen it can in recent years are more vexed issues. In Douglas Rushkoff's reading, this is a critical aspect of corporatism's essentially negative effect on our culture, that it 'reduces the myriad complexity of human need down to individual selfishness', and greed does seem to have moved on to a new level of intensity.[3] We have such examples before us as the corporate sector investing considerable time and effort in devising ways to avoid paying its fair share of tax – often bypassing this altogether by the adroit use of the many offshore tax havens scattered around the world, and under at least some measure of international protection. In the aftermath of the crisis, however, most Western governments have begun to investigate the possibility of placing restrictions on the practice, in response to public opinion angered at how banks in particular have been deploying it. In the boom years the public purse gained little from them, therefore, yet in their lean years we are required to bail them out – not exactly a triumph of public relations on the bank side.

Although corporate social responsibility (CSR) has become something of a buzz phrase in the business community, it seems notable by its absence in such practices, which are designed exclusively for the benefit of shareholders and their demand for the highest possible dividend for their investment (how serious companies really are about CSR is another question).[4] Commentators have been remarking for some time how much more aggressive shareholders have become, applying concerted pressure to managements who are felt to be too cautious in their market dealings – to the extent of driving them from office on occasion. Western governments turned a blind eye to the system when economic times were good (the 'light touch' approach particularly favoured in the UK and USA), when the business world felt itself strong enough to dictate terms to politicians. Now that those times have gone, and the public has recognised the extent to which the corporate sector has been evading its social responsibilities, governments can no longer afford to be seen to collude with it. For the time being at least, greed is not being identified with the public good. It remains to be seen whether it will be given its head again, however, if and when things start to pick up on the world's markets.

Modernity and the Western Lifestyle

What has life been like for the average citizen in the West in recent times? How might we say it has improved or, at any rate, significantly changed compared to previous eras? In material terms it would have to be agreed that modernity has largely delivered the goods. There is no doubt that the last few decades have been something of a golden age for Western consumers, whose disposable income has increased markedly as aggressive globalisation has brought the cost of many products down as well as increasing the range of what is available quite phenomenally. Whereas items like

29

cars were not so long ago considered luxuries in European countries, now the majority of households own one, and very often several. Washing machines, refrigerators, dishwashers, televisions, computers, all are now standard household equipment, and at least in the West it is expected that the full range of public utilities – water, electricity, sewage, rubbish collection, etc. – will be made available to all citizens (the developing world is another matter, but I will come on to that later). Exotic foods from all over the globe appear year round on supermarket shelves. Mass transport systems are in operation in all of the West's major cities, and transport networks are highly developed throughout most countries. Airlines, once considered the height of luxury, are now a standard method of travel – not just internationally, but also within the national borders of even smaller countries like the UK as regional airports proliferate. Cheap airlines have revolutionised travel and with that the general population's vacation habits, which now routinely run (even for weekend trips) to what until recently were taken to be very exotic locations. The population is undoubtedly more mobile than it ever has been, more exposed to other cultures and their ways, and more knowledgeable about the world (if also perhaps somewhat arrogant about its supposed superiority over other cultures because of its technological sophistication and amount of disposable wealth).

The population is also healthier than ever, with well-developed healthcare systems throughout the major nations of the West – although admittedly varying in cost, with America the least user-friendly in this regard. In educational terms too, the improvement in lifestyle has been very marked. Educational systems are generally well maintained, and university education, once the preserve of the moneyed elite, is far more open than it ever has been. At least in theory most Western governments are committed to the idea of mass higher education, and Tony Blair's mantra on his election victory in 1997 – 'education, education, education' – is one from which few would demur. The higher educational sector has expanded massively in terms of both student population and teaching institutions in the last few decades, and although gaining a qualification can still be a very expensive activity to lower-income groups (many governments having introduced quite substantial student tuition fees), participation overall has nevertheless increased across the social spectrum. Whether this upward trajectory will survive the credit crisis remains a tantalisingly open question, however, and one that all political parties will be anxious to monitor closely in the next few years given public expectations on this score. Support for the banking industry to prevent its collapse will almost certainly lead to cuts in public services as a way of balancing the books, and higher education is unlikely to be at the very top of a government's priorities under those circumstances. Markedly higher tuition fees are a distinct possibility, and in an economic downturn these will be anything but popular.

The most dramatic changes have come in the realm of technology, and the range of technological aids and gadgets available to the general public nowadays would have been unimaginable even just a few generations ago as regards their level of sophistication and generally affordable price. In communication terms life arguably has altered most of all: the volume of information to be found on the internet, for example, far outstrips anything previous generations were able to access – and the internet is within almost everyone's reach in the West now. Mobile phones facilitate contact from almost any point on the face of the globe, and enable information to be retrieved and downloaded on command, turning individuals into communication centres in their own right. (John Naish identifies the beginnings of a movement against this in the USA, with 'tech-no's', so called, deliberately disconnecting themselves, and he welcomes this; but there seems little evidence of this as a general trend.)[5] The hyper-individualism this has served to promote has created a climate even more conducive to technological innovation, which thrives on conspicuous consumption, and so the cycle goes on.

Politically, the West has embraced parliamentary democracy, where each citizen has rights that are protected by the state and also has access to the state's many official institutions. There is a universal franchise amongst adult citizens, and regular elections (every four or five years on average) to make sure that governments keep attentive to the public mood. Freedom of speech and the press – within certain constraints in each case, which can vary from country to country – are in principle guaranteed, as is freedom of movement, and opposition to the government is an accepted part of the political process. This is to describe the system in its ideal state, and it has to be acknowledged that it does not always work in quite that fashion. Many abuses do occur even in the most liberal of democracies; rights can be overridden and marginal political voices suppressed, for example – often in the name of national security in recent years (anti-terrorist legislation being a particularly contentious case in point since 9/11). Not everyone has shared in the increasingly affluent lifestyle of Western society, and not everyone has seen their human rights always respected and protected by the authorities: immigrant communities often experience considerable problems on that score. Broadly speaking, however, it would be true to say that the majority of the population in the West has seen its lifestyle alter for the better both materially and politically over the last couple of centuries, with the process speeding up considerably over the last few generations as technological innovation has taken off in a really big way. (What has also taken off in a big way is the availability of credit to take advantage of that booming innovation culture, but to more problematical effect as regards living standards, as I shall go on to discuss in Chapter 5.)

As mentioned above, however, the developing world is another matter altogether when it comes to improved lifestyles, and although it is tied into modernity in terms of globalisation and world trade (not least through the practice of outsourcing, a very mixed blessing), it has not necessarily had its fair share of the material benefits that are taken for granted in the West. Public utilities can be both inefficient and prohibitively expensive in much of the developing world, with no guarantee of constant clean water supplies or electricity, for instance, nor of the means to pay for them on the part of the poorer sections of the population. Shanty towns, of which there are no shortage in such countries, are not noted for the range of their amenities nor their quality of life, and they are growing more common around the major cities as the population increases and outsourced production from the multinationals draws people into the urban areas for employment (poorly paid though it almost invariably is). Education and healthcare systems are often rudimentary, and in extreme cases non-existent, with a consequent effect on life expectancy, which is generally far lower than it is in the West.

Nor has the developing world shared in the political benefits that have followed on from modernity: Western-style liberal democracy is by no means widespread in that sector, and older authoritarian models still hold sway in a host of countries, barring large swathes of the world's population from effective participation in the political process. Rights that are now taken to be standard in the West are often conspicuously absent in non-Western societies (freedom of speech, freedom of the press or even freedom of movement, for example), which still adhere to pre-modern practices a great deal of the time, despite being part of the globalised trade network. It is easy to forget that most of the world has not really experienced the full impact of modernity, and it may well be that it will pass them by entirely as modernity is found to be unsustainable. Progress as we have understood it will have to be reassessed, and it will most likely be the developing world which will suffer the most from the exercise – unfair though that manifestly is. Already low living standards there, of a kind that would not be tolerated in the West, could slide even further down the scale, and we have to wonder what effect this will have on the geopolitical order. What might desperation generate under such circumstances?

The Dark Side of Modernity

Modernity had its critics in the West even before postmodernism came on the scene, and it is worth considering briefly two of the most penetrating of these, Theodor Adorno and Max Horkheimer, the major figures involved in the 'Frankfurt School' of social theorists, and a major influence on the development of postmodern philosophy. Writing in 1944 as the Second World War was coming to its conclusion, Adorno and Horkheimer presented a very bleak assessment of what modernity had achieved, claiming that the reality was a long way from the promises offered by the ideal: 'In the most general sense of progressive thought, the Enlightenment has always aimed at liberating men from fear and establishing their sovereignty. Yet the fully enlightened earth radiates disaster triumphant.'[6] Enlightenment for these thinkers, the very ground of modernity, had a dark side which had led to the crisis for humankind that was the Second World War, and their projections for the future were not all that hopeful either. Modernity had created a world of totalitarian belief systems, deeply intolerant of each other, with Adorno and Horkheimer noting that, 'mankind has been divided up into a few armed power blocs' which inevitably came into collision with each other on a fairly regular basis.[7] As we now know, the defeat of Fascism, although then imminent, was soon to be replaced by the clash between the West and the communist bloc, thus continuing that tense state of affairs for the several decades of the Cold War. Then in the aftermath of that has come the conflict between the West and Islamism carrying on into the twenty-first century, and showing no signs of abating any time soon (for some, this is serious enough to be defined as a 'clash of civilizations').[8] Surveying the geopolitics of the last century or so, it would have to be said that the authors' air of pessimism about our prospects is not without foundation.

Even at this stage of the twentieth century Adorno and Horkheimer were complaining about the spread of globalisation and the adverse effect it was having on individuals. The main effect as they saw it was to trap the vast majority of us in the clutches of what we would now call a grand narrative:

> Only if the inhabitants of these power blocs become totally identified with them and accept their dictates as second nature while all the pores of the consciousness are blocked, can the masses be kept in the state of total apathy which makes them capable of fantastic exploits. Any decision-taking functions which still appear to be left to individuals are in fact taken care of in advance.[9]

This is what the authors call an 'administered society', where conformity is imposed on the individual regardless of which particular grand narrative he or she happens to have been born into:

The ticket thinking which is a product of industrialization and its advertising machine, extends to international relations. The choice by an individual citizen of the Communist or Fascist ticket is determined by the influence which the Red Army or the laboratories of the West have on him. The objectification by which the power structure (which is made possible only by the passivity of the masses) appears as an iron reality, has become so dense that any spontaneity or even a mere intimation of the true state of affairs becomes an unacceptable utopia, or deviant sectarianism.[10]

It is a line of argument which will be taken further by postmodern thinkers like Jean-François Lyotard and Jean Baudrillard, the gist of it being that modernity has degenerated into a repressive and authoritarian system and that we should be looking for ways to counter its baleful influence and reorient how our society is run. Preferably this should be on pluralist lines, with a far greater range of voices and opinions being given the opportunity to make themselves heard. The grand narratives of our time were to be called to account.

Some commentators found the *Dialectic of Enlightenment* defeatist and despairing in tone, with Jürgen Habermas (a latter-day Frankfurt School theorist himself), as a case in point, complaining that the authors, in this 'their blackest book', had 'surrendered themselves to an uninhibited scepticism regarding reason, instead of weighing the grounds that that cast doubt on the scepticism itself';[11] but we might regard that note of scepticism as more pertinent now than it would have been in the 1980s when Habermas was writing. Scepticism about the power of reason, the impetus behind modernity as a socio-political system, seems entirely justified by the chaotic course of recent events. Reason most certainly did not predict the breakdown of the modernist paradigm; nor, for the time being anyway, does reason seem to have any workable idea on how to deal with the effects of this. Both rational politicians and rational economists were caught completely off guard by a turn of events which ran counter to everything in which they had been taught to believe. They had felt themselves to be in control, but manifestly they were not – and that had to be a humbling experience that sowed doubts about one's ideology.

Neither does Habermas's contention that modernity is an 'unfinished project' sound as persuasive as it did back in the 1980s.[12] Habermas emphasised the political benefits of modernity against postmodernism's claim that these had now evaporated, and insisted we could build on these to construct a society more responsive to our collective needs. We could admit there were flaws in modernity without turning our back on the original project, or the theory that had brought it into being. For Habermas, the major postmodern thinkers are guilty of 'an irreconcilable anti-modernism', and he fears that this might succeed in obscuring the very real virtues of modernity, especially to an impressionable young audience.[13] He regards postmodernists as essentially backward-looking, identifying a 'neoconservative' strain in their thought and suggesting that 'they are merely cloaking their complicity with the venerable tradition of counter-Enlightenment in the garb of post-Enlightenment'.[14] Overall, he finds postmodern thought to be rather facile, more interested in attention-grabbing gestures than sustained intellectual analysis, and with little to contribute to public debate about the direction our culture should be taking. The pessimism that Adorno and Horkheimer pass on to their postmodern disciples is an impediment to improving the human condition, and is to be disdained.

Habermas remains firmly committed to the cause of rationality. The question we have to ask ourselves, he asserts, is 'should we try to hold on to the *intentions* of the Enlightenment, feeble as they may be, or should we declare the entire project of modernity a lost cause?'.[15] The answer from Habermas is a resounding 'yes' in favour of the intentions, because '[t]he thesis of a post-Enlightenment . . . is anything but convincing'.[16] But the question we have to ask ourselves now is: what should we do if those intentions lead not just to intellectual freedom, but to the phenomena of global warming and credit crunch? Is it possible to retain the political benefits (democratic polity, freedom of speech, movement and the press, for example), while ridding ourselves of the obsession with progress and consumption that seems to be projecting us into terminal crisis? We should certainly want to retain those benefits, and it could be argued that we have lost sight of them in the headlong rush towards expanding the economy, assuming this was all that really counted any more, what modernity was essentially about. It has to be acknowledged that globalisation, for example, has done very little for the cause of democracy, no matter what its supporters may care to claim – in most cases it has tended to reinforce the power of the ruling elite at the expense of the local working class, whose condition has often worsened both politically and economically. To some extent what we are now looking for is modernity minus its dark side, and that could prove to be no mean task – especially after several decades of unfettered capitalism.

If modernity is now failing, the reality unable to meet the promises made and the expectations aroused, where did the postmodern fit into the scheme? And how might we move beyond it? Those will be the concerns in the next chapter.

3

Beyond Postmodernity

Postmodernism has presented a significant challenge to the assumptions behind both modernism and modernity for some decades now, although its high point as a cultural phenomenon was during the 1980s and 1990s, when it became a very trendy term to use in both the media and everyday discourse.[1] Postmodernists attacked the authoritarian aspect of modernity as a cultural system, arguing that it suppressed dissenting views in favour of defending its overall grand narrative of economic, technological and political progress. This grand narrative was no less in operation in the communist bloc than in the Western democracies (both of whom claimed to have found the ideal political system destined to overcome all others), and postmodernists were concerned to reveal how repressive this had become across all areas of our lives, promoting conformity of belief and curbing dissidence wherever it appeared. Postmodern theorists felt that such all-encompassing grand narratives were beginning to break down in the later stages of the twentieth century, and events such as the collapse of the Soviet empire in the 1980s and the move towards a capitalist style of economic system in China seemed to provide solid evidence for their claims: Marxist theory, at least, was losing its hold. Change was well under way, and it was to be greeted with enthusiasm.

It seemed that totalitarianism was no longer a sustainable political position, and the line taken was that we were entering a postmodern world, where pluralism would be the new ideological paradigm – to the benefit of marginalised groups internationally, who would now be given a voice in public affairs that had been denied them in the past. Even Marxism could be brought into the mix in the form of post-Marxism, where the spirit of Marx was deemed to take precedence over the letter of his theories. Although some thinkers went on to reject Marxism altogether, the sentiments were still considered admirable by many on the left, even if the philosophy constructed on them now stood revealed as deeply flawed and in need of substantial reassessment (I will be going into the internal complexities of post-Marxism later in the chapter).

What postmodernists failed to appreciate, however, was the importance of the growth of religious fundamentalism around the globe (in all of the world's major religions), as well as the extent of the commitment to modernity's economic goals – as expressed, for example, through the spread of globalisation, which has turned the world into one large marketplace for the products of successive new generations of technology. In economic terms the world continued to follow a modernist line, with growth the only goal that really mattered to the majority of those in power. Unfortunately, the boom in international trade over the last few decades also had the adverse effect of dramatically accelerating global warming, which has to be seen as a direct consequence of modernity's relentless pursuit of progress. Trade increases consumption, which increases carbon emissions – and trade also increases global traffic, generating yet more emissions through air, sea and road transport.

While postmodernists have been right to challenge the grand narratives of modernity, their projections of what would come after these now look more than a bit questionable – certainly optimistic. They envisaged something like an internal reform of modernity, based on a reworking of its power structures to take account of a broader range of viewpoints – pluralism coming to the fore. Real postmodernity, however, is a far more chaotic affair than such theorists' analyses predicted, and the relevance of what we might now call 'classic postmodernism' to the actual collapse of modernity as a cultural paradigm needs to be examined.

For the time being no new vision or theory of how society should organise itself post-credit crunch has emerged, although older ones, such as theocratic religion and socialism, in various varieties, are opportunistically being recycled by some – with more success as far as the former is concerned than the latter (Islamism in particular has experienced a considerable revival worldwide). It will be instructive, therefore, to observe how classic postmodernism, the only really sustained critique of modernity we have had in recent history (although some claims might also be made for Islamism too, I suppose), shapes up to life beyond modernity. What sort of pluralism could we have in the aftermath of economic collapse, for example, when it would seem that only strong central government stands between most nations and a descent into social chaos? What will happen to globalisation as a system if governments become more involved in its operations (as it seems inevitable they must in the wake of the socially destabilising effect of the market's volatility)?

Postmodernism and the Critique of Modernity

Postmodernism was a concerted attack on the ideals of modernity, which it was claimed had become authoritarian and repressive over the course of the twentieth century, preventing other world-views from expressing themselves properly. It had become a grand narrative, and as such intolerant of all other outlooks, which were simply taken to be wrong-headed and in need of retirement. The critique took wing in the architectural world first of all, with the theorist Charles Jencks leading the way. Jencks's target was modernist architecture, or the 'International Style' as it had come to be known, with its strictly imposed conventions – straight lines, minimal ornamentation, extensive use of concrete and glass, preference for high-rise structures (all very much inspired by the work and theories of Le Corbusier).[2] As the name indicated, such buildings could be found anywhere on the globe, regardless of local vernacular styles which tended to be swamped by the sheer scale of modernism's productions. Modernity in its public guise had a distinct tendency to favour homogeneity, with one place being very much like another, an advertisement for the movement's grand narrative vision.[3]

The public could hardly avoid these kind of imposing structures from impinging on their daily lives, especially since they were to become the standard pattern for constructing not just office blocks and company headquarters, but also mass housing projects in a time of significant population growth. Pruitt-Igoe's equivalents were to be observed going up in almost any major city around the world, and as far as Jencks was concerned they led to the creation of a series of urban waste lands which brought out the worst in human nature, hence the recourse to vandalisation by some particularly disgruntled sections of the population:

> Good form was to lead to good content, or at least good conduct; the intelligent planning of abstract space was to promote healthy behaviour. Alas, such simplistic ideas, taken over from the philosophies of Rationalism, Behaviourism and Pragmatism proved as irrational as the philosophies themselves. Modern architecture, as the son of the Enlightenment, was an heir to its congenital naiveties.[4]

This was not to be construed as a defence of vandalism, but rather as an attack on poorly conceived social engineering out of touch with the public's real wants and needs. It was the top-down approach that most incensed Jencks, as it was to do in other areas with postmodern thinkers.

Jencks was a harsh critic of such overt standardisation and went on to call repeatedly for a radical change in architectural practice, based on taking into account the feelings of the general public as well as of other architects. His contention was that buildings should be designed to appeal to both cohorts, 'double-coding' as he conceptualised it.[5] Jencks argued the case for a style based on 'radical eclecticism', mixing elements from various periods so that the general public could be given something familiar with which to identify.[6] In practice, this has happened, and even become, rather ironically, something of an International Style in its own right – although one with a greater flexibility and room for manoeuvre on the architect's part than is to be found in the modernist version (it can absorb and rework local vernacular styles, for example). Eclecticism may well be demanded of practitioners now, but with the whole history of architecture to choose from there is no lack of choice to exercise creativity in one's selection of components: pretty well anything goes. For Jencks, this was enough to break free from the strictures of modernism, and he was tireless in its support, finding a social and political resonance in it which went well beyond the world of architecture.

Various other architectural theorists weighed in with critiques of the modernist movement. For some it lacked a human dimension – Donald Kuspit, for example, complaining of 'the tendencies of modernist architecture to annihilate all traces of humanness'.[7] For others, it lacked the saving grace of a sense of humour, being over-concerned with trying to impress and even overawe its users. Given the general severity of modernist architecture, these were not unreasonable criticisms. Las Vegas could even be held up as a model of how to create an urban landscape, based in this instance on very pragmatic commercial considerations, that the general public could both enjoy and feel at home in:

> The commercial strip, the Las Vegas strip in particular . . . challenges the architect to take a positive, non-chip-on-the shoulder view. Architects are out of the habit of looking nonjudgementally at the environment, because orthodox Modern architecture is progressive, if not revolutionary, utopian, and puristic; it is dissatisfied with *existing* conditions. Modern architecture has been anything but permissive: Architects have preferred to change the existing environment rather than enhance what is there[.][8]

In other words, architects were fixated with the need to 'make it new', Ezra Pound's clarion call to modernist creative artists everywhere.[9] Making it new was taken to override all other considerations, social or artistic. An ideological vision was being imposed on the public regardless of its response, and as with modernist aesthetics in general there was a decidedly elitist quality to this practice – the architects simply assumed they knew best and that the public were obliged to adapt to what they were given. No modernist architect would design something as messy and vulgar as the Las Vegas cityscape, no matter how popular it might be with the general public – and so much the worse, as far as the authors of the highly polemical study of American architecture *Learning from Las Vegas* were concerned. What was required, in their view, was more of a dialogue with public taste and a greater sense of humility on the part of architects when dealing with the public space. Purity of conception was no longer to be the basis of the architectural vision, instead quirkiness was actively encouraged – evidence of the 'slackening' that Lyotard, with some reservations (he worried that it might also constitute a slackening of the creative imagination), saw as characteristic of the postmodern ethos.[10]

It is only fair to record, however, that modernist architecture can still claim supporters into the twenty-first century, as Owen Hatherley's book *Militant Modernism* makes clear. The author emphasises the utopian and egalitarian side to modernist architecture, which sought to provide the masses with a brave new world far removed from the privations of their past. Even though the postwar modernist housing estates of his home town of Southampton had become 'shabby' by the late twentieth century when the author was growing up, they could still appear to him as 'glittering towers of science fiction'.[11] Such projects are often unfairly derided, Hatherley feels, and he wants us to recognise the still laudable socially conscious vision that lay behind their creation. The urban planners in question really did feel they were acting for the greater common good by banishing the sense of the past (as Le Corbusier had also felt before them). But the sad part was that the general public rarely seemed to share the planners' enthusiasm, and most of those glittering towers are now sunk into a state of fairly abject decay, the vision long since consigned to oblivion.

Modernism remains for Hatherley potentially counter-cultural, and what has replaced it architecturally leaves him cold: 'the Disneyfication of Britain continues apace', being his dismissive verdict on the turn towards postmodernism.[12] Such a kitsch conception of the past is most certainly not what Jencks had in mind, but it is salutary to remember that postmodernism does have its faults, that it can play to people's prejudices and fear of change: one can understand why Jürgen Habermas would make his charge of neo-conservatism against the movement. As Agnes Heller and Ferenc Fehér have also complained, 'the postmodern political condition is tremendously ill at ease with Utopianism of even a non-Messianic type, which makes it vulnerable to easy compromises with the present as well as susceptible to "doomsday myths" and collective fears stemming from the loss of future'.[13]

As we shall see in Chapter 7, Jencks's architectural theories have had a marked effect on postmodern aesthetics, but the reason for dwelling on them here has been to demonstrate the nature of the social concerns which inspired the postmodern outlook to develop. What Jencks succeeds in doing is showing just how grass-roots those concerns were, about things that affected all of us in our daily lives and that raised critical issues about the power relationships operating in our society. Thinkers like Jencks had identified a certain restlessness among the general population about the way their societies were being run, a feeling that they were being patronised by those in charge. In consequence, they were becoming less and less enamoured of the establishment and more motivated to question its authority. Again and again throughout postmodern thought we are to find anti-authoritarian sentiments being expressed forcefully, and pleas being made for top-down controls to be either eased or, even better, removed altogether. Postmodernists were consistently suspicious of power, and above all of those who wielded it. Power, as they saw it, was generally abused, and the full extent of this needed to be revealed so that we could start to reclaim some of the freedoms we had lost. Esoteric though their analyses could be on occasion, postmodernists were speaking for a wider constituency than just cultural theorists and articulating concerns that ran deep in society.

Interestingly enough, some theorists saw those concerns as emerging from the experience of previous economic crises, with the urban geographer Edward W. Soja, for example, arguing that,

[A]nother culture of time and space seems to be taking shape in this contemporary context and it is redefining the nature and experience of everyday life in the modern world – and along with it the whole fabric of social theory. I would locate the onset of this passage to postmodernity in the late 1960s and the series of explosive events which together marked the end of the long post-war boom in the capitalist world economy.[14]

What Soja is suggesting is that this particular blip in modernity's progress had sowed the seeds of doubt about what modernity was trying to achieve, showing how dependent the project was on the delivery of its economic promises for its acceptance. As we know, modernity recovered and went on to generate even greater booms than the post-war's had been, but theorists had recognised there was an underlying unease about the kind of culture that modernity had created. It was not just the booms which got bigger, the busts did too, and that had to raise increasingly serious questions about modernity's stability. An era of scepticism had begun, and this had significant political ramifications: authority could no longer count on uncritical support from the public, and postmodernism was signalling the gradual erosion of a consensus in Western society.

Postmodernism conceives of itself as a movement for liberation therefore, although it has to be conceded there is a certain amount of truth in the remark that it can take refuge in 'easy compromises'. It is very much a tactical movement, concerned to spread doubt and scepticism, and it will not appeal to those who like boldness of vision. One area in which it maintained a much more militant stance, however, was in its critique of Marxism, to which I now turn.

Post-Marxism

Post-Marxism attempted to give us a postmodern version of Marx, stripped of his authoritarian connotations, which had become entrenched over the history of communism as a political system – a fairly unhappy history overall as it appeared to most from a late twentieth-century vantage point.[15] What this meant for our approach to the thinker's work can be seen to good effect in a book entitled *The Postmodern Marx*, where the author, Terrell Carver, invites us to read Marx anew, putting aside that history which had created the notion of there being a unified body of theory, 'a single Marx', from which to draw revolutionary doctrine.[16] Instead, Carver argued, we ought to recognise there there are now 'multiple Marxes':[17] that he can be read in a variety of ways and communicate many different messages – if read with an open mind. This was to be a Marx for the age of pluralism, one that could be reinterpreted in the light of contemporary concerns, a Marx without ideological baggage. What the postmoderns wanted was dialogue with Marx rather than doctrinal pronouncements that could not be questioned.

In the hands of thinkers such as Ernesto Laclau and Chantal Mouffe, arguably the most influential of post-Marxist theorists, Marx was recast to take account of cultural changes which could not have been foreseen in the period when his theories were being formulated: Marx, as they saw it, was to be made relevant to what was actually happening now, as opposed to what Marxists thought should be happening. The concern of these thinkers was to maintain a socialist dimension to their thought, hence their commitment to protest movements against the established political order around the globe, but not to be bound by the dogmatic prescriptions that had come to characterise Marxist theory, particularly in its communist guise, by the later twentieth century. It was immaterial whether those movements conformed to Marxist criteria or not: the notion of a party line alienated Laclau and Mouffe, who were more interested in promoting resistance to the world's existing power structures than in upholding any idea of ideological purity. Their call for a move towards 'radical democracy', a concept which has attracted a considerable body of followers in political philosophical circles since they floated it in the mid-1980s, represented a rejection of institutionalised Marxism, which saw no need to change direction nor to reassess its basic methodological principles.[18]

In line with the postmodern ethos, radical democracy has proceeded to champion the cause of pluralism, which is not a concept a totalising theory like Marxism can readily encompass, since it raises the spectre of a loss of control over the political process by the centralised party system that the theory insistently advocates. In Marxist practice 'democracy' translated into the 'one-party state', and opposition of any kind was invariably classified as illegal and subsequently quashed by the party (as still happens in the few bastions of old-style communism left in the twenty-first century, such as North Korea and Cuba). Post-Marxists were particularly critical of the drive towards uniformity in communist states, which could only be maintained by repressive means. The ideological unity that such states were claiming to have achieved was in fact a sham – appearance only. The reality was a cowed citizenry, afraid to articulate its real opinion of the system.

Pluralism is now widely accepted as a political ideal, although in many cases little more than lip service is actually being paid to it: politically speaking, there is still a fairly narrow range of views being represented in the formal politics of most Western countries. As radical democracy would have it, a 'democratic deficit' applies (although one would have to say this does help to marginalise extremism by denying it much of a public platform).[19] Multiculturalism is this commitment's most obvious manifestation, but it has turned out to be something of a battleground in most Western countries, where grand narratives of nationhood (often backed up by strongly held notions of ethnic or racial superiority, no matter how spurious these may be in reality) can keep reasserting themselves. The extent to which multiculturalism has succeeded in challenging political grand narratives in general is very much open to question. There has even been a recognisable backlash in many countries, with fringe parties throughout Western Europe seeking to demonise the local immigrant population by appealing to deeply rooted prejudices in the host community. Neither does a commitment to multiculturalism imply that all cultures within a given country will have the right to set up their own systems – legal, political, educational, etc. – to contest those of the dominant culture. There are certain things, such as freedom of speech and women's rights (which are not always recognised in non-Western societies), that are not held to be negotiable, and compliance with the practices of the host culture is demanded, often on pain of legal penalty.

47

Nevertheless, multicultural pluralism continues to be the ideal championed by radical democratic thinkers, who see this as the way out of the trap of totalitarianism and centralization. This is firmly in line with the postmodern ethos which is always concerned to distribute political power as widely as possible, and to prevent the build-up of a dominant ideological bloc that will seek to marginalise dissenting voices (Lyotard even spoke of the need to 'wage a war on totality').[20] This is the positive aspect of the radical democratic creed; its negative is that it remains above all an academic discourse, with minimal discernible effect on practical political life – where 'radical' is the most abused of concepts these days anyway. It is a problem with postmodern thought overall, its political impact has not matched what it has achieved in areas like the arts and the media (as we shall see in Chapter 7): hence the need to find a way to go beyond it in order to deal with the situation in which the collapse of modernity has placed us.

In truth, neither radical democracy nor postmodernism offers a very specific programme for political action, relying as they both do on the accumulated action of little narratives – in essence, pressure groups with specific targets, such as environmental abuses – to destabilise the grand political narratives of our culture. Why we should resist is made abundantly clear, but not exactly what we should do to make that resistance consistently successful in the longer term. Little narratives work up to a point, and can score successes against the institutions of the grand narrative on occasion (the green movement has had its moments in this respect), but they cannot constitute the whole answer to adjusting to life after modernity – useful though they are in helping to change the climate of cultural opinion.

Jean-François Lyotard also contributed to the post-Marxist cause, but in a much more critical manner. As early as the 1950s he was raising doubts as to Marxism's validity in terms of the Algerian revolution then in full swing against the colonising French state, arguing that the theory was not really suited to the needs of a Third World country with little in the way of developed infrastructure.

Marxism's totalising tendencies were particularly taken to task by Lyotard, the notion that the theory held in all places and at all times regardless of whatever the local conditions might happen to be. The sheer difference between Algeria and an industrialised European country of the kind that Marx's theories had been designed for argued against their application in this instance for Lyotard, who could only see problems ahead if communism was forcibly imposed on the population:

> [T]he problem of helping Algerians to live is conceived and solved in terms of an individual or a small collectivity, a village, a family, a quarter. No consciousness can span the whole of society so as to pose the question of what that society is for itself . . . No one, no political group, no social class is able to build and propagate a new image of Algeria that Algeria might desire as it had desired independence.[21]

Marxism is committed to progress but it will accept only one road to achieving it, which implies that repression will be employed as and when necessary. The collective ideal will override any individual objections, with unity always the paramount concern of the communist party. The anti-authoritarianism that is so prominent in postmodern thought is already to the fore in these early writings by Lyotard, who will become increasingly critical of attempts to subjugate individuality and the little narrative. For this thinker, the specifics of each situation must always be taken into account and there can be no overall solution to the multitude of problems besetting humanity.

Lyotard's *Libidinal Economy*, written in the aftermath of the Paris *événements* (a particularly traumatic experience for radical leftists of Lyotard's persuasion), constitutes a vicious attack on Marx as a thinker, and one aspect in particular which very neatly brings out the modernist quality of his work. Marx was notoriously poor at meeting publishing deadlines, with *Capital* being delayed for years as its author went off on yet another tangent, continually adding to the work's length to the despair of both his colleagues and the waiting publisher. The gist of Lyotard's complaint is that Marx became consumed by the act of production, which of course is a common criticism of modernity, that the process takes over and turns human beings into its servants. As with modernity, the production, in this case of words and arguments, became almost an end in itself to Marx; a state of affairs which provoked some of Lyotard's most biting sarcasm, such as the reference to,

> something quite astonishing: the perpetual *postponement* of finishing work on *Capital*, a chapter becoming a book, a section a chapter, a paragraph a section, by a process of cancerization of theoretical discourse, by a totally pulsional proliferation of a network of concepts hitherto destined on the contrary to 'finalize', to 'define' and to justify a proletarian politics . . . We are able to support this, in these post-relative days; but for Marx (and therefore for Engels the impatient!), it must rather have been a bizarre, worrying fact.[22]

The extent of Marx's production can be gauged from the fact that Engels was able to put together other volumes of *Capital* from the collection of manuscripts left after Marx's death.[23] Marx himself was unable to bring the work to an end, to stop producing, to say 'enough'.

Post-Marxism is as much a reaction to modernity as to Marxist theory itself, therefore, as can also be recognised in the work of Lyotard's French contemporary André Gorz who was dismissive of the Marxist obsession with, and idealisation of, the working class. As far as Gorz was concerned, this class no longer existed in the form that Marxists traditionally had conceived of it, and it was time to consign it to history:

> That traditional working class is now no more than a privileged minority. The majority of the population now belong to the post-industrial neo-proletariat which, with no job security or definite class identity, fills the area of probationary, contracted, casual, temporary and part-time employment.[24]

Marxists had always seen workers as a homogeneous unit, sharing a common outlook, but Gorz disputes that such an interpretation can still hold by the later twentieth century – or ever will again, for that matter. It is yet another rejection of Marxist totalisation, which elevates conformity above pluralism and difference – precisely what Lyotard also finds so difficult to take about the theory, and then Laclau and Mouffe after him. The repressiveness of the notion of progress, which reduces the individual to the demands of the system, comes through very strongly in such critiques. Post-Marxism overall is an attempt to bring a human dimension back into politics and to liberate individuals from the overweaning power of doctrine.

Postmodernism and Religion

Postmodernism has also been conducting a dialogue with religion, although one would in the first instance assume it would be inimical to the entire concept of religious belief, a point made succinctly by the philosopher Pamela Sue Anderson: 'A straightforward account of the relationship between postmodernism and religion – as two Western conceptions – has been one of direct opposition and discontinuity. Whereas postmodernism undermines biological, cognitive and moral certainties, religions rest on them'.[25] Nevertheless, some claims have in fact been made for significant correspondences applying between the two areas. Both postmodernism and religion are suspicious of the Enlightenment world-view, that enthusiastic celebration of the power of reason and the cult of progress. The notion that reason can resolve all human problems is no more acceptable to the religious community in general than it is to postmodern theorists like Lyotard. The Radical Orthodox movement in theology sees common cause with postmodernism in this respect, with both of them taking up an oppositional stance to the Enlightenment grand narrative.[26] The postmodern insistence on there being limits to reason, symbolised by the 'sublime' (a topic I will be looking at in more detail in Chapter 6), also finds echoes in religion, with the concept of the divine, held to be essentially unknowable by humanity, being analogous. In both cases something impenetrable is felt to lie beyond reason, and human beings have no option but to admit the power that it holds over their lives.

Yet religion is also where postmodernism can come unstuck as a socio-political theory. The dramatic rise of religious fundamentalism across the globe has to cast doubt on the theory's confident pronouncements that grand narratives are steadily losing their authority, and that we have become a less credible age overall. The increasing political influence wielded over the last few decades by Islamism alone would give the lie to such claims, and the steady growth of Christian fundamentalism in the USA emphasises that this is a global phenomenon we are observing, one pan-religious in its scope. Judaic and Hindu fundamentalism merely add to the impression of a definite reassertion of religion as a force in our lives – and a force with a political agenda. Both postmodernism and religion may be concerned to bring down the Enlightenment grand narrative, but the critical difference between them is that religion is doing so in the name of yet another grand narrative, substituting faith where postmodernism wants scepticism to be in play. What is more, increasing numbers of people, across a range of religions around the world, are signing up for a particularly fundamentalist version of this, suggesting that postmodern theorists have badly underestimated the depth of the psychological attraction to grand narratives. This is something to be borne in mind in adjusting to life beyond both modernity and postmodernity: many will want a simple solution that harks back to pre-modernity – and that will not really be very helpful. Such uncritical belief in those in authority is not what the situation requires – quite the opposite: we shall need all the scepticism we can muster to keep authority in line. Secularism cannot be taken for granted; it will have to be defended against the encroachments of fundamentalism and the theocratic mentality, which are likely to become ever more assertive in a condition of crisis.

The Postmodern Enough

In its own way postmodernism was a form of 'enough': saying enough to top-down authority, party lines, religious fanaticism and to fundamentalism in all its many guises. What was recommended instead was scepticism and doubt and a far less doctrinaire approach to belief systems in general. This was especially so when it came to the arts. As an aesthetic, postmodernism invited us to rid ourselves of the modernist obsession with formal experimentation and the cult of originality, and to make greater use of what we could find around us in artistic history, the vast body of materials that had been built up by successive generations. Pastiche became the order of the day as artists sought to connect with their cultural past through appropriating its key stylistic features: in effect, to recycle materials from previous eras and recreate our relationship with them. While some modernist artists had also seen the virtue of constructing a dialogue with the past, one thinks of the development of the neoclassical style in music in the early decades of the century as a case in point, it was never an abiding concern for the movement in the sense that it clearly became for postmodernists.[27]

Postmodernism invited us to reconsider our relationship to the past therefore, and to accord it more respect than modernity generally felt it merited. It saw no need to cut ourselves off from our cultural heritage, and set itself against the iconoclastic approach favoured by the modernists where past practice tended to be regarded as a hindrance to the creative drive. The notion of progress, the supposed virtue of progress, was being contested, in the artistic realm as elsewhere, and it can be claimed that in the arts world the campaign was highly successful: modernism lost its aura among most of the new generation, who proved very receptive to the postmodern vision. Having said that, some theorists and artists now feel a need to advance beyond the modern-postmodern debate, as in the case of those who have adopted the label of the 'altermodern', a topic I shall be turning to in Chapter 7.

So much for the cultural dimension to the breakdown; next, we turn to the economic, starting with an assessment of where Marxist theory fits into all of this, since that is the theory which has long been predicting that capitalism eventually would come crashing down.

Part II

The End of Modernity? The Economic Dimension

4
Marx was Right, But . . .

Marx's economic theories decreed that capitalism would collapse once the working classes came to realise the full extent of their exploitation by their unscrupulous employers. When that came to pass, they would then rise up against the political system that supported the capitalists' interests and overthrow their oppressors, instituting the dictatorship of the proletariat where they owned the means of production and banished exploitation once and for all. Although communism did succeed in taking over the political system, and means of production, in large parts of the world over the course of the first half of the twentieth century (Russia, China and Eastern Europe, for example), capitalism itself never did collapse as Marx had forecast, despite a series of severe socio-political and economic crises in the form of wars and recessions. The Great Depression, for example, really ought to have ignited a rebellion, having revealed the glaring contradictions underlying the system. Marxist theorists have speculated at length as to why capitalism has nevertheless managed to hang on, and have come up with some ingenious solutions, such as the concept of hegemony. The details of the concept will be discussed below, but it enabled theorists to argue that the revolution Marx had prophesied had merely been delayed for a while, assuring supporters there was nothing wrong with Marx's actual projections or the theories that had generated them: the dictatorship of the proletariat was still on its way.

We now face the most dramatic challenge to the free market system since the days of the Depression, and potentially an even more serious one. The Depression could be glossed over as a one-off event, the product of a society lacking a truly sophisticated understanding of economic systems, proceeding more by trial and error than with the scientific rigour we have since developed. The Depression gave us something to learn from and to test ourselves against if anomalies arose. But to go through something similar after we have been repeatedly assured that our financial institutions are now all but foolproof against such a collapse, that we would never repeat those earlier mistakes, certainly not on that scale, has to raise doubts about the structure of the overall system itself. Marx suddenly looks remarkably prescient again, particularly his claim that the system would implode under the weight of its contradictions: what else is a credit bubble but a mass of ultimately unresolvable contradictions?

So we could say Marx was right; but he was also wrong – in terms of his predictions as to what would happen next. Generally speaking, what has happened in such cases, as in the Depression, is that there is general public support to save the system – some dissenters notwithstanding. The actions of most Western governments in the last year or so seem to bear that observation out. We have all the conditions currently that from a Marxist perspective really ought to be leading to a large-scale social revolution but not, apparently, the political will or popular impetus to do so (or enough of either anyway). Whether the desire to resurrect the system will continue to work this time around, as it eventually did after the Depression, is an open question, however, and there is a genuine fear of social breakdown being expressed in the media at present. If some political commentators are to be believed, that breakdown may even occur in the middle classes (hardly a revolutionary minded group normally), angered enough at the effect of the credit crisis on their pension arrangements, property worth, career plans, etc., to take direct action against the governmental system in protest. How likely such a response would be in reality is doubtful, but the mere fact of this being discussed at all indicates just how deep the disaffection goes about how our financial system is performing. Old allegiances and behaviour patterns cannot necessarily be relied on any more: we are clearly in unprecedented conditions which could give rise to many surprises.

The validity of the Marxist analysis of economic breakdown patently needs to be reassessed, as does also the issue of why it does not seem to be generating the revolutionary consciousness predicted by the theory. Slavoj Žižek's interesting observation in *The Sublime Object of Ideology* that there is a psychological disposition to collude in failing political systems, as in the case of the citizens in communist countries almost right up to the very end of the Soviet era, provides one answer deserving to be tested against recent events. As he notes, 'they know that, in their activity, they are following an illusion, but still, they are doing it'.[1] Part of that illusion was that they had overcome the capitalist instinct, which the subsequent history of the ex-Soviet bloc suggests was more than somewhat wishful thinking: Russia has in fact spawned a particularly ruthless form of capitalism since the demise of the communist system, something of a throwback to capitalism's anarchic early days when there was very little check of the entrepreneurial class's actions. In a recent novel by Jeanette Winterson, *The Stone Gods*, one of the characters makes the intriguing claim that '[c]apitalism is like Japanese Knotweed: nothing kills it off. If there were only two people left on the planet, one of them would find a way of making money out of the other.'[2] The implications of such a view for our cultural future are certainly worth speculating upon.

Marx and the Critique of Capitalism

Marx's critique of capitalism is impressive in its scope and it laid the groundwork for communism as an international socio-political project in the twentieth century. Even if that project proved to be very disappointing overall (although not entirely without its successes, as in radically improved literacy levels and life-expectancy in countries like Russia and China), it constituted a clear alternative to capitalism and helped to shape the way that its adversary subsequently developed. At the very least capitalism had to admit it had a worthy rival with a coherent belief system behind it that was genuinely capable of attracting widespread public support – drawing in both workers and intellectuals across a range of countries around the globe. Capitalism had to think how to present itself to best advantage in order to deflect the criticisms being levelled against it by its ideological competitor; it had to be able to claim its road to material progress was superior, and that it had the evidence to prove it.

Marx made it clear how much the industrial proletariat were suffering in order to maximise the wealth of the employer class, and the social history of the period largely bears out what he says: the discrepancy between the lifestyles of the upper and lower classes in Western society at the time was stark. This is caught particularly well in *The Condition of the Working Class in England* by Marx's erstwhile collaborator Friedrich Engels, which catalogues at length the appalling deprivation to be found in England's industrial cities, such as Manchester, describing how the workers were trapped in 'dwellings in which cleanliness and comfort are impossible', in streets of 'the most miserable and filthy condition' where disease (as in regular cholera outbreaks) abounded.[3] Government studies of the period painted a very similar picture. Such exploitation could not continue indefinitely, in Marx's opinion, without inspiring a violent reaction – and communism would be the reaction that brought about the dictatorship of the proletariat and thus the end of such cynical treatment. There was a pattern to history, a dialectic working through it, which was propelling us towards that goal, and the more widely the fact was recognised by the working classes then the quicker it could be brought to fruition. Marx's work was a call to arms in this respect: 'Let the ruling classes tremble at a Communistic revolution. The proletarians have nothing to lose but their chains. They have a world to win. WORKING MEN OF ALL COUNTRIES, UNITE!'.[4]

Marx's argument was that labour produced surplus value, which was then accumulated by the employer class. This meant that every worker was being short-changed for his or her efforts, with the consequence, 'that to an increasing extent his own labour confronts him as another man's property'.[5] The more that employers were successful in keeping wages down, as well as workers' hours up, then the greater the surplus value they could succeed in stealing from their unfortunate employees; thus the employers' hatred of any attempt, as in trade union activity (or occasional government initiatives, however tentative they may have been), to improve the workers' lot. The two classes were set in opposition against each other, a class war in Marx's interpretation, with the moral right being firmly on the workers' side – they were the ones systematically being exploited after all. Only when this exploitation was eradicated from the system could we be said to have a properly just society in which alienation did not figure, and this was to be the goal of the communist project, to wrest the means of production away from the elite so that all could share the value created, the public good triumphing over the private.

There is a distinctly utopian side to Marx's thought which assumes that, given the right conditions, human beings will act in good faith towards each other and that the class war will wither away as all the advantages of the collective ideal become apparent. It is the capitalist system which is held responsible for bringing out some of the worst features in human nature, and once this is overcome and we lose its insidious influence then our characters will alter for the better, putting social needs before the personal. Yet Marx at the same time admired the opportunities that system offered to improve the quality of human life through the agency of technological progress. As he insisted in *The Communist Manifesto*,

> The bourgeoisie cannot exist without constantly revolutionising the instruments of production, and thereby the relations of production, and with them the whole relations of society. Conservation of the old modes of production in unaltered form, was, on the contrary, the first condition of existence for all earlier industrial classes. Constant revolutionising of production, uninterrupted disturbance of all social conditions, everlasting uncertainty and agitation distinguish the bourgeois epoch from all earlier ones. All fixed, fast-frozen relations, with their train of ancient

and venerable prejudices and opinions, are swept away, all new-formed ones become antiquated before they can ossify.[6]

A climate such as this is ripe for change, and Marx considered communism to be ideally placed to take advantage.

The Soviet bloc certainly saw technological progress as the way forward in the construction of a new type of society, and in that sense it was just as much a part of the project of modernity as were its Western adversaries (one could even claim that the Trotskyist-Maoist notion of 'permanent revolution' was a logical extension of the modernist programme and its obsession with unceasing progress, its refusal to rest on its achievements).[7] Hence such phenomena as the 'space race' to prove one's technological superiority to the rest of the watching world, and thus score valuable ideological points (which at least initially, with the launch of Sputnik, the Soviet Union did). It was not progress that was wrong, simply the capitalist method of pursuing that objective where the benefits were unequally spread among the populace. The Soviets preferred elaborately planned schemes with a centralised management structure rather than the market-driven entrepreneurial method, which in their eyes encouraged greed and then abuse of the power that financial success almost invariably granted.

Marx's critique of the capitalist system is an extremely powerful one, and it continues to command respect even today – sometimes in the most unlikely of contexts. As Francis Wheen points out in his acclaimed 1999 biography of Marx, even investment bankers have been known to praise his insights on the workings of capitalism in recent years, and 'right-wing economists and journalists have been queuing up to pay similar homage. Ignore all that communist nonsense, they say: Marx was really "a student of capitalism"'.[8] He was to be praised for being a particularly astute commentator about both the strengths and weaknesses of the capitalist system, who could still be read with interest if approached non-doctrinally. For such readers, you could agree with large stretches of Marx without feeling this made any case for communism as the answer to social injustice. In a way, it constituted a form of right-wing post-

Marxism, and one less critical than most of the left-wing variety. But it was the 'communist nonsense' that inspired generations of radicals, and there is no doubt that when it took hold it did not easily give up its grip on adherents, who felt compelled to give the theory the benefit of doubt when there was any significant mismatch with reality – as proved increasingly to be the case.

Hegemony: Explaining Away Capitalism's Survival

As time passed and global revolution failed to materialise, Marxist theorists turned increasingly to the concept of hegemony to explain why this was so. Hegemony argued that the ruling class managed to maintain control of the rest of the population through making its values seem the natural ones to which everyone should aspire. Class position was bypassed by this method, which achieved its aims not through force (which always remained the means of last resort, as in the use of the army or police force), but rather through a culture's various institutional systems – such as education, the media and the world of the arts. The values represented in these systems were those of the ruling class, and the objective was to make the populace internalise these ('into the ideological experience of Meaning and Truth', as Žižek has described the highly devious nature of the process)[9] such that they were unaware they were even doing so – to the extent that they were also unaware that those values could be challenged and were not simply 'natural'. When such systems were successful, as capitalist systems in the West were tending to be throughout most of the twentieth century despite the rise of communism elsewhere in the world, then the populace could be considered as trapped in a condition of false consciousness – helping to uphold an ideology that was against their best interests. Thus the ruling class could hold them in their power with a minimum of fuss, little overt show of that power being necessary.

For such theorists as Antonio Gramsci, hegemony constituted a particularly subtle form of class warfare that was hard to counteract:

In reality the State must be seen as an 'educator', in that it aims precisely to create a new type and level of civilisation. Because of the fact that it operates essentially on the economic forces . . . one must not draw the conclusion that the events of the superstructure must be abandoned to themselves, to their spontaneous development, to a haphazard and sporadic germination. In this field as well the State is an instrument of 'rationalisation' . . . it works according to a plan, it presses, it arouses, it urges.[10]

In other words, the dominant class of the state in our era (the bourgeoisie, as Marxists saw it) seeks to saturate society with its beliefs and values, such that the populace is confronted by them at every turn, not just in the workplace. With the state pressing, urging and arousing us with such energy and efficiency it becomes very difficult indeed to interpret the world in a different way to the dominant ideology. We are constantly being bombarded by the official line, such that we are caught up in the consensus it manufactures and can barely recognise that this is what is happening to us. False consciousness works against the growth of political dissent, which is precisely the state's objective.

Various other theorists, most notably Louis Althusser, proceeded to build upon Gramsci's work to demonstrate how capitalism still managed to hold much of the West in its power, even in the face of a series of economic and political crises that should really have shaken the system's credibility to the core. That was the problem, however, the system *did* continue to survive, and, as the century wore on, increasingly to thrive: to thrive, as well, at the apparent expense of its ideological enemy, whose credibility steadily declined, even among its own supporters. As Althusser described it, the Ideological State Apparatus (the combination of the institutions which disseminated the values approved by the political establishment) very effectively kept the populace in line, such that the Repressive State Apparatus that lay behind it – the various forces of law and order – rarely needed to be invoked: instead, the dominant ideology was experienced as natural and adhered to by more or less everyone.[11] A certain amount of dissent could be tolerated, to give the impression of freedom of expression, as long as it did not pose any really serious threat to the ruling ideology – licensed dissent, in other words, that the system could easily monitor and contain.

The long-awaited final crisis of capitalism never quite seemed to arrive, therefore, and that had to raise doubts about the validity of the theory that was claiming the inevitability of its collapse – and the longer the delay, then quite obviously the higher the incidence of doubt. There was a limit as to how long you could persuade even those sympathetic to the idea that the end was just round the corner if you could only keep faith. Althusser's reading of capitalist ideology was that it screened us from the real state of affairs, the exploitation taking place all around us on a systematic basis; it was *'a "Representation" of the Imaginary Relationship of Individuals to their Real Conditions of Existence'*.[12] So successful did he make the process sound, however, that it was difficult to see how we could ever break through it and bring the system down. Capitalism seemed to have cracked it as far as wielding power was concerned, making repression seem like normality: 'the school (but also the other state institutions like the Church, or other apparatuses like the Army) teaches "know-how", but in forms which ensure *subjection to the ruling ideology* or the mastery of its "practice"'.[13] Marx had predicted that the concept of the state eventually would wither away as communism took hold, but ironically it was Marxist theory that seemed to wither away as the twentieth century progressed.

Perhaps, as post-Marxists kept insisting, there wasn't a pattern to history after all – and, without that, Marxism lost much of its rationale as a social theory. As Gilles Deleuze and Felix Guattari put it, 'universal history is not only retrospective, it is also contingent, singular, ironic, and critical';[14] in other words, there is only a pattern if we work backwards. It was hegemony's manifest failure as a theory to rescue the notion of an unfolding pattern which helped to inspire the development of post-Marxism, as in Laclau and Mouffe's spirited dissection of its chequered history in *Hegemony and Socialist Strategy*.[15] Some went on to argue that 'Marxism is not a "science of history"' either, which prompted some interesting questions.[16] If there was no pattern then why sign up to fight the class war? If it was not a science then why accept its reading of what was happening over any other, or its predictions either? The emphasis on the 'event', by such as Lyotard, the sheer unpredictability of what would happen next, represented a rejection of the dialectic: 'It is time to get rid of the illusion that universal history provides the universal tribunal, that some last judgement is prepared and fulfilled in history.'[17] If the future was entirely open, merely a succession of indeterminable events, then Marxism had no claim to superiority over other social theories, and that was the line taken by the leading post-Marxists.

Some post-Marxists were positive about the theory's apparent fall from grace – Laclau and Mouffe, for example, who thought it could be revised and still act as an inspiration to those fighting social injustice:

> We are living . . . one of the most exhilarating moments of the twentieth century: a moment in which new generations, without the prejudices of the past, without theories presenting themselves as 'absolute truths' of History, are constructing new emancipatory discourses, more human, diversified and democratic.[18]

But for others, such as Lyotard and Michel Foucault, the openness of the future was a reason to discard Marxism altogether, with the latter dismissing the theory's 'revolutionary promise' as meaningless outside its nineteenth-century context.[19] The world had changed and deterministic theories no longer had any intellectual purchase to speak of: that was the message of a new generation of sceptical thinkers. We had come to realise in the interim just how messy history and human behaviour in reality were, how far removed from grandiose theoretical projections such as Marx and his disciples had indulged in.

The financial crisis certainly seems to have conformed to Lyotard's conception of the event – 'the impact, on the system, of floods of energy such that the system does not manage to bind and channel this energy . . . the traumatic encounter of energy with the regulating institution'.[20] The financial world was overwhelmed in much the way the concept intimated, and for all concerned it was an undeniably traumatic experience to discover just how power-less they actually were, anything but the masters of the financial universe they had liked to believe themselves. Marxists would want to claim that their theory had predicted such an event would occur, that capitalism's internal contradictions finally had caught up with it and generated the full-scale breakdown they always knew it would; although, as just discussed above, the time lag involved does make one wonder how useful the theory really is as a socio-political guide. But more to the point, the crisis suggests unpredictability as much as anything – not so much a dialectical pattern that was unfolding, rather something much closer to chaos. I would argue it was more like being confronted by the sublime, a force which conforms to no known pattern or set of predictions, or to human manipulation either. It is a notion I will be exploring in more detail in Chapter 6.

Žižek: The Problem of Collusion

Žižek's interpretation of hegemony is more intriguing than standard Marxist accounts, because it implicates the population of communist countries in the system's survival – although in a very sympathetic way as far as the general public is concerned, recognising their lack of any real political power under such regimes. The problem was, as Žižek pithily summed it up, that in communist states,

> we have a circular definition of the People: in the Stalinist universe, 'supporting the rule of the Party' is 'rigidly designated' by the term 'People' – it is, in the last analysis, *the only feature which in all possible worlds defines the People* . . . [T]he People always support the Party because any member of the People who opposes Party rule automatically excludes himself from the People.[21]

Anyone within a communist state realises that they will have to work very hard to carve out any sense of meaningful political exist-ence within such a heavily regulated system (especially if they are not in the Party), and that this may well involve stretching cred-ibility quite a bit – perhaps even to the point of having to develop a schizophrenic personality. Failure to do so might even threaten one's survival. As one might expect, this will call for more than a certain amount of ingenuity in how an individual sets about constructing his or her relation to the Party as a member of the People.

Žižek succeeds in giving us a very persuasive psychological explanation as to how even very poorly functioning political systems, such as the Yugoslavia that he was brought up in, can generate at least a semblance of loyalty and commitment among those who have to suffer from its imperfections. In Žižek's reading, the system depended on the general public identifying with it enough to gloss over its easily identifiable and, in terms of daily life, often extremely frustrating faults. This is indeed what happened in much of the Soviet empire as a way of trying to prove to oneself that you had some degree of control over your existence, that you were more than just a mere pawn in the ruling communist party's ideological game. Whereas Marx had contended that the working class was largely oblivious to the fact they were reproducing the dominant ideology in their daily lives (essentially the line also taken by Althusser), Žižek sees a different attitude developing under communism: 'they know that their idea of Freedom is masking a form of exploitation, but still they continue to follow this idea of Freedom'.[22] For an individual to admit to the complete failure of the system was to imply the complete failure of his or her own life too. To defend the system, even half-heartedly as so often was the case, was to gain at least some feeling of empowerment, of having a stake in what had happened and how the state had developed, no matter how qualified it may have been. It may have been an illusion, but it was an illusion providing a certain amount of psychological comfort for many who had no other means of expressing themselves politically under a totalitarian system: an 'enlightened false consciousness' as Žižek described it, paradoxical as that may sound.[23]

Once any political system manages to establish itself, no matter how authoritarian it may be, it is capable of eliciting such support as this, and we have to allow for that possibility in the current economic crisis also: that modernity will exert at least a residual pull on the public's loyalties no matter how obvious its failings have become or how dire its performance. It may be a failed system, but it is *our* failed system, and it is psychologically very difficult to detach ourselves from it – never mind to admit that we may have been living a lie for most of our lives. Public nostalgia for the boom years of modernity cannot be discounted as a significant factor in our response to the credit crunch: conspicuous consumption still has its devotees, and they will be highly receptive to arguments offering them anything like a return to normal service. Enlightened false consciousness actively, and possibly more than a little desperately, will be seeking reinforcement for its illusions.

Capitalism as Knotweed?

Is capitalism to be treated as something like Japanese knotweed? As so deeply embedded in our make-up that it can never be entirely expunged from social experience, no matter how hard we may try? Or no matter what crises happen to befall it? That would be to say the urge to exploit is always a factor in human affairs, and there is a wealth of historical evidence that this is indeed so, even if the urge has not always revealed itself in a specifically capitalist manner. Capitalism in many ways has constituted a more benign method of channelling the competitive instinct than other forms found throughout history, such as war and conquest. Which is not to say that it has not involved human suffering, as it patently has (war and conquest on occasion too), but in relative terms it could be said to be preferable to other forms of human exploitation – even if I agree this is the most grudging of testimonials to offer on its behalf.

Yet there is another way of looking at this issue, which is to accept that the exploitative urge may well be deeply embedded in us but that it is nevertheless subject to control, and need not be allowed completely free rein. Japanese Knotweed may well be ineradicable, but at the same time it does not rule our lives, and can at least be contained – as long as we do not encourage it. So, we might argue, can the exploitative imperative within us that has manifested itself in modern culture as free market capitalism. We do not have to accept it as our fate for capitalism to have no limits placed on its expression, as has been the approved policy for some time now around most of the globe in the wake of Friedmanite economics, any more than we would, for example, with the urge to violence, which is certainly at least as much encoded within our nature (male anyway).

Perhaps we need to look again at models such as the Chinese, where capitalism is a state-directed phenomenon with very clearly defined objectives and targets. There is probably too much of the command economy method about this for comfort, certainly for the West (although it would probably better be defined as planned). But in the current climate we cannot afford to go back to the hands-off approach favoured by most Western governments of late, and should acknowledge that a degree of centralisation is a necessary element in running any economy. The trick has to be to prevent centralisation from turning authoritarian. In the West at the moment we have certainly moved past the mixed economy, where government schemes co-exist with the free market, to something which might even be described as 'semi-command', at least as far as the banking sector and money supply is concerned. Neoliberals do not like the mixed economy, and are even less enamoured of the semi-command: as Simon Tilford of the Centre for European Reform (a London-based think-tank) has complained, '[w]hat we risk seeing . . . is more regulation, less competition, more state intervention and rising opposition to immigration. All this bodes ill for Europe's economic future.'[24] Yet if we have to rescue the banks then surely we should have some kind of say, through elected politicians, in how they are run and what their trading policies should be. (I will be returning to the issue of the command economy, its pros and cons, in Chapter 8.)

We can conclude that Marx's diagnosis was largely right about the nature and likelihood of economic breakdown in the capitalist sector therefore, but not about its aftermath. So what was the diagnosis of those inside the market system as to its future? That forms the next topic.

5
Diagnosing the Market: Fundamentalism as Cure, Fundamentalism as Disease

D espite the credit crunch, there are still arguments being put forward in support of the unregulated free market by some economists. Their line is that the market must be left free to correct itself (the notion of the 'invisible hand'),[1] and that eventually it will do so, regardless of how bad the crisis appears to be at present, leaving the market a leaner and more efficient organism than it was before: the 'survival of the fittest' in publicly visible operation. The market will cure itself of any disease that may arise. It is accepted by such thinkers that some companies which have overstretched themselves will go under, especially if this has led to them being dramatically overvalued in terms of their share price. The dictum that the stock market can go up as well as down is taken very seriously by neoliberal economists, who see it as simply part of the natural order of things that there are cycles of boom and bust, and that the human cost of the latter just has to be borne, much like other natural phenomena such as the weather. We have no alternative but to respect the autonomy of the market and adapt ourselves to its patterns as best we can: first and foremost we are *Homo economicus*, so that is our destiny.

From this perspective, for governments to intervene in the market is to corrupt the mechanism of the invisible hand and, by providing a safety net, to encourage recklessness on the part of both corporations and investors – the condition known as 'moral hazard' (defined by John Maynard Keynes as the 'voluntary default or other means of escape, possibly lawful, from the fulfil-ment of the obligation' undertaken by the market participant).[2] Instead, the line of reasoning goes, institutions should be fully exposed to risk, knowing they will have to take the ultimate responsibility for the consequences of their actions – such as the loss of their money if they make rash or ill-chosen investments. For market fundamentalists, there can be no failure of the market itself, merely bad judgements by misguided human beings who must then pay the penalty of financial loss – and, it is assumed, learn from their mistakes in consequence. Moral hazard under-mines the efficiency of markets.

Whether such arguments still hold up if the entire banking system faces collapse will now be explored. This was thought to be imminent at the worst point of the crisis in 2008, and is still a distinct possibility if the situation worsens again, as it all too easily could: we might just wonder what aftershocks to our financial earthquake could still be in store for us. Yet even economists who are critical of the actions of banks and hedge funds in bringing about the crisis can argue that all that is needed is a measure of reform rather than any wholesale reassessment of how banking operates. In this latter camp are such eminent figures as the Nobel Prize-winning American economist Paul Krugman, whose views can be analysed as representative of the pragmatic approach to economic crisis. The question that now arises, however, is whether pragmatism is a realistic response to a potentially apocalyptic situ-ation which subverts traditional economic wisdom; whether it is a diagnosis going deep enough. Is it really just a case of making a few adjustments and then springing back to normal? Of 'fixing' global finance, as one commentator insists is a perfectly possible project if we all put our minds to it?[3] Or are we facing something far more fundamental? Many commentators are starting to gravi-tate towards the latter position, that we are dealing with a disease which lies beyond the market's ability to cure, one embedded in the market's DNA as it were, and I shall be exploring such views later in the chapter.

Moral Hazard

Much has been made of the concept of moral hazard recently, with fundamentalists claiming this is what government intervention in the workings of the market creates. The fundamentalist position is that we must be prepared to take risks in the market, but also accept that if these go wrong we are willing to pay the resultant penalty. Taking risks is an integral part of playing the market, and all banks and investment houses have incorporated this into their business strategy. Without risk, the wisdom goes, there can be no hope of making a substantial gain on the market, and that is precisely what all investors are looking for, to maximise their gains – preferably by making some killing in the market at the expense of their competitors. Stock markets have always worked this way, but what has changed in recent times has been the degree of risk that organisations were prepared to take in pursuit of ever-larger profits on their investments. Traders have been inspired to take greater risks by the advent of the bonus culture, which offers huge rewards for being bold in the market. Bonuses regularly amount to far more than the wages being paid in such jobs, reaching levels which spur traders on to new and more daring levels of speculation with their companies' assets in order to boost their own bank balances as well as their employer's.

The problem with this system, it has since transpired, is that it has been very light on failure, which seems to carry few penalties. Much to the public's disgust, bonuses have continued to be paid even in the aftermath of market meltdown, despite government insistence that they should not be, the argument being that this is now an expected part of employment practice in the financial sector and that staff will leave if this is is not forthcoming (not such a bad thing, many in the general public would probably think, perhaps also wondering who else would want to take them on). The only way in which penalties have come into play has been in job losses when firms have not been rescued by public money, as with Lehmann Brothers and some other hedge funds which have gone to the wall. In banks, however, the practice has tended to be

continued, even when it is public money that is propping the industry up – as it appears to be in most cases now in the Western world.
Many of the senior staff have maintained their positions despite the
crisis (or left on a generous pension or pay-off), although significant
job losses have occurred much lower down the food chain with sala-
ried staff who never shared in the bonus culture to any significant
degree. Responsibility for creating this situation is something most
bankers have studiously avoided admitting; apologies tend to be
at best vague, and very general (sorry that it has happened rather
than that they were instrumental in causing it). A few high-profile
cases notwithstanding, most of the top management is still in place
– public disapproval notwithstanding. If moral hazard has revealed
anything, it is just how little moral conscience exists in the upper
echelons of the financial sector: they seem to feel under little obligation for having been offered a handy 'means of escape' from their
desperate predicament.

Yet it is hard to see why there is so much objection to government
involvement in the market when we accept it so readily in so many
other areas of our lives. One rarely hears arguments that having
a police force makes us more careless and eats away at our moral
fibre. Yes, there is an encroachment on our personal freedom in
such cases, certain restrictions on what we can and cannot do, but it
is compensated for by the greater sense of security that all of us feel
in our everyday lives. It is a mark of a civilised society, moreover,
that it does have safety nets to protect its citizens from misfortune,
which can befall anyone at some point in their lives, even if there is
always disagreement between the left and right ends of the political
spectrum as to how extensive these should be, and whether they
should always be under government control. Some on the far right
do claim that safety nets lead to a culture of dependence, the equivalent of moral hazard one could say, but all Western societies have
adopted them to some degree, and there is general acceptance that
there must be a measure of them in place.

Similarly, there is a recognition that government-backed regulation is to the public benefit when it comes to things like health and
safety (as in food and drug acts or workplace codes). Again, this

does not make us reckless, rather it adds a further layer of security to our lives. Regulation can become excessive and bureaucratic, and we should campaign against it when it does, but the principle of it is still worth defending. For the market to go unregulated, as fundamentalists demand, goes against everything we have learned about how society works: without rules and regulations, and some official body to back them up, things can all too quickly descend into anarchy. Not everyone can be trusted to act consistently in the public interest, not everyone has a properly developed moral conscience: they may be a minority, but they are a minority the rest of us need protection against.

Hedge Funds: For and Against

So what mechanisms do exist to effect an internal cure of market problems? For the true believer, hedge funds are necessary to the health of the system, providing a corrective to the inflated claims often made by companies in order to push up their share price and make them more attractive to investors. Hedge funds are investment vehicles where managers play the market using money deposited by their client body. Since those deposits are required to be very substantial, it is essentially a wealthy person's pastime. Being largely outside the regulatory framework of the financial sector gives hedge funds considerable freedom of action, as a recent detailed study of the phenomenon makes clear:

> With the freedom to trade as much or as little as they like on any given day, to go long or short any number of securities and with varying degrees of leverage, and to change investment strategies at a moment's notice, hedge fund managers enjoy enormous flexibility and discretion in pursuing performance.[4]

Hedge funds are therefore well placed to test the truth of the claims being made, and it could be argued that they performed that function highly effectively in the early days of the current crisis by drawing attention to the very significant overvaluation of many companies – particularly banks caught up in the sub-prime mortgage network (as most of the world's major banks subsequently have turned out to be). The banks themselves were hardly going to admit to their overvaluation: that was not in their own interest, since it would act as a deterrent to investors – public image is all in these situations. It was possible to make a case for hedge funds almost as the conscience of the market under those circumstances.

The other side of hedge funds, however, is their ability to destabilise. Markets can be volatile at the best of times, but frantic hedge fund activity can create panic among the investment community. As Andrew W. Lo, the author of the study mentioned above, notes:

> [U]nlike banks, hedge funds can decide to withdraw liquidity at a moment's notice, and while this may be benign if it occurs rarely and randomly, a coordinated withdrawal of liquidity among an entire sector of hedge funds could have disastrous consequences for the viability of the financial system if it occurs at the wrong time and in the wrong place.[5]

The invisible hand is not always in evidence in such cases, and real damage can be done, not just to individual companies but to the overall operation of the market itself, which can often take a long time to recover from the resulting turmoil. When it came to the credit crunch, therefore, hedge funds did not just help to reveal its existence, they also helped to create it – certainly to make it worse than initially it was. Hedge funds were, for example, deeply implicated in 'short selling', betting against a fall in a company's stock market value with stock temporarily borrowed from its owner (usually a brokerage house), the understanding being that if the price falls then the short seller pockets the difference between the new price and the old. It was a practice that clearly got out of hand once the market started to slump, turning into one of the main reasons why so many large corporations proceeded to run into serious trouble. The effect was to drive stock market prices down across the board, casting hedge funds in the role of villains and prompting several governments – most notably the American and British – to take action against the practice.

Yet short selling is entirely consistent with the market fundamentalist ethos, which positively encourages such predatory activity (as it would appear to most outside observers, certainly to non-market players), by demanding as unregulated a framework for financial dealings as it can get away with. That means it has its defenders in high places, with the chairman of the UK's Financial Services Authority, a regulatory body set up by the government, referring to the practice as a 'necessary and desirable underpinning to the liquidity of the London market'.[6] There were few checks on short selling until well into the crisis, not until it became abundantly clear that it was undermining rather than underpinning liquidity. The longer-term health of the market is not a concern of short-sellers, immediate gain is, and they will pursue that objective single-mindedly whatever the cost to competitors. Again, moral conscience does not loom particularly large. A market dominated by hedge funds is therefore a market heading for trouble: it is an example of market fundamentalism at its anti-social worst, especially since a downturn in the market is to the benefit of funds which have bet on this eventuality coming to pass. We enter something of a mirror-image world at such points, with failure turning into a source of economic success – for some, anyway. For most of us outside the inner circle of the market this can only appear a bizarre state of affairs, almost the opposite of what we think the market is actually there for.

Interpreting the Credit Crisis

As one might expect, the credit crisis, or 'crash' as it is also being dubbed, has generated a string of interpretations from the economics community, and books have been coming out steadily in its wake. I will now consider some of the most important of these. One of the most thoughtful responses has come from Paul Krugman in his book *The Return of Depression Economics and the Crisis of 2008*. The fact that this is an expansion of an earlier book, published in 1999 and outlining the potential dangers to the world economic order revealed by the Southeast Asian economic crisis of the later 1990s, indicates that Krugman is an acute observer of the scene whose prescience is to be admired. That the lessons of the earlier situation had not been taken to heart clearly pains the author, who had warned us back then that it would be 'foolish' not to reconsider how we were running the global economic system:

> At the time, I thought of it this way: it was as if bacteria that used to cause deadly plagues, but had long since been considered conquered by modern medicine, had reemerged in a form resistant to all the standard antibiotics . . . Well, we were foolish. And now the plague is upon us.[7]

The plague metaphor is only too apt, since the current crisis has been transmitted from country to country with amazing speed, encountering almost no meaningful resistance on its way. No country has proved immune from the problem, and none has been able to insulate itself from the likelihood of further attacks – and such events have been occurring with depressing regularity over the last couple of years.

Krugman's original study looked at not just the Southeast Asian crisis but the series of crises that had marked out the 1990s, such as in Mexico and Argentina. Although emphasising that politicians had to shoulder at least some of the blame for creating the conditions for crisis, Krugman is also very critical of international speculators, such as George Soros, for their role in preying on weak economies and thus destabilising the world political order. Soros is notorious for his role in humiliating the British government over its financial policy in 1992, forcing an effective devaluation of the British currency in the process as the UK was forced to withdraw from the EU's Exchange Rate Mechanism, and I will be considering his role in the debate in more detail below.

Krugman tries hard to be rational and pragmatic about the economic 'plague' we are now suffering, but on occasion a note of genuine unease creeps into his analysis:

> We're not in a depression now, and despite everything, I don't think we're heading into one (although I'm not as sure of that as I'd like to be). We are, however, well into the realm of depression economics.[8]

Depression economics turns out to be a situation of falling demand, to the extent that it begins to lag very significantly behind each country's production capability – the obvious implication of which is that unemployment soars and then tax revenues fall, dragging the economy even further down. The first step in dealing with this state of affairs, Krugman argues, is to 'get credit flowing again and prop up spending':[9] in other words, to go back to the prescriptions that Keynes recommended for combatting the Depression (and subsequently put into practice in the Roosevelt administration's New Deal programme). As various governments around the globe have been discovering, however, this is far easier said than done – even when the banks have been taken into what is effectively public control (as has happened particularly widely in the UK). Stimulus packages do not always have the desired effect, either on the banking community or the general public, no matter how upbeat politicians may try to sound.

It also has to be noted that the instinct of most conservative politicians in such instances is to rein in on government spending rather than increase it, on the grounds that it is simply manufacturing problems for subsequent generations if huge budget deficits are run up now – the long-term being sacrificed to the short-term, future generations to the current one. Such arguments are certainly being voiced regularly around the West at present. This policy does little to prompt individuals to spend either, and the general tendency is for savings to increase instead. On that latter point, however, we now face the interesting prospect in an era of banking collapse of such savings not being so safe as we had always assumed they were in the past, adding a further layer to public anxiety.

Krugman nevertheless is confident that we can work our way out of the crisis of 2008 if we apply the primary lesson the last depression taught us, which is to do our utmost to deploy the spare capacity for production of goods and services that a major economic downturn brings in its wake – making a virtue out of adversity, as it were. Rather daringly, he argues that 'there *is* a free lunch, if we can only figure out how to get our hands on it'.[10] Ultimately, any solution will have to come from the realm of ideas, with Krugman maintaining that the problem is not really a structural one in the economic system itself: 'I believe that the only important structural obstacles to world prosperity are the obsolete doctrines that clutter

79

the minds of men'.[11] It is an optimistic conclusion, and one which most of the West's political class will be only too glad to embrace, but it does make some questionable assumptions – such as that a credit crisis is not evidence of a structural problem, or that world prosperity is an unproblematically sustainable objective in terms of both resources and the environment.

I would want to argue instead that what we are now facing up to *is* intrinsically a structural problem – a structural problem lying at the very heart of modernity as a socio-political project, and which has become more pronounced with time until it cannot be ignored any more. It is an entire ideology that needs to be addressed, the ideology of constant material progress, not just some abuses of it that have momentarily distorted its otherwise socially unexceptionable operations. When it comes to using resources, such as fossil fuels, which contribute very significantly to global warming, then there manifestly is no such thing as a free lunch; even green energy does not give us that, although it is undeniably cleaner overall, if untested on the larger scale as yet. Energy usage in the name of maximising world prosperity has consequences – and fairly drastic ones as we are somewhat belatedly coming to realise.

Krugman is a subtle thinker with a deep and impressive understanding of the global economic system, but it has to be noted that his conclusion hides the bigger picture from us. Economic goals can no longer be divorced from their environmental impact, and that impact can only become more adverse if we think it is just a matter of reforming the existing economic system and then carrying on with business much as before. We have to recognise that spending more means warming more, and that every credit bubble plays its part in exaggerating the problem by encouraging greed and excessive consumption: a growing GDP is a warning sign as much as anything else (anathema though that may be to the average politician). There can be no quick fix for modernity, and we need to acknowledge the fact sooner rather than later. Even if the economic system is patched up, modernity's internal contradictions will not go away – at some point they will return to haunt us.

Others have been more inclined to see the crisis as a systemic failure. Gillian Tett, for example, refers scathingly in *Fool's Gold* to a financial system that had become 'detached from the rest of society', rewriting the rules for its own benefit with scant regard for the public interest.[12] It is not an attractive picture she gives us of what has been going on behind the scenes in the industry, and she can hardly contain her astonishment that this was ever allowed to happen, that no-one in responsible positions could seem to recognise the dangers their increasingly byzantine trading practices were creating: 'Were the bankers mad? Blind? Evil. Or were they simply grotesquely greedy?'[13] The answer is a bit of each, but for Tett the larger problem is that the system itself was deeply compromised internally, 'as a result of flawed incentives within banks and investment funds, as well as the ratings agencies; warped regulatory structures; and a lack of oversight'.[14] Failure on an epic scale it would appear.

Tett plunges us into the mysterious world of credit derivatives, a product destined to play a critical role in precipitating the crisis. Derivatives involve trading in the risk on loans, with other parties agreeing, for a fee, to take on the risk (of default, etc.) from the lender. The risk can even be split up and traded on to others in turn, and it can develop into quite a complicated chain of liability. Even for an experienced financial journalist this is at best 'murky' territory, and it becomes evident over the course of her researches that it was so for most of the rest of the financial world too.[15] The history of derivatives in our era begins to sound very much like a detective story, with Tett searching for clues as to how and why the product came to gain such a hold on the financial community that it could go on to generate the chaos that ultimately it did. Derivatives as such were not a new idea and go well back into financial history, but it was not until the later twentieth century that they began to attract such sustained attention from finance houses and for conditions to emerge favouring experimentation with their form. With the pressure to deregulate growing steadily stronger, lucrative new markets soon arose and derivatives proceeded to become ever more sophisticated, eventually constituting a very substantial part of the business of the financial sector. As Tett points out, however, they were not entirely predictable in terms of their operation: 'The crucial point about derivatives was that they could do two things: help investors *reduce* risk or create a good deal *more* risk.'[16] Just how much risk they were capable of creating, and on what scale, we have only latterly come to recognise. Innovation is one thing, but laying waste to the entire global economic system is something else again: as Tett points out, giving derivatives' developers their head went on to 'fuel a boom beyond all bounds of rational constraint – or self-discipline'.[17] A case of modernity in overdrive, we might say.

One of the most damning points to come out of Tett's book is how divorced the financial sector had become from the everyday world by the twenty-first century. Finance had turned into a highly abstract subject that barely seemed to touch on the lives of the general public, a hard science in the eyes of its practitioners that only the professional elite could hope to make any sense of, being all but impenetrable to outsiders (even most financial journalists it would seem in retrospect). This tended to dissolve all sense of social responsibility on the part of the players, with the result that they began to see their industry as a law unto itself, above both politics and the public interest.

Fool's Gold is a depressing book in many ways in revealing just how much power had been ceded to the financial community by politicians and regulators, and in particular to the industry's teams of bright young whizz-kids, whose innovations became so complex that almost no-one outside the teams themselves could quite understand how they actually worked. Even the higher managements involved had only the sketchiest idea of what these departments of their business were doing. Sadly, despite the occasional qualm on the part of the higher-ups, that did not stop those schemes from being almost universally adopted by the major banks and financial houses, and then pushed hard to investors who were led to believe they were witnessing nothing less than a revolution in trading practices.

What one insider called the 'group-think' at work inside banking houses meant that once a process like this got under way it became very hard to halt. [18] Dissenting voices tended to be brushed aside as old-fashioned, naive, or just plain disloyal to the cause, especially when huge profits started to materialise in the derivatives markets as the new products caught the imagination of both traders and investors. Soon everyone wanted to jump on the bandwagon, confident in the claims being made that risk had been minimised to the point where it was hardly a significant factor in investment any more. (The highly respected, as well as highly successful, American investment fund manager Warren Buffet was one such sceptic of the new methods, going so far as to describe derivatives as 'financial weapons of mass destruction', but even he was ignored.[19] 'These guys are *dinosaurs*' was a not untypical response from the converted to those resisting the onward march of derivatives).[20]

Even more sadly, however, for the general public it did turn out to be fool's gold at the end of the day. Risk had not been tamed once and for all; indeed, it had reasserted itself with a vengeance, leaving a trail of devastation in its wake. As Tett bleakly concludes, '[a] new era of finance has dawned – albeit not one that most bankers had ever expected, far less wanted, to see'.[21] But it is not the bankers who will have to pick up the pieces of the 'shattered global markets' proclaimed in Tett's subtitle: rather it is the general public who have been left to cover the almost unimaginable (unless you think naturally in trillions) bundle of toxic debts resulting from the industry's excesses. It is hardly an example of social justice, and it is small wonder that there is widespread public anger at the outcome (tempered to some extent by a sense of resignation that there seems to be no alternative way of protecting one's savings).

Tett suggests a horrified fascination with the way everything slipped so comprehensively out of control in the financial world, and with the generally woeful response of everyone involved in the affair – bankers, brokers, hedge fund proprietors, regulators, politicians, all seemed inadequate to the task at hand, blinded by their faith in free market economics to the severity of the crisis brewing right under their noses. Ultimately, she decides it is a lack of social responsibility that is the most important source of the crisis, resulting in the market coming to be viewed by the financial industry as an end in itself rather than a means to improve the human lot. (The unwillingness of banks in the UK to join together as a consortium to cover the debts of a failing peer and thus openly demonstrate their social responsibility, as was suggested by negotiators on several occasions during the crisis [and did happen in Germany in 2007], speaks volumes: the competitive instinct was simply too deeply embedded in the institutions to recognise the public relations value that such a gesture undoubtedly would have had.) The human dimension had been lost sight of in the hectic scramble for growth, progress, innovation – the key objectives of modernity that we had been taught to regard as sacrosanct, as being beyond all questioning as to their validity. This was modernity reduced to its basics, and it was not a pretty sight: 'a terrible, damning indictment of how twenty-first century Western society works', as Tett feels compelled to observe after her journey into the desperately murky depths of cyberfinance.[22] By any standards, the system had failed us.

Philip Augar, too, puts the blame squarely on the system that was allowed to develop in financial centres such as the City of London, which prided itself on being the world leader in this respect:

> 'Alpha' is shorthand in the City for supercharged profit and 'chasing alpha' is what Britain's bankers, investors and corporate chief executives did in the last two decades of the 20th century and the opening years of this millenium, culminating between 2003 and 2007 in an orgy of leverage and reckless growth plans . . . It seemed too good to be true and it was.[23]

Again, we have teams of bright young things being given their head in the scramble to make a killing in the market, with rational constraint and self-discipline being cast to the wind: 'The financial services industry was on a roll, and it was neither fashionable nor, in the heat of the moment, considered credible to question its business model.'[24] The City of London in particular became derivatives-happy, and in a trading context considerably less regulated than its American counterpart (successive British governments doing their best to turn the City into the international capital of finance as a way of boosting the national economy) the financial business boomed as it had never done before. Funds flooded into London in unprecedented quantities.

The industry really did feel that it had discovered the ultimate free lunch: risk of default on loans was now felt to be a condition belonging to the past, with a bright new, apparently all-but-risk-free future opening up for banks and credit institutions. That huge fees also accompanied the frenzied trading going on in these products as they circulated round the globe only helped to accelerate the boom, the bonus culture coming into its own. The British economy did appear to prosper in consequence, and the government could congratulate itself on the apparent success of its 'light touch' approach to the City. The official line was that the boom-and-bust cycle was essentially over, and that we could now depend on the City to deliver lasting financial success. But, as Augar concludes, this 'was shown in 2007–8 to have been a mirage, an alluring figment of the imagination that had shimmered during the bull market years but then evaporated'.[25] To keep up with the market-speak, we now found ourselves with a very different cross to bear.

Critical though he is of the City, and convinced that it was guilty of a system failure in this instance, Augar still believes it can be resurrected after the crisis, if in a less powerful form than before. When that happens, it can then resume being a significant contributor to the national economy, if not perhaps on the scale the government had hoped. That does depend on whether the lid can be kept on greed, however (as Augar remarks elsewhere, '[t]he money paid to brokers is a social and moral disgrace'),[26] and on the market's gravitational pull towards chasing alpha. Augar feels we can exonerate many of the leading financial executives' actions on the grounds that they could hardly refuse to adopt the same policy in a bull market as their competitors, that their shareholders would not accept a cautious approach when others were apparently piling up vast profits by going for broke. But that is the root of the problem; alpha is always going to cast a spell in the market, and it encourages herd-like conformity rather than rational calculation. Who would bet against this happening again if the markets were once more set free? Perhaps the system failure goes even deeper than Augar thinks.

Paul Mason is no less scathing of the financial sector's practices at the latter end of the boom years, as his book's title *Meltdown* would suggest, although he thinks the blame goes far wider than that:

> People in the finance industry may act like they are the masters of the universe, but that is, in a way, because the rest of us have let them take that role . . . The responsibility for what happened must lie, as well as with any banker found to have broken the law, with regulators, politicians and the media who failed to hold them up to scrutiny.[27]

It is not just the system which has failed, therefore, but the entire social apparatus lying behind it, and in Mason's view that just has to change: 'Basically, neoliberalism is over: as an ideology, as an economic model. Get used to it and move on.'[28] Taking neoliberalism to be a particularly purist interpretation of economic modernity, I can only agree.

Mason's is an unashamedly apocalyptic vision, in which we are said to be witnessing nothing less than 'the collapse of free-market capitalism'.[29] He confesses to being a lifelong sceptic of the economics of the free market, and is clearly quite happy to be observing and recording its demise (an 'extinction level event' as he gleefully reports a fund manager describing it in the darkest days of the crisis),[30] while also registering his impatience with the political class for failing to recognise that this is what is actually occurring and then altering their policies to fit. Rather like generals who fight wars on the experience of the previous one, generally with disastrous results, politicians, in league with the financial industry, are operating on the basis that this is simply yet another instalment in the 'boom-and-bust' cycle with which we have become so familiar in modern times, and that it can be 'fixed' as it has been before. Mason is of a radically different opinion, criticising what for him is a 'fatal . . . attachment to the old ideas and strategy' that must be shown up for the false consciousness that it is, 'a whole era of financial hypocrisy' as far as he is concerned.[31] From his perspective it is simply so much wasted effort trying to salvage the neoliberal market system, and he tears into those who continue to think it is with some gusto.

Mason's solution to moving past neoliberalism, drawing on the work of the controversial American economist Hyman P. Minsky, is to nationalise the banks and turn the industry into the equivalent of a public utility. Money and credit have to be accessible to all if our kind of society is to function properly, just as water and electricity are: we cannot allow ourselves to be held to ransom by speculators in such areas; the public interest must take precedence. (One might put in the qualification that, although credit should be accessible, we should be careful not to let it get out of hand, as it clearly did just before the crash in the UK to the extent where total household debt was running 50 per cent higher than the nation's GDP – a situation just asking for trouble if the market faltered.) Hedge funds and investment banks could continue to exist under the new setup, but would be kept strictly separate from the main banking system; this is what Mason refers to as '[t]he Minsky alternative – a socialised banking system plus redistribution'.[32] This would be the first step towards achieving a greater sense of social justice in our culture, rather than allowing self-interest to dominate as it has been doing under a neoliberal dispensation. As Mason points out, capitalism can take many forms, and there is no reason at all why we should feel we have to persevere with the neoliberal version. Again, I can only register my wholehearted agreement.

Larry Elliott and Dan Atkinson also have an apocalyptic vision to communicate in their analysis of the crisis, *The Gods That Failed*, but adopt a tone of mockery against those who have brought the global economy to its knees: 'We call these people the New Olympians, so named because of their remoteness from everyday life and their lack of accountability and because of the faith to which they subscribe.'[33] The New Olympians have gained power on a false prospectus, gulled us with 'exotic securities' and generally treated the public with open contempt.[34] Elliott and Atkinson concede that if the New Olympians had delivered improved living standards across the board then there would at least be room for some debate as to whether we agreed with their objectives and methods, but the critical point is that they have failed to do so. Instead, '[c]hronic financial instability and the prospect of, at the best, years of sluggish economic activity as we pay off borrowings of a debt-burdened society are the fruits of their guidance'.[35] We shall have to get used to the waste land for quite some time yet.

Elliott and Atkinson do not believe the financial system can be reformed from within, and reject all claims by politicians to that effect. We simply cannot trust a sector run by characters who, in one of the authors' more knockabout phrases, 'aren't all quite human'.[36] Real reform would mean bringing the New Olympians 'back under democratic control' and specifying very precisely what they could and could not do.[37] They propose a movement called 'New Populism', which would involve such principles as 'the subordination of finance', and an emphasis on personal security and social stability at the expense of the alpha culture:[38] in other words, for the establishment of a more egalitarian society in which everyone's democratic rights were respected and protected. They also advocate smaller banking firms, a separation of the savings and investment arms of banks, tighter credit controls, official licensing of derivatives and increased taxes on hedge funds and the like. Overall, the objective is to reduce the importance of the financial sector in British life, and thus the national dependence on it, which to Elliott and Atkinson has been a singular piece of political misjudgement. It is their hope that if this were done then it might even inspire a shift of personnel away from finance and back to more socially useful occupations.

Graham Turner feels that the crisis has come about because 'governments have . . . resorted to house price bubbles to drive economic recovery', this being their remedy for the loss of revenue suffered by the corporate sector moving so much of its production to the developing world. [39] Turner pictures a world chronically out of balance, with neither workers nor developing countries receiving a fair share of the benefits of globalisation. He is not against free trade as such, just the unfair way it is being conducted, with corporations holding almost all the power in their hands: 'Free trade is a positive, but not when companies abuse it and use it as an excuse to cut costs and boost profit margins.'[40] It has been this corporate determination to keep driving down production costs, the market fundamentalist mentality at its most ruthless, that has created the conditions for crisis. Unless governments take a firmer line on this, then bubbles will continue to bedevill us. Probably the most intriguing figure in the debate over market fundamentalism, however, is George Soros. Here we have someone who has been consistently critical of the fundamentalist ethos, despite having prospered very substantially from it in his role as a hedge fund proprietor – most famously, as previously noted, in terms of the UK government in 1992, when he manipulated the crisis over the exchange rate of the pound to his considerable advantage (as much as £1 billion it has been claimed). Given his eminence, and even notoriety (think of Krugman's sideswipe at his activities), it is worth dwelling on Soros's interpretation of the crisis in some detail: his is clearly an inside voice.

Soros has been one of the most successful market players of recent times, clearly benefitting enormously from the deregulated market; yet he has also repeatedly called for greater regulation by governments, believing the market to be an inherently unstable organism only too prone to boom-and-bust cycles which are not in the wider public interest. His interpretation of the current financial crisis, *The Crash of 2008 and What It Means*, is that it creates the need for a 'new paradigm' as far as the markets are concerned, otherwise we are condemned to experience periodic recurrences of the 2008 crash.[41] The new paradigm would be based on the recognition that, in Soros's uncompromising words, 'the global financial system has been built on false premises'.[42] Coming from someone in Soros's position this is a somewhat startling claim, and he does not hold back on the criticism of his financial peers: 'One cannot escape the conclusion that both the financial authorities and market participants harbor fundamental misconceptions about the way financial markets function.'[43] Those misconceptions multiplied to create the crash of 2008, when, in Soros's withering assessment, '[e]verything that could go wrong did', and we are now wrestling, largely unsuccessfully to date, with the consequences.[44]

The suddenness of everything going wrong caught even Soros, a long-term sceptic of market fundamentalism, by surprise, as evidenced by the fact that his book on the event is a hastily assembled expansion of its first edition, entitled simply *The New Paradigm for Financial Markets* (the new edition's subtitle), which came out in the year of the crash itself.[45] Soros has a larger overall objective than to berate his peers, and that is to call into question our assumptions about the relationship between knowledge/thinking and reality; then to demonstrate how the falsity of many of those assumptions has led to distortions in the market. His original worries about the inherent dangers involved in our misunderstanding of the world become spectacularly vindicated by the situation of crash into which the first edition of the book arrived. So there is an important philosophical dimension to the book, particularly since Soros insists that the misconceptions that distort the workings of the market are endemic to humanity and thus present in all the projects we undertake. For this thinker, we overreach ourselves on a regular basis, and it is high time we took some action over this trait.

The gist of Soros's argument is that there is a mismatch between our knowledge and our expectations, and that when these become confused, as they almost invariably do, we end up with problems – such as the bubble which has now overtaken us. When we play the stock market we do so in the expectation that the stocks we buy will prosper, but that is no more than a hope – we cannot know they will. This may seem self-evident, and it is a well-established philosophical principle that we cannot claim knowledge of the future (the point cogently made long ago by David Hume),[46] but economists continue to promote the idea that the market can be understood, as in 'rational expectations' theory. Soros is dismissive of this theory and its belief that 'financial markets are self-correcting and tend towards equilibrium', and sees it as the root of what is wrong with the current market system.[47] Economists posit an abstract system whose patterns can be predicted (with a certain amount of leeway), whereas the reality is a host of individuals mistaking their hopes for actual knowledge and risking their funds on that basis. What is thought to be predictable is in fact a mass of contingencies, and we have been deluding ourselves over this state of affairs for generations. Under such circumstances it is little wonder we have found ourselves the victim of a 'super-bubble' that threatens to overwhelm us. [48]

Soros freely admits to running 'an aggressive hedge fund' for many years until his retirement, and perhaps that has to raise some doubts as to his analysis, or the motivations behind it.[49] We might well question the sincerity of someone who exploits the system fairly comprehensively before calling for a new paradigm: 'the contemporary world's best example of a financial poacher turned would-be gamekeeper', in Martin Wolf's rather acerbic assessment.[50] Soros further owns up to being a serial 'short-seller', now considered to be one of the most destabilising practices on the market. We might also suspect that we remain vulnerable to those of similar mentality, who may be more likely to admire Soros for his cleverness in playing the system for so long with such success rather than to heed his criticisms and amend their ways, to identify with his poaching rather than his conversion to gamekeeping. Soros is quite capable, for example, of boasting how much money he made by driving companies into liquidation, presenting this as shrewd business practice rather than predatory behaviour of a venal kind.

What Soros has been successful in doing, however, is calling our attention to the degree of uncertainty and indeterminacy which applies in the everyday workings of the market – in my terms of reference, the 'economic sublime' (as I shall go on to explain in more detail in Chapter 7).[51] Economists have tried to pretend that such indeterminacy did not exist, to insist that rational expectations dictated the market's development instead, but that is no longer a sustainable position; instead, in Soros's damning words, rational expectations is 'a make-believe world that bears no resemblance to reality', and we have to face upto the the implications of that.[52] Hearing such views being expressed by such a high-profile, and in his heyday utterly ruthless, speculator is a sobering experience.

Soros is a great admirer of Karl Popper, in particular of the latter's notion of the 'open society' (he has even founded an Open

Society Institute). For Soros, the open society is an idea not just worth defending but using as a blueprint for his new paradigm – a paradigm that would extend to our political as well as our economic life. Political life, too, has suffered from a mismatch between expectations and reality, with Soros citing President George W. Bush's invasion of Iraq as one of the most disastrous consequences of this disjunction in recent years. What political life seems to have lost sight of, in Soros's opinion, is 'standards of honesty and truthfulness', and he takes these to be 'explicit requirements for an open society'.[53] An open society would be one that honestly recognised human limitations, acknowledging that there is no such thing as perfect knowledge of reality, but committed all the same to understanding it as best we can for the common good: 'What is imperfect can be improved.'[54]

Soros wants us to strive for this kind of improvement, arguing that postmodernism represents a capitulation to the limitations of reason rather than a recognition of the need to take more care in discriminating between our knowledge and expectations. While I think this underestimates not just the subtlety of postmodern thought, but also the moral imperative that lies behind the best of it (Jean-François Lyotard's work, for example, with its persistent concern to find workable grounds for judgement in a relativist universe)[55] Soros is to be applauded nevertheless for insisting that human psychology must be taken into account in a social science such as economics. It seems astonishing that modern economics consistently has marginalised this factor, choosing to present itself as a hard science instead, a claim which hardly bears scrutiny after Soros's remorseless dismantling of its pretensions. The fact that, as he points out, even most regulatory bodies in the sector do not understand the new raft of practices that have emerged in recent years (such as securitisation and credit default swaps) really ought to alarm us quite profoundly: you can hardly cure what you are unable to diagnose. If professionals do not understand what is going on (and given that nearly all major banks have been left with very substantial toxic assets as a result of participating in the new practices, we can see how widespread a phenomenon this is), then where does that leave the general public? If those running companies like Lehmann Brothers cannot spot dodgy ideas, if they are capable of being sold essentially worthless financial products by their peers, then what hope can there be for the private investor?

Caught in the Spider's Web

Collectively, what such analyses of the crash as the ones discussed above succeed in doing is making us aware how untenable neo-liberalism is as a position now: when one of the most successful hedge-fund proprietors in history such as George Soros asserts that 'financial markets . . . cannot be left to their own devices', then we surely have to sit up and listen.[56] The call for a return to properly-monitored regulation is becoming ever more insistent, the need for it ever more evident as the institutional failures mount up across the West: that is a common feature of the narrative arc of the interpretations of the crisis. Another recurrent feature is a general sense of unease about the removal of the separation between the investment and savings arms of banks (the Glass-Steagall Act that ensured this in America from the Depression onwards was repealed a decade ago, although banks had been expending a considerable amount of ingenuity in finding ways round it for some time before that). While this freed up more capital for traders to speculate with, it also meant everyone's savings were being put at risk. It is unlikely that the general public realised that this was happening, and even more unlikely that they would have agreed to it if asked. Few of us think of putting money in a savings account as equivalent to playing the stock market, but in effect that is what it has become in recent years thanks to deregulation. (When government ministers in the UK encouraged us to have accounts in several banks rather than risk getting caught out in the failure of one, on the grounds that our savings could only be guaranteed up to a certain amount in such an event, the advice had the unfortunate side effect of making saving sound like spread betting.) If we are to have any confidence at all in banks then the division between investment and saving needs to be reintroduced as soon as possible, and not just reintroduced but monitored extremely closely: the public interest surely demands no less.

Neoliberalism has been an excuse for giving greed free rein, and it will be a long time before the global economy recovers from the binge years and the super-bubble that, rather like Frankenstein's monster, it generated. Whether everyone in the financial sector will heed Paul Mason's advice to 'get used to it and move on' is another issue however, especially if and when some 'green shoots' of recovery do start to emerge. Greed is not so easily kept down: the monster is nothing if not resilient. It is unlikely that the financial services industry will be able effectively to police greed on its own ('group-think' militating against this), so we can only really move on if constraints are introduced from outside that curb the potential for it to be expressed. For the foreseeable future we are in no need at all of financial 'innovation', that is yet another area in which it is time to say 'enough' – especially since the system has become, in Gillian Tett's well-chosen image, 'a vast opaque spider's web' that defies comprehension.[57] (Analyses of the crisis do tend to harp on about just how little the industry overall understood about the products they were dealing in, especially senior management.) A sense of proportion has to be brought back into financial life, a recognition that modernity in overdrive can only end badly at some point, that there is more to life than growth and more growth – or speculation and more speculation either. The lure of alpha has to be firmly resisted: going for broke is no way to run a civilised society.

Soros claims to be introducing a new paradigm, but the theory behind it, 'reflexivity' as he calls it, is descriptive rather than prescriptive, starting from the premise that 'financial markets are always wrong'.[58] Reflexivity asks us to revise our world-view, to beware of taking risks based on misconceptions, to try our best to police this side of our nature; but its message of caution is, sadly, hardly likely to appeal to professional market-players for whom '[a]lpha at all costs', as Philip Augar has dubbed it, remains the guiding principle.[59] At the very least, however, there is now a substantial body of work letting the general public know that without meaningful regulation we shall not be able to pull ourselves out of the mess that market fundamentalist-led greed has landed us in. The momentum for root-and-branch reform of the financial sector just has to be kept going: the diagnoses overwhelmingly point us in that direction, calling for an end to the entire project of 'chasing alpha'.

Perhaps the most striking aspect of the crisis, however, is how it seemed to catch nearly all the major players in global politics and finance off their guard (I say nearly, because there were some dissenting voices, although little heed was paid to them by those in positions of power). No-one at the top seemed to recognise that the system was, to quote yet another recent account, little stronger than a 'house of cards'.[60] Right up to the very brink of the crisis itself politicians and financiers were confidently predicting the brightest of economic futures, and congratulating all those involved for having engineered such a happy state of affairs. Gordon Brown's now notorious Mansion House speech of 20 June 2007, just as he was on the verge of taking over from Tony Blair as the UK's Prime Minister, has to stand as one of the most ill-judged of recent political history, and will no doubt live long in the annals on that basis. It was almost embarrassingly fulsome in its praise for the City of London ('I congratulate all of you here on your leadership skills and entrepreneurship'),[61] and claimed that its success had been a direct consequence of the light touch policies adopted by the Labour government over the previous decade – administered, of course, by its Chancellor during that entire period, one Gordon Brown. We were now living in, it appeared, the best-of-all-possible economic worlds, and should know whom to thank for our good fortune.

The irony of the event is, however, stunning: within a matter of weeks the Northern Rock bank had to be rescued by the UK taxpayer and the credit crunch was well and truly on. [62] A better example of a grand narrative imploding would be hard to find: why should any of us believe anything we are told about the economy by those who had got it so spectacularly wrong that they believed the opposite would happen to what actually did? It was a Titanic moment, recalling Thomas Hardy's powerful poem on that subject, where ship and iceberg are brought together by forces outside human control, or even knowledge:

Alien they seemed to be:
No mortal eye could see
The intimate welding of their later history,

Or sign that they were bent
By paths coincident
On being anon twin halves of one august event,

Till the Spinner of the Years
Said 'Now!' And each one hears,
And consummation comes, and jars two hemispheres. [63]

If the Gordon Browns of the world could not see the iceberg coming, if they believed that we were now proof against icebergs anyway, how can we have any confidence in their pronouncements about the underlying strength of the real economy, or projections about the imminent arrival of the green shoots of recovery? If, '[f]or those prepared to look', as one financial journalist put it, Northern Rock 'had long been an accident waiting to happen', why were so few in positions of power prepared to look?[64]

Most of the books about the crisis turn it into an exciting drama, with a cast of characters, assorted politicians and financiers, in varying states of confusion about how to act, most of the time giving the impression they were stumbling around in the dark ('faction' treatment duly arrived in *The Last Days of Lehmann Brothers* on BBC2, September 2009). Some acquitted themselves quite well under trying circumstances, most rather badly;[65] but it is not really about the actions of particular individuals, it is about the belief system behind them, and this had simply crumbled, its contradictions being starkly revealed by the test it had been set. We now had not just a credit crunch to deal with but a credibility crunch also. 'Are we really so much cleverer than the financiers of the past?', the Governor of the Bank of England, Mervyn King, had somewhat provocatively queried just before the crunch occurred;[66] but even he must have been shocked to discover just how unrealistic the industry's image of itself and its abilities turned out to be.

Where Has All the Money Gone?

What was also shockingly unrealistic was the industry's belief as to how extensive the assets were that had been accumulated by the exercise of those abilities in the boom years. Huge profits were reported during the boom years, then, quite suddenly, huge losses. There was a particularly hard crash that shook everyone, market players or not, leaving them bewildered as to how to make sense of it all. A question that is constantly being put by members of the public since the crisis broke is: where has all the money gone? If it has been lost, where has it been lost? The idea that trillions of pounds, dollars and euros (etc.) have just vanished into thin air, a financial Bermuda Triangle as it were, is difficult for the general public to comprehend: the feeling persists that it must still exist somewhere or other, that someone must have gained by it, whether by ethical means or not. Yet the sad truth is that it has just vanished, and that tells us some uncomfortable truths about the concept of value, as well as the flimsiness of our economic structures.

We are often assured by politicians that we should not worry overly much in an economic crisis because the underlying economy is fundamentally sound and will see us through to safety. But the relationship between the real economy and the stock market is deeply problematical (in Soros's view, based on yet another set of unfortunate misconceptions). Countries may still be producing goods and have enough people in employment to constitute a market for those goods, as well as for imported ones: that is the prospective free lunch identified by Paul Krugman as our eventual salvation. But so much of business life depends on perception, and that has a negative as well as positive side. Companies are worth what investors think they are worth (and the same goes for national economies). If their share price falls then they lose much of their power in the marketplace, and that can be a very difficult process to reverse. The perception may be true or false (rumour and Chinese whispers can play their part in this), but as long as people believe it then it will dictate how events unfold: diagnosis will follow perception.

What this means is that even a small drop in profits – just a few per cent will do – sends out the wrong message as far as the investment community is concerned (modernity being all about constant, unremitting, improvement) and tends to trigger even larger falls as investment is withdrawn or dries up. In a real crisis such as the one we are currently living through, confidence evaporates rapidly and the result is a nosedive in share prices. This is a situation which triggers short selling, the scourge of bear markets, thus adding to the general sense of panic. Banks have seen their market value dramatically cut over the last year or two to the point where some of them are only worth a fraction of what they were in the boom years: HBOS in the UK, for example, saw its valuation drop from £36 billion to just £4 billion between 2007 and 2008 alone.[67] The message is that the money is only there if it is thought to be there, if the company is thought to be worth it; if not, then it is gone, as if it had been nothing more than an illusion all along – perception rules. Just as it is an illusion that your house is really worth a certain amount of money because that is its current market valuation: it is actually worth what someone else is willing to pay for it, and that is most certainly a figure which can go down as well as up (with the threat of negative equity kicking in, as it has done for many home-owners over the course of the crisis). Property has no intrinsic value, although that tends to be what most of us believe, and also what we have been using as the justification for obtaining ever larger amounts of credit to fund our ever more conspicuous consumption. As Graham Turner has correctly pointed out, 'house price inflation is a zero sum game. Society as a whole does not benefit from a rise in house prices.'[68]

In so many ways the market system is a gigantic illusion, which only continues to work if everyone believes in it. Share prices are built on faith as much as anything, on what we would like the situation to be, or become; that is, on our most optimistic diagnosis. This is particularly so when the product being sold is a service rather than something manufactured. (The religious metaphor is a powerful one here, since religions too are critically dependent on belief for their existence, and this can wax or wane in response to unpredictable psychological shifts in individuals.) Company assets invariably lag behind what their shares collectively add up to, meaning they are always susceptible to a run being made on them if perceptions suddenly change. Banks can easily go under when that happens – as it has many times in the past, most notably in the Depression when there was an almost wholesale collapse of the sector, with governments being less inclined to step in as quickly and decisively then as they do now. It is only the injection of huge sums of public money, and the guarantees accompanying these, that has prevented this re-occurring in a string of cases of late in countries such as the UK. The situation is all the more problematical given that so many banks have ended up with substantially more money out on loan than they have assets to cover at any one time (an astounding £500 billion more in the UK by 2007, for example).[69]

The threat of such a run hangs over the banking system, in the knowledge that once it starts in one place it is likely to spread uncontrollably as the public, quite understandably, loses its nerve and quickly starts to withdraw its deposits. On the day after Northern Rock's liquidity problems were reported on the TV evening news, customers withdrew £1 billion, for example, leaving the bank reeling and hastening government intervention. The effect, again, is much like the spread of plague, and even the most heavily capitalised bank will experience problems when that proceeds to happen. Unfortunately, it has been an inevitable side effect of the recent crisis that most banks are now badly under-capitalised instead – in large part because of the complacency generated by the belief that derivatives had radically reduced credit default risk and that they could therefore ramp up their speculation, a diagnosis which has proved to be quite spectacularly wrong. Hence they are even more susceptible to such an event than before. Toxic debt abounds throughout the system globally, with new examples coming to light regularly; indeed, the full extent of this is still unknown, and that exacerbates banking vulnerability very considerably. Regaining public trust under such circumstances is going to be a very tall order.

There, Or Not There?

Ultimately, the answer to the question 'where has all the money gone?' is that it was never really there in the first place – which is not a very comforting piece of news to contemplate. As Paul Mason pointedly notes, we have to remember that this more generally applies to banking: 'If we all drew our money out of the bank at once we would find it was not actually "there", and had been lent to somebody else on terms that meant neither we nor the bank itself could get it back immediately.'[70] While all of us probably are aware of this somewhere in the back of our minds, it is still a sobering thought (another example of Žižekian enlightened false conscious-ness perhaps?). It makes banking seem like a sleight–of–hand operation rather than something we can put our full trust in: just how much of a chance are we taking by putting our money in an account? We might also like to ponder on the fact that, as of legisla-tion passed in 2004, American banks are permitted to have a ratio of debts to capital of 40–1;[71] the more you look into it, the further proof you are given that the money really is not there.

Value is not intrinsic, therefore, hard though we may try to con-vince ourselves that it is. It is a lesson we are coming to realise, more than somewhat painfully, over the course of the financial crisis – in tandem with that of the financial markets being equivalent to a large confidence trick by which we have all foolishly allowed ourselves to be taken in. As Larry Elliott and Dan Atkinson remark, we let 'banks behave in a way that would be considered fraudulent in any other walk of life – to lend out money that does not exist'.[72] Unless the market is constantly expanding and share prices going up, then it cannot really meet its short-term obligations: there is precious little room for error. Banks cannot even loan out money that is not there if they do not have ready access to credit to give the impres-sion it is there – at which point the pyramid just collapses. As for the real economy, that may be little more than rhetoric: as things cur-rently stand, our economy is trapped on the market rollercoaster, which means it is worth whatever the market happens to say it is at any one point. Politicians can talk this up as much as they like in a brave attempt to allay our fears, but the real economy has very little power when confronted by the machinations of the market.

If market fundamentalism could sell shares then they would be doing abysmally at present, their value effectively in freefall, beyond the aid of any financial innovation to arrest. Perhaps the very idea itself needs to be jettisoned once and for all? That will form the consideration in the next chapter.

6

Forget Friedman

The doyen of the neoliberal, and thus market fundamentalist, cause was Milton Friedman, one of the most prominent members of the internationally renowned 'Chicago School' of economic theory. For Friedman and his followers the most effective – perhaps the *only* effective – market was the least regulated, and he campaigned tirelessly for this doctrine over the course of his life, starting with his influential book *Capitalism and Freedom* in 1962. Friedman was also a fanatical proponent of small government, believing that its role should extend little further than securing law and order and laying down basic guidelines for the conduct of our economic life. This was 'government as rule-maker and umpire' as he described it, and anything stronger than that was an unacceptable infringement on our personal freedom.[1] Friedman advocated that 'government power must be dispersed. If government is to exercise power, better in the county than the state, better in the state than Washington', on the grounds that this left the individual free to move elsewhere if he or she did not agree with the policies being developed and implemented locally.[2] What is wrong with the current system, he feels, is '[t]he very difficulty of avoiding the enactments of the federal government'.[3] America has a strong tradition of individualism and self-help going back to its frontier days, and along with that a reflex suspicion of big government which keeps reasserting itself in the political arena – for all that America is now the most powerful government in the geopolitical order. Friedman is very much speaking from that tradition, and recommending its values to the whole world.

At the time he wrote *Capitalism and Freedom*, however, Friedman was very much out of step with the ideological ethos of the times, which favoured highly centralised, interventionist-minded government, with quite complex welfare schemes in operation in most countries (less so in America than Europe perhaps, but huge government-directed social projects such as President Lyndon Johnson's 'Great Society' could still emerge there and count on widespread public support). The Cold War, with the West confronting the Soviet bloc and China, all but demanded such a style of self-consciously 'big' government to maintain one's position in the international order. But the climate was soon to change, and Friedman's subsequent impact on political life in the closing decades of the twentieth century was to become very considerable. His doctrines were adopted by such internationally high-profile political leaders as President Ronald Reagan and Prime Minister Margaret Thatcher, as well as promulgated by powerful global institutions like the World Bank and the International Monetary Fund (IMF), who insisted that Friedman-style economics, with its privileging of the private over the public sector, were put into play by any country receiving their aid. 'Government', Friedman pronounced, 'can never duplicate the variety and diversity of individual action', and when it tries the effect is to 'replace progress by stagnation'.[4] That was certainly the view held by the World Bank and IMF. In the event many countries did turn out to require their aid, and found themselves being turned into large-scale economic experiments in consequence – often at some considerable social cost.[5] It is essentially Friedmanite doctrine that lies behind globalisation and that has informed banking and investment practices in recent years, a neoliberal consensus as to how the world should be run, and he is still a source of inspiration to many economists and politicians, even in the aftermath of the credit crisis.

What we have to do now, if we want to survive that crisis and reconstruct the world's economic order in a more just and humane fashion, is to forget Friedman and everything he stood for economically and politically, because the bankruptcy of his ideas has been dramatically exposed. Governments cannot stand idly by while the banking system and the stock markets collapse, because these are not just abstract issues about the systems involved for academics to debate at their leisure, in economics departments or elsewhere, but the very basis of our social existence. Neither is it a solution for the individual simply to move elsewhere when things go wrong like this, as Friedman advocated: not when every economy is as intimately interconnected as we now find they are (thanks in large part to the enthusiastic adoption of his ideas). It is now widely accepted that governments are under an obligation to do all they can to prevent such collapses – although the extent of the intervention is still a matter for discussion and negotiation across the Western world, and will no doubt continue to be so for some time to come yet. The public sector has come back into its own again, after some years in the wilderness as a result of the aggressive application of Friedmanite policies, and that is a welcome trend to note.

It has become clear, too, that small government is unable to provide the level of security a developed nation state requires in conditions of severe economic crisis – conditions that go well beyond standard 'boom-and-bust' episodes. Iceland stands as a grim warning of what can happen when governments do not have the power to protect their citizens against economic mismanagement on the grand scale. Friedman is espousing what amounts to a purist form of modernity in the economic realm, and his ideas have to be taken apart to reveal how philosophically threadbare, as well as politically dangerous, they have proved to be, and why it is essential for them to be shunned by future generations. It has to be made absolutely clear that any return to Friedmanite policies would be socially disastrous. Friedmanworld is not a safe place for the average citizen to be: self-help and individualism will not take you very far when Depression strikes or your savings disappear into a financial sector black hole. What Friedman saw as freedom in the economic realm has turned out instead to be far more like anarchy, a landscape stalked by nasty predators restlessly seeking out the weakness of their peers in order to take maximum advantage: given the opportunity, *Homo economicus* can turn into a very unpleasant being. We would not countenance these conditions in our social lives, that is why we accept the existence of police forces to maintain law and order and protect us against the evil and ruthless, also armies to guard against any outside intrusion, so why should we in our economic? And especially so since these two are so closely intertwined.

The Market Rules

For Friedman, the market is a largely autonomous entity that must be left to its own devices if it is to work properly, and government is at best a necessary evil which must be kept to a bare minimum – that persistent American dream. In a very real sense the market represents humanity's destiny to Friedman and his followers, an arena of freedom where we can express ourselves to the fullest in seeking to further our own interests, where our character will be strengthened by the tests it is set in the act of competing with others on a regular basis. The free market has an almost mystical significance to this thinker, constituting the ground of our political freedom:

> Historical evidence speaks with a single voice on the relation between political freedom and a free market. I know of no example in time or place of a society that has been marked by a large measure of political freedom, and that has not also used something comparable to a free market to organize the bulk of economic activity.[6]

When government interfered with the market's freedom, as in regulating its trading practices, then it curbed our political freedom also, and the Friedman camp found that intolerable. In Friedman's view this was what had happened in the Depression; we had lost a significant part of our political freedom when the Roosevelt government introduced regulations into the American market in response to the economic crash (in Friedman's revisionist reading that was the major cause of the Depression's length, government tampering rather than market failure). Friedman wanted to overturn that

105

process. For a significant part of the world's political class the equation of economic and political freedom soon became an article of faith, helping to inspire the dramatic expansion of the world's financial industry in the closing decades of the twentieth century and then even more explosively into our own. Neoliberalism was to hold centre stage for several decades.

The effect of Friedman's theories was to make the market seem the most important aspect of human experience, what we should all be aspiring to make our mark in. All those who opposed it, such as communists and assorted socialists, were deemed to be against the cause of personal freedom and castigated accordingly in the available political forums and the media. The Republican Party in America and the Conservatives in the UK in particular became impassioned crusaders for Friedman's ideals, and set about restructuring their societies to incorporate them. They may not have turned into small governments when in power (although they continued to claim this was their ultimate aim), but they most certainly reduced government's role in the financial world. Restrictions on banking houses, for example, were swept away in a bid to intensify financial speculation, the belief being that this would jump-start sluggish economies (as most Western economies were in the early to mid-1980s). The decline of communism only seemed to add weight to such arguments, giving the free marketeers even more licence to pursue their unashamedly expansionist goals, the line being that the Western political system had won out, and that economics had been the driving force behind this triumph. In effect, it was neoliberalism that was the geopolitical victor, and its cause was to be pushed even harder from now on.

Ideologically speaking, in this period the market came to rule, exercising a profound hold over global, and particularly Western, culture, and anything standing in its way ran the risk of being dubbed evil. In the eyes of Friedman-inspired politicians, to be anti-free market was to be anti-freedom itself. '[O]nly certain combinations of political and economic arrangements are possible', Friedman claimed, so 'a society which is socialist cannot also be democratic'.[7] Even left-wing parties took fright, and started campaigning on a market-friendly ticket – New Labour in the UK, for example (which has since had to pay the political price for that support). The effect of such consensus was to entrench the market culture even more firmly in the public consciousness. For all but a few fringe political groups in the West the market had gone beyond criticism: it was simply humankind's natural setting.

Friedman did not invent neoliberalism, but he stands as one of its most eloquent advocates and provided much of the intellectual impetus for its growth, turning himself into a potent symbol for the new ideological regime. It was a regime temperamentally opposed to the notion of safety nets, not just in the market but almost anywhere at all in our lives, on the principle that these could only hamper the growth of entrepreneurialism (Friedman was even against compulsory pension schemes, or professional licensing of occupations). To forget Friedman would be to forget everything done in his name, and that is precisely what I feel we should be doing as we head into life after modernity. So forget Friedman, forget small government, forget the fundamentalist-style free market, forget neoliberalism, forget financial 'innovations', forget the entrepreneur as cultural hero.

The Economic Sublime

One of the most pressing reasons for forgetting Friedman is that we have now entered what might be termed the 'economic sublime': the condition in which we genuinely do not know what will happen next, or what the effect of our actions will be on future events in the economic realm. Postmodern theorists such as Jean-François Lyotard emphasised the critical role of the sublime in human affairs, arguing that we had lost sight of this under the dispensation of modernity, with its belief in humanity's ability to exert control over the environment by the development and application of a rationally ordered technology of increasing levels of sophistication. Modernity was in fact largely about putting into practice and extending such forms of control. We still tend to regard technology, drawing on the findings of cutting-edge science, as our saviour, and to expect it to provide us with increasing power over our world at both the collective and individual level. The permanently connected individual has become a cultural ideal, and we are expected to enter into the spirit of this by purchasing all the constantly changing technology that will enable us to maintain that condition. Upgrading has become a way of life, a means of demonstrating our faith in the ideals of the system – and we are given the opportunity to do so on a frequent, one could even say rather relentless, basis.

The sublime, in contrast, represents everything that lies beyond our understanding, and, crucially, beyond our ability to control. It is conceived of by philosophers as a realm of unknowability where we become painfully aware of the limitations of human reason; as Lyotard described it, the best we could hope for when confronted by the phenomenon of the sublime was to be able to recognise and acknowledge those limitations: 'The differend cannot be resolved. But it can be felt as such, as differend. This is the sublime feeling' (a differend being the disjunction between two discourses founded on incommensurable world-views).[8] The sublime was what modernity had been steadfastly refusing to acknowledge, but postmodernists were insisting we could no longer avoid doing: the condition where reason fell short, and would always fall short.

Enlightenment thinkers such as Immanuel Kant had certainly been very aware of the sublime, but as modernity developed, and with it a growing confidence in the power of reason to improve the human lot generation by generation, it was not something that was going to be dwelt on too much.[9] The concentration was going to be on where we could show ourselves capable of exercising dominion, of manipulating the environment to our material benefit. It would not be until postmodernism came on the scene that the sublime began to attract renewed interest. Postmodernists like Lyotard regarded it as a salutary experience to be confronted by the sublime, especially, as he noted, 'for us Westerners, haunted as we are by the passion of the will'.[10] It was bewildering to discover that we could not always impose ourselves on situations, as modernity consistently encouraged us to believe we could, to find instead that our will could be frustrated, perhaps even permanently. Modernity had been a celebration of the force of human will, but now we were being asked to consider the implications of being less powerful, possibly far less powerful, than we had supposed. Although metaphysical in nature the debate resonated far more widely than that, raising awkward questions about our perception of ourselves as a species.

How we cope with the economic sublime looms up as one of the key issues in life after modernity. It has become depressingly clear that the system can only be managed up to a certain point, and that the profusion of variables involved renders it deeply unpredictable – hence the emergence of bubbles that have such a destructive effect on our life. (As Paul Mason wryly remarks in his exposition on how 'off-balance sheet companies' – in particular 'conduits' and 'structured investment vehicles'– operated in the financial industry, 'I have seen MPs slumped with their heads in their hands trying to understand these entities, so bear with me if you are having trouble.'[11] One has to wonder how many members of the senior management in the industry had similar trouble but did not dare to admit it for fear of losing face.) This is not the kind of news most politicians will want to hear, since competence in economic management is one of their primary claims to fitness for office. Governments in the West tend to rise or fall on their ability to demonstrate, or at any rate to claim, such competence. 'It's the economy, stupid', as President Bill Clinton summed up how to win elections, and few Western politicians would disagree with the sentiment. Yet we have to admit that we have drastically overestimated our understanding of how economic systems, particularly in an unregulated free market form, actually work – or how they can go horribly wrong. From a postmodern perspective, this is yet another example of having overreached ourselves, of having overestimated our abilities.

What has largely been ignored by the economic community has been the factor of human psychology, which really does raise the spectre of unpredictability on the large scale. Some economists are coming round to recognising the importance of the psychological dimension, with George A. Akerloff and Robert J. Shiller, for example, echoing Keynes in identifying the importance of the 'animal spirits' in explaining 'why the economy takes rollercoaster rides' such as the one through which we are going.[12] For these two commentators, 'economic crises . . . are caused by changing thought patterns', and policy-makers really ought to be taking these into account.[13] Yet the assumption stubbornly remains among most economists that players in the market act in a rational manner, weighing up the pros and cons of their actions according to a considered analysis of how the system overall is operating and how they can maximise this to their own particular advantage. This has meant ignoring bubbles that had occurred in the past, and they have been traced back at least to the seventeenth century and the speculation that took place then in tulip bulbs in Holland.[14] (A more dramatic example from not long afterwards was the South Sea Bubble of 1719–20 in the UK. The losses there were enormous, with, as an example, Sir Isaac Newton losing £20,000. Shares in the South Sea Company were trading for £1,050 at their high point in June, 1720, but had fallen to £175 within 3 months, precipitating many bankruptcies.) Most pertinently, it meant turning a blind eye to the recent dotcom bubble of the 1990s and the panic that went along with it when it proceeded to burst.

Plainly, the dotcom bubble was not an example of coolly calculated rational behaviour by well-informed individuals and companies, but more on the lines of a bout of madness which temporarily took hold of both the entrepreneurial and investment community. As a keen student of bubbles, Charles P. Kindleberger, has reminded us, we should regard rationality as 'an a priori assumption rather than a description of the world'.[15] The conduct of market players may bear out that assumption some of the time, but on fairly regular occasions we find ourselves dealing with, as the title of Kindleberger's book has it, 'manias, panics, and crashes' instead; the product of outbreaks of what Alan Greenspan, the chairman of America's Federal Reserve Board from 1987 to 2006, has called 'irrational exuberance', which serves to 'drive up prices to nonsensical levels' until the euphoria fades (often quite suddenly).[16]

The dotcom bubble was just such a mania based on the promise of getting rich quick on a new business model generated by the very newest technology, and caution was thrown to the wind as start ups proliferated to meet the demand for appropriate-sounding ventures – often based on the flimsiest of pretexts, with little in the way of market research behind them. In the event, the vast majority of them were found to be wildly overvalued (Greenspan declaring himself quite bemused by 'the looniness of the stock prices' at the time)[17] and failed to deliver the expected returns – quite spectacularly so in some instances.[18] Instead of rational calculation, what the market revealed during the dotcom bubble was a mad rush fuelled by sheer greed, with everyone involved desperate to corner their share of what was being touted as a financial bonanza. At such points investors tend to be 'swept away by the current', as Philip Augar has described it, rather like being caught up in a tsunami[19] – not the kind of image that free marketeers would care to cultivate, one suspects.

The fall-out from the dotcom bubble was considerable in terms of lost investments, but the system nevertheless managed to weather it – which has often been cited as evidence of the fundamental robustness of the market economy. Everyone took a deep breath, and then started looking around for the next new thing. For many it turned out to be the derivatives market – which just invites an ironic aside. As the financial journalist Alex Brummer pithily observed: 'Never ones to heed a lesson, the banks, fresh from burning their fingers in the dotcom boom, had marched straight to the enticing world of sub-prime lending [one of the main catalysts for the expansion of the derivatives market], barely stopping to pass "Go"'.[20] And it really did appear to be more like a game than anything else in this period, with a distinct lack of reality as to how investors were acting: 'possibly the most absurd money game ever', as one disenchanted insider described the scene developing from the 1980s onwards.[21] Nowhere was this more evident than in derivatives' trading, the guiding principle of which seemed to be, as a bemused Brummer concludes, nothing more sophisticated than 'pass the parcel'.[22] Unfortunately for us all, it is we as the general public who have been left holding the parcel in the aftermath of the banking collapse, with no-one else left to pass it on to: we have made our way methodically from mania to panic to crash.

One cannot depend on absolutely every bubble being absorbed in the way of the dotcom of course, which is what fundamentalists tend to imply will happen, conveniently forgetting the Depression (unless you choose to espouse the Friedman line of the American government being the real villain in that instance). What the dotcom episode amply demonstrated, however, was that investors' behaviour could be very irrational indeed, and that a herd mentality could take over on occasion, with potentially dangerous consequences for the general health of the market. A recent psychological study has indicated just how irrational such behaviour is capable of becoming, in reporting how, in situations like playing the market, most people will follow the advice of those who sound the most confident – even if those advisers have a poor record of tips behind them. (If we were all the '[s]avvy economic naturalists' that Robert H. Frank recommends us to be when it comes to assessing stocks, we would not be taken in by such a spiel, but greed and our expectations have a way of overriding our logical side.)[23] In other words, the hard sell appeals to the investor mentality, which wants to be convinced that its expectations will come true – another example of how Soros's misconceptions keep reinventing themselves. As the *New Scientist* report on the study noted, however, this also means that we can be swayed by the loudest voices on topics such as global warming, an area where deniers in particular tend to adopt a very confident pose in their campaign to persuade us there really isn't a problem.[24] It is depressing to think how effective mere rhetoric can be in such cases.

The dotcom bubble was not exactly an advertisement for the unregulated free market system therefore, running counter to the picture it wanted to present to the public of shrewd investors making prudent use of their resources, under the guidance of highly vigilant financial advisers of proven competence and strategic vision. Such professionalism was meant to impress the public, but it was at best superficial, with mere confidence often masquerading as knowledge. The more unregulated that system has become, the more that governments have adopted a hands-off approach to the financial sector as the Friedmanites have consistently demanded they should in favour of 'the variety and diversity of individual action', then the more likely the creation of bubbles has become in turn.

Herd psychology seems an extremely poor basis for our financial existence, especially when combined with gambling (the rather less glamorous term for risk).[25] While it is true the market will generally correct itself after such behaviour is punished (although not necessarily all that quickly), the knock-on effect for society at large can be drastic. Just how drastic, the current bubble is now making us realise – lost jobs, blighted career prospects for the young, collapsing house prices, a credit squeeze, fear over the safety of one's savings, to name only the most obvious effects on individuals and families. Add in national bankruptcies, as I shall be discussing below in the case of Iceland, and the magnitude of the event becomes all too obvious. Bubbles make us recognise the existence of the economic sublime, but they are an expensive, and socially very damaging, way of doing so: almost as if we are tempting the sublime to reveal the extent of its superiority over us. To our collective dismay, the sublime has yet again duly obliged.

Iceland: Surviving Market Fundamentalism

Iceland has been one of the worst victims of the credit crisis, and its fate constitutes a dramatic warning of the dangers that come along with the unregulated market: the economic sublime in devastating action at national level. In effect, the country went bankrupt, its banks and leading business figures having wildly overextended themselves in the world's markets, borrowing with abandon during the boom years to buy up an impressive range of companies in several other countries: as one British newspaper reported it in suitably apocalyptic-sounding fashion, 'The party's over for Iceland, the island that tried to buy the world.'[26] When the crisis hit, its banking industry simply did not have the reserves to cope and it went under, throwing the country into economic and political turmoil.

For Iceland it was something like the perfect financial storm: the currency collapsed, the stock exchange plummeted (at one point in October 2008, it was 93 per cent down on its pre-crisis high), and the government had to take over the country's three major banks. In political terms it was a doomsday situation that caught the country completely unprepared (the 'Icelandic disease', as one commentator went on to call it, 'whereby a banking sector outgrows its host economy'),[27] eventually bringing down the government and casting an entire political generation into disrepute. This was a nation after all which, according to a UN poll, was the world's 'best country to live in' as recently as 2007; by 2008, with both unemployment figures and inflation soaring just to add to the general misery, that must have seemed like a particularly grim joke to its citizens. Market fundamentalism had revealed its darkest side and claimed a notable victim.

Highlighting the interconnectedness of the world financial order, other countries went on to suffer from the collapse of the Icelandic banking system; many public institutions in the UK, for example (such as local government bodies), had opened accounts in Iceland in recent years to gain the benefit of some of the highest rates of interest then being offered on the world's financial markets. In retrospect – always an easy thing to say after a crisis, I concede – such rates should have given investors some pause for thought, but the ethos of the time hardly encouraged that, and many were only to happy to be 'swept away by the current' yet again. When Icelandic banks threatened to default on those accounts, it rapidly led to a political crisis between the two countries. The UK government was moved to threaten to freeze Icelandic funds held in British banks until restitution was made to British account-holders, and relations between the two states subsequently became very embittered. One wonders if the future might hold out the prospect of 'credit default wars' between desperate states.

The vulnerability of small countries to the unpredictable swings of the unregulated market registered particularly strongly in Iceland's case, and it now has to confront the problem of reconstructing itself economically, having seen its financial sector laid waste almost overnight. From possessing one of the West's most buoyant economies and highest standards of living, it now finds itself facing a very uncertain future which it has very little real power to shape to its own advantage. It is hardly well placed to weather any future downturns that may occur – and these clearly cannot be ruled out as things stand, no matter how much the West's politicians may try to reassure us that the worst is probably over. Beware the hard sell in this area too.

There is no denying that Iceland's standing as a nation has been badly damaged by recent events. Having to negotiate huge loans from other countries (Russia and a Nordic consortium, as well as the IMF) just in order to keep functioning as a nation state does little to promote national wellbeing. Nor does it encourage the populace to remain rather than deciding to emigrate to improve their individual situation: emigration from Iceland was reported to have doubled over the course of 2008–9. Foreign workers (mainly from Eastern Europe) have also been leaving in droves now that the currency has lost much of its value, thus affecting their remittances home.[28] For a country with meagre natural resources this is no mean problem, and there are many others in a similar position around the world who have just as much cause to be worried about their future in the current climate of uncertainty (Ireland, for example, is in notably poor shape, its 'Celtic Tiger' image now badly tarnished after its explosive growth ground to a halt). Economic vulnerability can so easily translate into national vulnerability: political sovereignty does not mean much with a ravaged economy around one and poor prospects for its recovery.

Economics after Friedman

What we need to campaign for in the aftermath of modernity, therefore, is an economics of enough: a recognition that it is not always necessary, or even desirable, to have more of everything in material terms, nor endless technological advances (many of which, as we have found out, do little to improve the quality of life in any really meaningful sense). An economics of enough would also be a recognition that our energies can, and should, be directed in other ways than in seeking greater economic gain, that value can be construed in

a variety of ways other than the purely economic. Social utility will
have to come into the equation far more than it has been doing in
recent decades, especially with the phenomenon of global warming
to be borne in mind. Products that lead to any significant increase
in carbon emissions will have to be very carefully monitored, and
even on occasion banned for the public good. The profit motive
alone must no longer be allowed to dominate our thinking on such
matters, nor the concerns of shareholders to dictate company policy
as to what is put for sale on the market – organisational carbon
footprints have to be taken very seriously from now on. The short-
term mentality that demands the quick dash for profit, regardless
of circumstances, must be overcome, and we really do need to start
conceiving of business in a different way. Even more importantly,
businesses have to start conceiving of themselves in a different
way, as something more than just profit centres run for the benefit
of managements and shareholders; they too will have to distance
themselves from a market fundamentalist past if they are to regain
public confidence.

More than anything else we have to rid ourselves of the notion
that political freedom is a subsidiary aspect of market freedom, that
it is in fact dependent on it and cannot exist without it. Friedman
may have sold that idea to a generation of politicians, but its limitations have now been starkly exposed and we have to think again.
We cannot cede control of the market to the financial sector if its
success or failure determines how our society is able to operate –
especially if it is largely made up of untrustworthy, and deeply
selfish, 'New Olympians' hazy as to what their 'innovative' staff are
getting up to in their name. Politics cannot be kept separate from
the economy, and the latter cannot be the dominant partner in the
relationship, as the Friedman-neoliberal camp has wanted. Market
freedom cannot be absolute, any more than political freedom can
be. There have to be checks and balances, various constituencies to
be accommodated, negotiations to be conducted: it must not be a
free-for-all in either case. We might be able to rely on the goodwill
of most of our fellow-citizens, but we cannot rely on the goodwill
of all, so opportunities for the exercise of anti-social greed have to

be minimised – which means markets cannot be left to their own devices. Friedmanite economics generates the opposite state of affairs, and it just has to go.

If we manage to forget Friedman, then where do we go next? One interesting suggestion as to the style that economics should adopt as a discipline post-Friedman and post-credit crisis has been floated by Richard Bronk in his book *The Romantic Economist*. Bronk thinks it is possible to use the insights of creative literature and literary studies from the Romantic era in order to construct a different approach to economics, which in his view is mistakenly thought to be essentially rationalist in orientation. The key is to make greater use of the imagination and intuition, which means that we should treat economics as being at least as much an art as a science. Unless economists recognise this then their projections will continue to be as problematical as they have been of late, with Bronk declaring himself 'intrigued . . . by the intermittent power of economics to explain and predict, and also by the frequent mismatch between the way economists model economies and the way markets actually work in practice'.[29]

Economics as a discipline, Bronk decides, is essentially theory-driven, and the divergence between theory and practice, predictions and actual behaviour, is a major motivation behind his project, leading him to pose some very searching questions to the economics fraternity:

> Why do economists rely on relatively static equilibrium models to make predictions, when markets and economies are so clearly dynamic and characterised by massive uncertainty, relentless innovation and perpetual novelty? And why do economists make the assumption that economic agents are motivated only to maximise (within given constraints) the satisfaction of their preferences and optimise their trading possibilities on the basis of rational expectations? For the most part, the entrepreneurs and investors I met seemed to know so little about the future to which their preferences and expectations related that they had no real way of optimising anything but their own salaries.[30]

Bronk's concern is to help us come to understand what really goes into creating those preferences and expectations, and just how far away we are from the utilitarian approach recommended by most economists. Romantic literature and philosophy will give us a new narrative by which to view our economic life, a narrative at variance with that favoured by such as Friedman, Rational Choice Theory and its 'attempt to validate the assumption of market rationality and a tendency on the part of individuals to maximise returns'.[31] To that end Bronk wants to replace *Homo economicus* with *Homo romanticus*, pictured as a 'self-creating, sentimental, sympathetic and imaginative social animal', who recognises the futility of basing our economic life on mathematical modelling and an extremely narrow conception of human nature.[32] The interaction of emotion and reason means that we are much more complex beings than Rational Choice Theory allows – and, critically, far less predictable as subjects for modelling exercises than mainstream economics assumes.

The principal lessons we are to learn from Romanticism, Bronk contends, are that there are no universal answers to human problems; that utilitarianism is severely limiting as a basis for our ethics; that self-creation is a necessary and desirable part of our individual development; and that imagination is at least as important as reason in making sense of the world and in the planning of our lives. Despite Bronk's expressed dislike of the postmodern world-view, there is nothing here with which the average postmodernist would wish to disagree: the overall concern is to challenge the notion of a grand narrative based on rationality, and to emphasise the critical importance of the little narrative in human affairs. Romanticism from this perspective is a counter to the culture of modernity, with its belief that the world can be brought under human domination by the power of reason working through the agency of science and technology.

Bronk is critical of mainstream economics because it does make the assumption of there being universal answers to economic problems, envisaging the world as one vast market operating under the same rules and principles, with local considerations left out of account. This is the globalisation ideal of course: modernity as our destiny, both economically and politically. Bronk, however, is adamant that we do have to take local factors into account, insisting that national contexts matter a great deal and must be respected. Globalisation does not have to mean homogenisation in his view: there is scope for difference in economic affairs. This is the line taken by the Varieties of Capitalism school, who draw attention to the institutional differences between countries such as Germany and the USA, and how these help to shape national economies. As the editors of an influential volume of essays on the topic put it: 'Our premiss is that many of the most important institutional structures – notably systems of labor market regulation, of education and training, and of corporate governance – depend on the presence of regulatory regimes that are the preserve of the nation-state.'[33] The end-result of those regimes is that nations tend to be more efficient in certain activities than others, and can turn their particular specialisation into a 'comparative advantage' on the world market. To erase these differences would be to put that comparative advantage at risk, and that may even mean arguing the case for that bugbear of the market fundamentalists, the welfare state. Thus we find Isabel Mares asserting in her chapter in the collection that 'social policies can offer distinct institutional advantages to employers' and that 'the benefits provided by social policy outweigh the costs of social policy to firms',[34] conclusions completely at variance with neoliberal dogma, which insists that the corporate sector will only thrive if left unfettered.

Although Bronk feels the Varieties of Capitalism school still assumes a unity of purpose in nations as to overall economic goals (to maximise one's gains in competition with others), he is in general agreement with their commitment to diversity of method. We do not have to go down the globalisation route, nor accept the primacy of the Anglo-American model of the market. Bronk is at pains to demonstrate the wide range of opinions to be found in the economics world at present, particularly in its academic side where much interesting work is being done. Rational Choice Theory has come under a lot of attack in academic circles of late, and Bronk is part of that trend, seeing a clash of views here that is an updated version of that between Romanticism and utilitarianism in the nineteenth century. William K. Tabb divided modern economic thought into two main types, 'A mode' and 'B mode', the former being mathematically oriented, the latter historically and socio-logically based.[35] While Bronk questions whether the division is as sharp as Tabb indicates, there seems little doubt that the A mode is more conducive to making predictions, and the sad fact is that the mechanistic model derived from this has come to prevail in political life. Given the imperatives behind modernity, it is not hard to see why this would be so: growth has to be quantified, and the cult of progress positively revels in statistics.

Another suggestion as to how economics should develop post-crisis, this time with a specifically American bias to it, comes from Kenneth and William Hopper in their book *The Puritan Gift*. As they see it, the problem is that the country's management class has lost touch with the ethical basis of American culture, which the authors locate in the lifestyle of the early Puritan settlers. The discipline and sense of responsibility associated with that group is no longer informing business practice, and the result is the economic disaster that has now overtaken the West. The situation will only be rectified if management starts adhering once again to the 'gift' bequeathed to us by the Puritans.[36] Whether this would be enough to save us from the cult of progress remains to be seen; the effect might just be to initiate a new and more efficient form of modernity, which would be of no help in dealing with global warming. We might also wonder whether Puritanism can still speak to such a multicultural nation as the USA has become, but the appeal for greater discipline in the conduct of the financial industry is well worthy of support: a strong dose of moral probity is certainly long overdue.

As Bronk's appropriation of literary studies for economics suggests, it could well be that we have much to learn from the world of the arts when it comes to readjusting our values in the aftermath of modernity – as well as from postmodernism's role in construct-ing an aesthetic which opens artistic practice out to a more general public. That is the argument to be pursued in the next chapter.

Part III

Beyond Modernity

7
Learning from the Arts: Life After Modernism

The area in which postmodern thought arguably has had most impact is in the arts, which has led the way in calling into question the grand narratives associated with modernity – such as that of modernism. Modernism is a varied phenomenon (most commentators now speak of 'modernisms' instead, stressing its diversity),[1] but whatever form it took tended to include a commitment to originality and experimentation – in effect, to the notion of progress. The past was to be treated as largely irrelevant: the goal for the modernist artist instead was continually to develop original forms and styles. In this respect modernism was also intensely competitive: as Peter Gay has put it in his large-scale survey of the movement, 'perhaps half the joy of making a radical picture or house or symphony must have derived from the creator's satisfaction to have bested the opposition'.[2] That is a trait central to modernity, especially in terms of its commercial aspect, where besting the opposition is the route to the holy grail of increased market share.

Postmodernism has offered a sustained challenge to this mindset, through, for example, Charles Jencks's concept of double-coding, an idea that has been widely adopted by postmodern artists. It has become common practice in literature, painting, music, etc., to cultivate eclecticism, making use of elements from both the past and the present in order to challenge the norms of modernity.

Postmodern artists have resolutely refused the instruction always to 'make it new', thus instituting a clear divide between themselves and the modernist aesthetic. The degree to which postmodern theory and practice have succeeded in their critique of modernism, and whether this gives us anything substantial to build on in other realms of ideas as to how we might confront and potentially destabilise an ideological paradigm, will now be scrutinised.

The Postmodern Aesthetic

Just as it has become common for theorists to talk of 'modernisms' perhaps we should also talk of 'postmodernisms', stressing diversity there too. As an aesthetic concept postmodernism varies quite considerably from creative artist to creative artist, and from one art to another, but, as with modernism, certain key features and ideals tend to recur nevertheless. First of all there is a recovery of lost forms and styles, those modernism had claimed to supersede – realism in literature and painting, for example, or tonality in music. Modernism had argued it had become inauthentic to use older models and that creative artists who did so were merely being lazy, refusing to push themselves to make new discoveries and develop new ways of depicting human experience in a period of accelerated social and political change. Postmodernists begged to differ and deliberately sought out older styles, even if they did approach them with a certain amount of irony, aware that they could not do so innocently without any knowledge of their historical import. The point was, however, deliberately to resurrect what modernism had been so determined to reject. Thus we find the novelist John Barth making a persuasive case for a return to plot and storyline in fictional narrative, claiming that this was the only way to move out of what for him was the 'literature of exhaustion' of late modernism, where such features had all but vanished.[3] There was a 'used-upness of certain forms or exhaustion of certain possibilities' to be noted about such work in his opinion, and this attitude needed to be tackled.[4]

For Barth, this desire to overcome creative 'exhaustion' became something of a crusade, as he could see no other way of continuing the tradition of literature without instigating such a move, or of maintaining the interest of the reading public: modernism had become a trap of diminishing returns, with Samuel Beckett constituting a glaring example of how this could impoverish literary activity if persisted in. Beckett's drama in particular had become sparer and sparer over time (and it had never been all that expansive in the first place, as witness *Waiting for Godot's* bleak landscape), until eventually he was offering us plays without words (*Act without Words I and II*), and even plays without any characters at all (*Breath*).[5] To follow the path of Beckett, in Barth's view, was to run the risk of ending up with nothing at all to say, and to him that was a clear dereliction of the author's duty to society at large – as well as of his or her own talent. Beckett, Barth complained, had 'become virtually mute, musewise' in his late period, and could therefore provide no role model for aspiring writers.[6] Although this judgement underestimates the power of Beckett's minimalist works, which still retain the power to make the audience think deeply about profound issues even now in the aftermath of postmodernism, Barth's frustration at how little scope this left for the imagination was certainly shared by many other writers, who similarly came to regard modernism as a creative cul-de-sac. Many came to feel there was a sense of sterility in late modernism in particular.

What postmodernists proceeded to do was strive to reconnect with the general public, making a conscious effort to give them material they could identify with in terms of their past experience: as Barth confidently proclaimed, it was time 'to rediscover the artifices of language and literature – such far-out notions as grammar, punctuation . . . even characterization! Even *plot*!'.[7] The charge of 'easy compromises' seems particularly mean in such cases, when the 'compromise' was with a public who were genuinely bemused by what most creative artists were doing and could find little point of contact with it. This enterprise often meant deliberately blurring the line between high and popular art, as well as engaging in dialogue with the past – which in the main modernists had disdained to do, preferring the new, original and unfamiliar instead. It was double-coding in action, and it became fairly standard postmodernist aesthetic practice.

It was a practice that was largely effective: not every postmodern artwork reached a mass public, but many did, becoming popular successes in the process. Umberto Eco's *The Name of the Rose*, for example, combined detective fiction (with copious references to the classic Sherlock Holmes series), semiotic theory (very deftly done, as detectives are always hunting for signs, or clues, after all) and the conflict between Aristotelian and Platonic aesthetics into a critically acclaimed and best-selling novel that subsequently went on to further success as a Hollywood film starring Sean Connery.[8] Minimalist composers such as Steve Reich and Michael Nyman drew sell-out audiences on concert tours, with their rhythmically insistent music for small groups recalling jazz and rock more than the classical tradition in which they had been trained. Nyman became even more widely known through his many film scores, with Philip Glass also being very prolific in this field, bringing the minimalist style to the attention of a mass public.

In the domain of advertising, the postmodern aesthetic had a particularly dramatic impact, so much so that critics began to complain it had turned into a cliché. Thus we had Gilbert Adair's observation that,

> The past (mostly the recent past) has been transformed into a mammoth lucky dip. All you have to do, if you are a maker of TV commercials or pop promos, a designer of shop windows or record sleeves . . . an architect, a painter, even a marketing entrepreneur, is plunge in and scoop out whatever happens to address your particular need . . . Nothing, *absolutely nothing* . . . need seem dated or outmoded.[9]

The point was well taken, but what it indicated was that postmodernism had managed to strike a chord with the general public, providing material they both liked and felt comfortable with. It had achieved something that modernism had very rarely experienced – widespread popular acceptance. Postmodernism, in this realm at least, did not alienate the public, as had tended to be the fate of the modernist aesthetic much of the time; in fact, postmodernism could be fun, entertaining the public with its wit and cleverness – as in the areas identified by Adair.

For the philosopher and art critic Arthur Danto, the later twentieth century had seen a clear break being effected from the history of art in a way that had freed up the artistic imagination. He believed that we had entered,

> the Post-Historical Period of Art, and there is no reason for it ever to come to an end. Art can be externally dictated to, in terms either of fashion or of politics, but internal dictation by the pulse of its own history is now a thing of the past. . . . [T]he Post-Historical Period is a post-narrative period of art. . . . [W]e face the future without a narrative of the present. We live in the afterwash of a narrative which has come to its end . . . [T]he master narrative of Western art is losing its grip and nothing has taken its place. My thought is that nothing can.[10]

What Danto had picked up, in the work of Andy Warhol among others, was a rejection of received authority, in particular the authority encoded in modernism as an aesthetic, and that the art-world had been propagating vigorously for the greater part of the twentieth century. Artists were no longer necessarily being driven on by controlling overall ideas, such as the demand to make it new every time around or to best the opposition by one's radical gestures: faithfully copying a Campbell's soup-can hardly seemed like adhering to the Pound ideal. Instead, a new generation was beginning to opt out of what had become all but a party line on how to approach artistic production. As a result, styles and subject matter were becoming ever more varied: 'art has become pluralized', as Danto enthused.[11] Difference was coming more into play, and practitioners had stopped conceiving of themselves as exponents of a tradition – or of a specific tradition anyway. Whether that attitude turned into another narrative in its own right, as some would claim (even Lyotard worried a bit about such a prospect), is an interesting question, but there is no denying how widespread the desire became to escape from what for many was the straitjacket of modernism.

Lyotard also emphasised the freedom to be gained by breaking with modernism and projecting oneself into a post-historical zone where tradition has no remit:

> A postmodern artist or writer is in the position of a philosopher: the text he writes, the work he produces are not in principle governed by prees-tablished rules, and they cannot be judged according to a determining judgment, by applying familiar categories to the text or to the work. Those rules and categories are what the work of art itself is looking for. The artist and the writer, then, are working without rules in order to formulate the rules of what *will have been done*.[12]

Artistic creativity need not provide reinforcement for a grand narrative, therefore, and can instead be deployed to undermine it, as Lyotard is convinced is the effect the postmodern is having on the modern. By extension this is what Lyotard wants to happen in the realm of politics too: for the mass of us to stop playing by the rules, which benefit only the elite who formulate them and then go on to make judgements on their basis. The grand narrative is only as strong as the belief invested in it, and its hegemony can be destabilised and eventually dismantled by the pressure applied by little narratives. This was what the Soviet Union and its sattelites discovered to their surprise in the 1980s, when their legitimacy simply crumbled – in most cases, to paraphrase T. S. Eliot, not so much with a bang as a whimper.[13] Both modernism and modernity only stand for something if we allow them to do so: their power vanishes when our support is systematically withdrawn, when they are subjected to some truly determined scepticism.

The Altermodern

The desire to move past modernism, and the inhibiting effect it can have on the creative artist, can also be seen in the development of the concept of the 'altermodern', which formed the theoretical hypothesis behind the Tate Triennial exhibition at the Tate Britain Gallery, London, in 2009. For the Triennial's curator Nicolas Bourriaud,

> [t]he term 'altermodern', which serves both as the title of the present exhibition and to delimit the void beyond the postmodern, has its roots

in the idea of 'otherness' (Latin *alter* = 'other', with the added English connotation of 'different') and suggests a multitude of possibilities, of alternatives to a single route.[14]

The postmodern may have claimed to have been the champion of the 'other' and the 'different', but for a thinker like Bourriaud it remains something of a prisoner to the past, overly concerned with positioning itself against modernism and modernity, with engaging in polemic. What is needed now, he believes, is a more definite break with tradition (which modernism in its day had successfully engineered, without necessarily carrying a mass audience along with it, however). Bourriaud goes on to argue that the desire for such a break to be made, and for a new perspective to emerge on artistic activity, is already being expressed throughout the creative community:

> Numerous contemporary artistic practices indicate . . . that we are on the verge of a leap, out of the postmodern period and the (essentialist) multicultural model from which it is indivisible, a leap that would give rise to a synthesis between modernism and post-colonialism. Let us then call this synthesis 'altermodernism'.[15]

The concern is to escape from the orbit of both modernism and postmodernism, in order to foster an artistic practice which offers us 'a positive vision of chaos and complexity'.[16] The art that is constructed according to these principles has for Bourriaud, echoing Gilles Deleuze and Felix Guattari's work, a 'nomadic' quality, with the artist moving around freely 'in space, in time, and among the "signs"' of the world, not being tied down to the demands of any particular 'ism'.[17] (Bourriaud emphasises elsewhere the importance of the exchange of information that takes place between artist and audience in this new practice.)[18] The implication is that modernism and postmodernism have been locked together in a binary relationship which demands a particular kind of commitment on the part of the creative artist. To be modernist or postmodernist is to have an ideology to uphold, and for Bourriaud that is to be restricted in terms of the exercise of one's imagination; the altermodern is not to be conceived of as an 'ism' in any traditional sense. Even more so than Danto, Bourriaud wants art to become 'post-historical' and cut loose from the narratives that have dominated the past.

Whether it is possible to escape so completely from the alleged problems of the past (as we have seen, modernism is still capable of attracting support in the new century) is a moot point. Bourriaud's claims notwithstanding, the altermodern is still to a large extent defining itself against what went before in attempting to be simultaneously beyond the concerns of both modernism and postmodernism – at the very least to be *neither* modernism *nor* postmodernism, with all the ideological baggage they bring along with them, but in some sense an uncategorisable position that confers freedom on both the artist and critic. Yet it would have to be pointed out that uncategorisability is a vain ideal in most cases; philosophers and critical theorists will always find connections and correspondences – that is one of their primary goals in life, to provide us with a sense of context. What is interesting about the altermodern project, however, is precisely the strength of that desire to go beyond, to gain a greater measure of freedom for the creative imagination, to create a genuinely new perspective on the world and the various forces that go into shaping its ideologies.

The drive to locate and communicate that perspective will no doubt become even more powerful now that the world's socio-economic system has run into such extreme difficulties and there is a general concern to rethink the way our world is ordered. Somehow, economically as well as aesthetically, we have to find a new method of organising our activities, and we must look at as many cultural discourses as possible for inspiration as to how to set about doing this. The altermodern is the kind of movement we should be paying attention to, and its call for a more nomadic approach to art resonates politically as well, given that traditional political ideologies are having such difficulty coping with the collapse of modernity (not surprisingly, given that they are products of modernity, formed by its ideals).

Lyotard contended that modernism and postmodernism were bound together in a cyclical relationship, destined to keep succeeding each other over time, and it is possible that the altermodern might qualify as a new sequence of modernism under this dispensation, which Bourriaud does seem to be hinting at.[19] This is not to be critical of the postmodern phenomenon: it cannot be expected that any aesthetic theory, no matter how loosely assembled, can go on indefinitely, especially one as polemically motivated as postmodernism always has been. Eventually, the target of one's critique fades into the background and one's agenda begins to lose its force and momentum in consequence. Modernism may have become authoritarian, but it was initially in good faith as a reaction against long-established traditions such as realism. In its day it was just as post-historically inclined, and we do need to remember its revolutionary side in any discussions of its legacy. What Peter Gay has called 'the lure of heresy' did have an invigorating effect, on the wider world as well as the artworld, in its 'sheer act of successful insubordination against ruling authority'.[20] This aspect of the modernist ethos would need to be stressed if we are heading beyond the postmodern, and it sounds as if Bourriaud wants to recapture that sense of discovery for his new project, of breaking free from a restrictive narrative. Perhaps we are now far enough away from modernism for that to be possible.

Responding to Bourriaud's conception of the altermodern, Okwui Enwezor extends the debate to consider the various ways that modernity and modernism have been interpreted and developed around the postcolonial world. He identifies a growing reaction there against 'supermodernity' (a term coined by Marc Auge),[21] this being the European model which has held the stage for several centuries, constituting the standard against which all other types of modernity are to be measured.[22] Enwezor goes on to argue that, in Africa particularly, we are now witnessing the emergence of a new kind of modernity with far-reaching implications for both politics and aesthetics:

[S]ituations of modernity in Africa are *aftermodern*, because, having no relation to history-making, its modernity can only emerge after the end of the modern. Such modernity, more than in other parts of the world, would be based in large part on a project of disinheriting the violence of colonial modernity . . . This modernity, it is hoped, is one that will emerge at the end of the project of *supermodernity*. It will perhaps mark not only an ideal of the altermodern, but will initiate a new cycle of the *aftermodern*.[23]

Enwezor's is a salutary voice, reminding us that we have to be aware of the political history of modernity and what it symbolised, thus of postmodernity too. For the postcolonial world modernity is inextricably tied up with its hated colonial heritage, and many countries there now feel motivated to strike out from that in both their political and artistic development. Perhaps even the altermodern is too Westernised a concept for their needs, although the two concepts spring from the common desire to escape from the 'isms' of recent Western history.

Just what the aftermodern means for Africa, Enwezor suggests, can be recognised in work such as that of the South African photographer Guy Tillim and his images of 'inconclusive projects of modernisation' around the African continent:

> His photographic project is an expression of the hope that showing the decaying legacy of colonial modernity in Africa is not an attempt to mourn the loss of some great past, but a possible *tabula rasa* for a future composition. It disarms and dispossesses the colonial inheritance[.][24]

Bourriaud thinks of the altermodern in a similar manner, as a tabula rasa for artists to go to work on to register the complexities of their time, minus the ideological demands made by supermodernity. In effect, the altermodern-aftermodern aspires to be modernity without the grand narrative, or the dark side we spoke of in Chapter 2; Enwezor even speaks of it as proof of Habermas's claim that modernity is an 'unfinished project' (although in a different way than Habermas intended, one suspects).

Postmodernism and its Downsides

Both Adair and Bourriaud identify weaknesses in the postmodern aesthetic, and it is worthwhile exploring these in a bit more detail to consider what we can take from the theory in the new cultural climate that is emerging. Postmodernism does not desire to make things new, rather it concerns itself with recycling what is already there, with the reassembling and pastiche of existing materials that most audiences will recognise. While that does offer a challenge to the norms of modernism, one can wonder whether it leaves much of a legacy to build on. How long can we go on recycling, ransacking the past as it were, without the law of diminishing returns settling in? For one critic of postmodern architecture, for example, it was characterised by nothing more than 'the conscious ruination of style and the cannibalization of architectural form'.[25] Although this is a harsh assessment, there is a grain of truth in it none the less. Then perhaps it could be said of double-coding that it just turns into a way of playing up to the audience's prejudices rather than inviting them to rethink these? The lack of invention noted by Adair can become a drawback if all it does is succeed in reinforcing the status quo even further. Postmodernism can be very backward-looking, and perhaps, as Adair implies, rather superficial too, a stylistic gesture as much as anything, and one that can become rather vapid. Pastiche soon becomes tiresome, no matter how cleverly it may be done. Having called modernism into question, it is not entirely clear where postmodernism can go next: that is above all the problem with which Bourriaud is wrestling. It is the problem that looms even larger now that modernity itself has effectively imploded, leaving us in an ideological vacuum.

Yet I would argue there are still several things we can take from postmodernism as an aesthetic theory that can be turned to account in the situation after modernity. The attitude of scepticism that postmodernists have adopted towards established authority and authority figures is certainly worth retaining in the new climate, as is their scepticism towards the whole process of making it new. We have not been critical enough of those driving modernity relentlessly on, even though it has put both the planet and our financial systems severely at risk. The cult of progress may have given us global warming, but economic growth and the health of the market still obsesses all the major world economies (perhaps even more so

133

in the aftermath of the crisis), with besting the opposition remaining a high priority. Making it new through financial innovation has turned into a global social disaster, and the fact that the products generated were incomprehensible to all but a few adepts recalls modernism at its very worst – as if obscurity was proof of intellectual depth. Then, too, we could use some double-coding in our financial systems, since they affect all of us in a major way, the general public as well as the whizz-kids in the financial institutions. If only in its development of a sceptical mindset, postmodernism has provided an object lesson in how to call a grand narrative's authority into question. From a tactical point of view it has much to teach us, its downsides notwithstanding.

It is also worth reiterating that the call for nomadism made by the altermodern camp is derived from postmodern thought, so there is already a sense in which the postmodern is being appropriated for the new battle. For Deleuze and Guattari nomadism was similarly a way of preventing oneself from being tied down in 'isms', of keeping one's options always open. Nomads have no home territory and can flit easily from one place to another as they see fit:

> [E]ven though the nomadic trajectory may follow trails or customary routes, it does not fulfill the function of the sedentary road, which is to *parcel out a closed space to people*, assigning each person a share and regulating the communication between shares. The nomadic trajectory does the opposite: *it distributes people (or animals) in an open space*, one that is indefinite and noncommunicating.[26]

Nomads only occupy territory temporarily, never being 'sedentary' for very long, and for Deleuze and Guattari this became a model for intellectual life. You did not submit to established authority and defend positions come what may, as from their perspective Marxists repeatedly were required to do as reality failed to match up to their theory (the trusty hegemony defence we considered earlier); instead, you retained your right to move on and thus demonstrate your intellectual independence. To be nomadic was to be beyond the reach of grand narratives, and that is the condition to which the altermoderns are aspiring; to be, in Deleuze and Guattari's terms of reference, aesthetically 'deterritorialized', beholden to no-one or no particular theory.[27]

Lessons of the Postmodern

The altermoderns want to take us beyond the postmodern and its perceived limitations, possibly to reintroduce an element of experimentalism into artistic practice (something that has been downgraded in importance in the postmodernist camp). But they have also clearly learned some very important lessons from it, the upsides of postmodernism, such as the need to steer away from a dominating central authority and to keep one's options open in the creative sense. While the postmodern aesthetic has developed some distinctive features – double-coding, dialogue with the past, revival of older styles and modes, erasure of the boundary between high and popular art, etc. – it has done so with a fairly light touch in the main. Modernism often has a rather severe quality to it that can be alienating to its audience – its practitioners too, to some extent. Architecture arguably exemplifies this trait best of all, in its obsession with geometric regularity and distaste for ornamentation. Thus we find Le Corbusier referring to '[t]he necessity for order', and insisting that '[t]he regulating line is a guarantee against wilfulness'.[28] That last word very clearly brings out the sense of there being a party line in modernism, and a party line which will be enforced: it is all so very serious, and more than a bit sinister.

Postmodernism, can be very playful, however, and this has certainly helped to win over a wider public for its efforts. While I would not exactly describe postmodernism as populist, it is capable nevertheless of exerting a popular appeal, and its palpable concern to connect with its audience is a trait that has been much appreciated. Its sheer irreverence to the authorities in its field has been both refereshing and liberating (wilfulness and irregularity becoming the order of the day), and this is a characteristic that does resonate more widely throughout the public realm. What we might call the arrogance of modernism has been undermined, and even if the altermodern wants to recapture some of the experimental quality of the modern as an artistic practice, it does not sound as if it wants to repeat the arrogance as well. Being radical for its own sake has lost much of its attraction, and I would argue that is a good thing.

These are very general points, and it cannot be claimed that every postmodern work achieves the aesthetic's ideals. The return of plot, storyline and characterisation, for example, has not always meant the return of intelligible plot, storyline and characterisation. Such exponents of the literary postmodern as Donald Barthelme and Robert Coover can be baffling enough in their way;[29] David Lynch's film and TV work can lose the viewer in its complex and often wildly digressive plotlines – not to mention its often downright strange characterisation (the 'Log Lady' in *Twin Peaks* memorably enough). Future generations will no doubt break the postmodern down into various strands and subsets, as has been done already with modernism, and some will be seen to have been more approachable than others. But the underlying imperative of the postmodern, to be free of an authoritarian prescriptiveness, will surely remain a consistent feature, as will playfulness with the elements of one's medium and a desire to keep the audience at the very least entertained (even baffling postmodernism achieves this to some degree: the audience for Lynch's TV series, *Twin Peaks*, was as much a popular as an intellectual one).[30] Possibly the main lesson to be learned from the postmodern critique of the modernist aesthetic is just how powerful, and destabilising, irreverence towards, and mockery of, the objectives of, established authority can be. That is something well worth carrying over into the political domain: making authority look ridiculous can pay big dividends.

Whether experimentalism begins to come to the fore in art practice again or not, the postmodern aesthetic has taught us how fruitful it can be to make the greatest use we can of the material that is already around us: fruitful not just for the artist but for the audience as well. The virtue of recycling is a theme that runs through the postmodern movement – it is certainly what informs green politics and the ecological awareness it has been instrumental in creating in the general public in recent years. Admittedly, recycling is not the necessity in the arts or the realm of ideas that it is in our daily life, where the intensity of our interaction with technology generates dangerous levels of both carbon emissions and credit requirements; but it does help to foster a climate of opinion receptive to a green agenda, and a recognition that new does not always mean better. In other words, it invites us to rethink the ethics of our throw-away culture with its fetish for upgrading. Postmodernism points the way towards the change of consciousness that needs to be made in facing up to life after modernity.

Aesthetic Value: Political Value

One of the claims being made here is that it would be socially beneficial if much of the energy being channelled into creating more economic value were instead directed into artistic activities – the intention being to reorient our concept of value such that we were less obsessed with the economic realm. Perhaps we can aim for a post-historical state of mind in that realm as well as the artistic? An interesting, and highly successful, experiment in this regard is *El Sistema*, the scheme set up in Venezuela a few years ago, subsequently winning government approval and backing, to bring musical education to the country's disadvantaged youth. The main public face of this project has been the Simón Bolívar Youth Orchestra, which has gone on to create quite a stir in the concert life of the West with its spirited and enthusiastic approach to the classical repertoire. Although the orchestra may well turn out to be a commercial success in the longer run, that is not the purpose as such of the scheme. Clearly, what we have here is an example of an aesthetic goal being pursued for its social effect, with the underlying assumption that it could be applied on a large scale and become a general ideal to which anyone in the society could aspire.

The idea has since been adopted elsewhere – in the UK, for example – so there has been a recognition that this may have wider implications for our culture. Given significant official support on the Venezuelan model, it would be possible to develop a range of such activities to encourage us to think beyond the consumer culture and its emphasis on the commercialisation of our lives: a commercialisation which, as a host of commentators – from econo-mists through to scientists – has made very clear, is threatening to cost us our future. That is a topic to which I shall be returning in Chapter 9, after first considering how politics will have to change if they are to be effective in the new cultural dispensation.

8
Politics After Modernity

Politics after modernity will have to take a different form, and espouse a more flexible set of attitudes, to that in operation beforehand. For one thing, it has become clear that the doctrine of small government, so beloved of the Friedmanite school, has been found to be fatally flawed. The more we leave our economic system to be dominated by self-interest, then the more vulnerable we are likely to become collectively – right down to the level of our personal savings. Whatever the market fundamentalists may say, self-interest is not always in the public interest when it comes to economic activity. Interventionism in the market by the nation state will become more common in the immediate future, and has to be accepted as a valid tactic by all political parties rather than attacked on doctrinal grounds: a new kind of consensus has to be created on this issue which transcends the left-right divisions of our immediate political past. Regulation of the financial sector has to become much more rigorous and be subject to strict monitoring, otherwise managers will simply fall back on moral hazard, leaving the public to pick up the bill for their extravagances. The days of deregulation as a way of life have to be regarded as over; otherwise we run the risk of most of the world's nation states going the way of Iceland. Governments have to stand between us and the market – which is after all a human construction not a given of our existence as the fundamentalists like to claim – tempering the greed that the market is all too prone to generate in participants, the siren call of alpha. Markets can be constructed in a variety of ways, it does not have to be a Friedmanite free-for-all that prevails: we have tried that experiment and have no need to repeat it.

Governments also will have to cooperate far more than they are generally inclined to do, rather than seeing themselves as perpetual opponents jostling for power and advantage over each other. The Chinese government has even suggested that we should be developing a global economic currency to take over from the American dollar, the reserve currency of choice at the moment. Politically this is a very contentious notion, and it would be immensely difficult to reach agreement on it, but it does sum up a growing recognition around the world that it is dangerous to be dependent on any one nation these days, that somehow we have to start thinking supranationally rather than nationally when it comes to economic life. Economic stability cannot be found in isolation, no matter how powerful the state. The success of the euro shows it is possible to overcome old ways of thinking on economic issues, to transcend currency nationalism, and we need a lot more of that to happen.

Big government brings its own set of problems in its wake, however, and structures will have to be put in place to prevent any drift into authoritarianism – as can only too easily occur. There may be a tendency as well to reintroduce the notion of the command economy (which as we have seen still exists in modified form in China, and a few other isolated outposts of a bygone political age such as North Korea and Cuba), and this will be have to be kept under very careful scrutiny. It is one thing for big governments to save us from economic collapse, another for them to take over absolutely every function of the economy and leave little scope for any personal initiative at all. Individual greed lies at one end of the spectrum, the command economy at the other, and a properly democratic system would ensure that we avoid both conditions, maintaining a dialogue between the respective arguments for them rather than sliding into one or the other and becoming stuck there indefinitely. That leaves a significant role for all the institutions outside the formal political framework – the media, education, the arts, for example – to contribute creatively to an ongoing debate of 'greed versus authoritarianism': a reverse form of hegemony, we might say, with those institutions keeping a sceptical eye trained on government and making sure that the public is kept informed of their findings. As the expenses scandal in UK politics in 2009 revealed, politicians are as prone to greed as anyone, and the press are manifestly acting in the public interest when they bring this to light. (Although it is also interesting to note in passing that this affair seemed to generate more passion in the British public than the market crash did, as if this was on a scale that could be grasped and thus easier to reach ethical judgements about. The amounts being discussed were truly minuscule in comparison to banking misjudgements, but caused a public furore none the less.)

It has to be considered, too, how the economic crisis might affect West-East political relations, since much of the authority the West has in the ideological realm is derived from its championship of modernity and that system's success in generating material and technological progress. When that ceases then so does the West's claim to cultural leadership, and the implications of that state of affairs for geopolitics have to be explored. It could well be that rising superpowers such as China and India will become progressively more assertive in world affairs – as they are already trying to be in a bid to reflect their growing economic sophistication, hence China raising the issue of the reserve currency system in the first place. Any such moves could create an interesting new set of global tensions if the new powers continued to operate according to the principles of modernity. It could also be that non-Western ethnic minorities living in the West will seek to become more independent in terms of their lifestyle, taking their lead from such an alteration in the balance of power. Multiculturalism may well turn into even more of a political battleground than it currently is in the West, and the arguments involved require careful consideration – especially when they tend towards theocracy, which has long since fallen out of favour as a political mode in the West. Whether other means of demonstrating cultural leadership than through economic progress can be developed, with humanity's general benefit in mind, is also an issue that deserves close attention: value need not be seen, as it has been in recent times, as an exclusively economic preserve.

Currency and Sovereignty

It is a central principle of the market fundamentalist creed that all currencies have to be in competition with each other, and that their value should be determined by the workings of the market, the cut and thrust of open trading, rather than fixed by governments. Currency crises to this constituency are evidence of the market doing its job properly, being signs of healthy competition reflecting the real worth of individual currencies rather than what vain governments claim they are for purposes of status. A strong currency tends to win respect on the world stage, and attracts investment on the grounds of stability, so governments have always been keen to give that appearance – sometimes on spurious grounds. From the neoliberal perspective, however, regulation can only lead to trouble at some future point and so is to be resolutely avoided.

Until recently, most countries guarded their national currency jealously and saw it as integral to their political sovereignty – indeed, to their national identity. The advent of the euro, however, has at the very least given some pause for thought on this issue. The UK has so far refused to enter the eurozone, holding on to the notion of the symbiotic relationship between national sovereignty and national currency (the 'national currency idyll' we might term it), but the majority of Western Europe has taken the plunge and joined forces in what has turned out to be a very successful regional currency that can more than hold its own on the world stage. The newer members of the EU, in the main countries from the old Soviet bloc in Eastern Europe, are not yet all included in the eurozone but they definitely aspire to it, indicating the high regard in which it is held. It is an assumption of those countries that the euro tends to stabilise, rather than put constraints on, national economies. Britain increasingly is looking out of step with events on the global economic front when it comes to the currency question, and it is noticeable that the euro has been outperforming the pound for some time now (which is not to say that the euro is safe from speculation).

The symbolic import of the creation of the eurozone is considerable, because it demonstrates the possibility of flexibility as regards the concept of sovereignty – a flexibility which will have to become more widespread in the aftermath of modernity as everyone comes to recognise their essential interdependency. No country can pretend any longer that it has meaningful control over its national economic destiny, or that its own currency is proof against global market turmoil. In fact, small countries which maintain their own currencies are extremely vulnerable to market conditions (think of Iceland), and can hardly avoid becoming progressively more so in the current climate of instability. There is a definite argument that a move towards more regional currency zones like the euro would be to most countries' benefit. While it seems unlikely that we will see a world currency come into being, the Chinese recommendation that we develop a world reserve currency is at least worth some speculation.

The Rise and Fall of the Command Economy

The command economy is a seductive idea in that it implies rational planning on the large scale, with a clear set of socially beneficial objectives to aim for and no unpredictable market to disrupt its operations: at least in theory there should be no bubbles arising from this system. The reality has been somewhat different, and the track record of command economies over the course of the twentieth century has been less than impressive. Communist regimes invariably adopted this practice, regarding it as the way to break with the capitalist order, with its reliance on entrepreneurialism and individualism.[1] Command economies could be quite successful in wartime – almost all the countries involved in the Second World War, for example, adopted a form of command economy (or at the very least a heavily planned one), not being prepared to rely on the market in such an extreme situation. Their performance in peacetime, however, has been another matter, generally very poor. The Soviet bloc and China could deploy that form of planning to good effect when it came to military matters, and projects such as the 'space race', but were unable to guarantee a regular supply of even the most basic consumer goods that any advanced society requires. Shortages – of standard food items like fruit and vegetables, for instance – were a common feature of these regimes, and eventually created internal pressure for change, especially since the West was forging far ahead in material terms as the twentieth century advanced.

Yet we may well have to revisit the concept of the command economy in the world after modernity, because we can no longer afford to leave ourselves quite so reliant as we have been on the vagaries of the free market. As I noted in Chapter 4, we have gone well beyond the concept of the mixed economy in the response to the financial crisis to date. Western governments, including the American, have been intervening in the market to a degree unheard of in recent times, and we certainly can speak of an administered economy at the moment – quite heavily so when it comes to the financial sector. One could imagine this edging ever closer to the command format if the financial sector were to run into any deeper trouble than it has so far, so perhaps we should be considering the concept's pros and cons more closely.

Command economies may not produce the level of wealth that their free market counterparts do, but they tend to be more stable (despite, as Timothy Dunmore points out in his study of the Soviet phenomenon, a certain amount of internal competition occurring in the hierarchy of command).[2] They are also more reliable when it comes to long-range planning compared to the free market, which is constitutionally short-termist, far more concerned with immediate gains (although one could argue, and neoliberals do, that this process leads to better long-term benefits than a command or planned economy is ever likely to achieve, by creating more opportunities to take advantage of along the way). The sheer excitement generated by the market is also missing when we shift to the directly administered system, but we do have to ask ourselves whether that is the ideal basis for a national economy. We also tend to judge command or planned economies by the communist models, which lacked any properly democratic context for checks and controls. (Although it is worth noting that it has been provocatively suggested that multinationals function in a manner that mirrors the command economy, exercising a high degree of control over smaller suppliers and minimising competition within their own area.[3] It is certainly the case that few governments have the power to take on the multinationals and ask them to change their methods.) There is no reason why those forms could not exist within the democratic political model, and they would most likely be more efficient there than under the one-party structure: as noted before, wartime can bring about the kind of consensus required to make a success of this approach, so we know that it is possible. This need not be seen as a permanent situation either; the dialogue between elected democratic governments and the market will go on.

Despite the actions of governments through the crisis, there is still considerable resistance to such intervention in the workings of the market. For many on the political right, any intervention at all is to be deplored – there is fierce opposition being voiced to this in the USA, where critics are even claiming that it is a betrayal of the American way of life, socialism in all but name. Anything that hinders our development as *Homo economicus* is anathema from this perspective, and that means keeping government firmly in the background. Yet it is imperative that such arguments be faced down. It is a myth that the free market is the best way to run an economy, or that without it there can be no democratic freedom. The lesson the crisis has taught us is that economies will have to operate on a spectrum running from mixed to semi-command (depending on the overall state of the financial sector at any one point), and that we simply cannot afford to indulge the fantasies of the free marketeers. Government is not an option in the running of an economy, it is a necessity – and its role has to be more than just mere umpire.

A Changing World Order?

China's call for the development of a new world reserve currency, one not tied to any particular nation as at present, is an indication of a changing world order. It represents a clear challenge to Western hegemony in the financial sector, and is therefore politically loaded. If such a currency did emerge it would constitute a significant blow to the prestige of the United States in particular, which would most likely cause it to lose much of its geopolitical authority and power. Admittedly, there is a big gap between floating such an idea as this and convincing the rest of the world to accept it, but it is a politically highly symbolic proposal that hints at growing confidence in the non-Western bloc as regards their economic future vis-à-vis the traditionally dominant West. The West cannot go on assuming it will always be able to set the global economic agenda as if by natural right, especially not after such a graphic illustration of how unreliable its financial sector can be as the credit crisis has just provided.

There is an inherent problem in the emergence of China and India as global economic powers, however, and it is that they will seek to pursue the goals of modernity – continual technological progress and rapidly improving living standards across the board. Although their economies have a long way to go yet to reach Western standards overall, the sheer size of their populations gives them massive room for growth, plus considerable pressure from the masses to deliver this as quickly as possible. If these two countries go down the modernity route then we can look forward to accelerated global warming, probably very accelerated, and the prospect of yet more globally destabilising credit bubbles. (Alan Greenspan is also concerned about the impact of such expansion on global inflation, but this seems far less of a worry than the other two prospects. What he describes as 'yet more inflationary tinder' will enflame more than just the inflation rate.)[4] The West is in an awkward position over this issue, because it would be hypocritical to deny other cultures the opportunity to develop technologically as we have been doing for several centuries now. Yet the more these cultures proceed to do so then the larger the eventual crisis we are building up for ourselves on a global scale: resources are not infinite, particularly when it comes to energy, and the market's weaknesses as an engine of growth have been ruthlessly exposed of late. On both counts,

problems cannot help but loom up as the Chinese and Indian economies expand, as they are primed to do.

Such expansion is of course contingent on the global financial
crisis being resolved, but Martin Jacques has argued that we are
entering into a period of 'contested modernity' owing to growth
outside the Western world, which he is confident has the impetus
to continue.[5] In Jacques's reading of this phenomenon, China is to
the fore:

> The West has thought itself to be universal, the unquestioned model
> and example for all to follow; in the future it will be only one of several
> possibilities . . . The bearer of this change will be China, partly because
> of its overwhelming size but also because of the nature of its culture and
> outlook. China, unlike Japan, has always regarded itself as universal, the
> centre of the world, and even, for a millennium and more, believed that
> it actually constituted the world. The emergence of Chinese modernity
> immediately de-centres and relativizes the position of the West. That is
> why the rise of China has such far-reaching implications.[6]

In similar mode, Fareed Zakaria foresees a move towards a 'post-
American world', arguing that this is not a case of 'the decline of
America but rather the rise of everyone else'[7] – and by 'everyone
else' he specifically means the non-Western community. Socially
and politically this form of modernity will be very different from
the Western version, yet it will be no less of a strain on the planet –
modernity cannot help but be that, however it is structured. (Okwui
Enwezor has noted how modernity's 'make it new' principle is still
apparently in play among the Chinese urban planning authorities,
who 'are simply unsympathetic to any idea that cities like Beijing
need to be historicised' and are demolishing old neighbourhoods
wholesale to replace them with tower blocks and skyscrapers.[8]
Apart from the regrettable loss of heritage, this is also a markedly
carbon emission-intensive programme.)

It is therefore encouraging to note that China has announced
plans to develop its solar and wind power sources very considerably, setting a target for 2020 of producing 20 per cent of its energy
needs from renewables.[9] Whether this will be enough to offset its

economic growth during that period remains to be seen (and China is already overtaking America in terms of total carbon emissions, with the inherent capability far to outstrip it). It is always worth remembering that governments often set ambitious targets in this area and then fail to meet them: the track record for the major players is quite poor, with a variety of lame excuses invariably being offered – generally before even more ambitious targets are then put forward as if to compensate. Given China's potential economic and technological expansion, we can only hope that it manages to break the mould in this respect.

Another problem that has recently been identified in this area is that continually expanding internet use (at least in part a product of the rapidly growing economies in countries like China and India) is beginning to put world electricity resources under considerable strain, raising again the prospect of increased carbon emissions as energy use goes up. It is clearly a sign of progress that non-Western cultures are able to access this system more extensively than they were able to in the past, but, as always, progress does not come without various complications in its wake – and those complications are not ones we can choose to ignore. There seems to be no prospect of internet use declining either: servers, search engines and advertisers are as committed to growth as modernity always has been, and will want traffic to increase for the benefit of their balance sheets. The expansion of the Chinese and Indian economies offers precisely that opportunity.

China may yet manage to escape the worst effects of the credit crisis because of its highly centralised political system, which gives it much tighter control over market activity than its Western counterparts have, thus in theory not being so unpredictable. (The system also promotes a very high degree of saving on the part of the population, which is allowed little in the way of investment opportunities, thus giving the authorities even more flexibility compared to the West: put simply, they are not as dependent on access to credit.) But this state of affairs cannot be relied upon for ever: commentators tend to suggest that acceptance of this degree of control is crucially dependent on rising living standards, and would have difficulty surviving any massive economic downturn.[10] In such a situation, the masses could well turn against the Communist Party, which has made economic improvement its central priority and effectively the basis of its governing legitimacy. There is also the problem of the Party's authoritarian nature, which in its denial of the value of pluralism is not the best way forward for political life after modernity. There is a need for more checks and balances, more scope for dissent and the creation of little narratives to our political systems than the Chinese presently admits, in order to counter the greater centralisation that has to occur to guard against the excesses of the free market.

Lacking its totalitarian political heritage and ideology, the Indian system allows greater scope for independent entrepreneurial activity than the Chinese currently does. While it did pursue a planned economy in its earlier history, nowadays, as Fareed Zakaria has summarised it, 'India's growth is taking place not because of the government but despite it. It is not top-down but bottom-up – messy, chaotic, and largely unplanned'.[11] But that carries the dangers we have seen come to the fore in the West in recent years when entrepreneurialism has been given its head – overheated markets, environmental blindness (or even outright denial) on the part of corporations and investors, indiscriminate use of energy and finite resources, all of these adding up to a recipe for yet further crisis.[12]

Again, the factor of scale needs to be taken into account: massively increased entrepreneurial activity in a country of over a billion population, and rising rapidly, could easily push us past several key environmental and economic tipping points. The country's environmental record already leaves much to be desired, although one always has to sympathise to some extent with the plight of developing nations trying to catch up with the West. Much of the poor practice with regard to the environment in emerging economies like India merely mimics what happened here in the earlier stages of industrialisation, which was an environmental disaster for large parts of the West (remember Engels's reports in *The Condition of the Working Class in England*, for example). The West came very late, and often more than somewhat reluctantly, to ecological consciousness, and its moral authority in that area is questionable. In that context, it would have to be said that the renewed enthusiasm for nuclear power in countries like the UK (as an alternative to fossil fuel-derived energy) raises some very awkward questions about our commitment to protecting the environment. The nuclear industry's record on that score is less than impressive, but the alluring prospect of growth seems to have the capacity to shorten memories – particularly among politicians, who are being very bullish about the return of nuclear.

Political Parties After Modernity

One of the most pressing demands of the collapse of modernity is that the internal ethos of the political party requires radical reassessment. In the first place, parties must lose their obsession with economic growth and the cult of progress. It is the headlong pursuit of those goals, alpha politics, that has landed us with the problem in which we are now mired, and they cannot go on being seen as all-purpose solutions – or the main focus of formal political life either. Too much of Western politics consists of jostling between parties as to who it is can claim to be best suited to delivering improved living standards, with little consideration of how these will impact on the environment or whether this is a sustainable project in the longer term. The electorate is rarely invited to think past the economic – and on the grounds of climate change alone it really should be.

I suggested earlier that political parties ought to spend more time developing a moral agenda to take us into the new cultural climate emerging in the wake of modernity, and that is something the major parties in Western society have been very deficient in doing in recent history. Even the left, which at one time did have a wider social vision that went beyond the economic, and prided itself in doing so, has in the main succumbed to market worship, often being all but indistinguishable from its right-wing opponents in this respect. Green issues, for example, are generally given official support, and included in party platforms when elections come around, but rarely given any very significant funding. The rhetoric is there, yet little of real substance ever seems to happen, despite the repeated warnings we are receiving from the scientific community and the environmental lobby about the implications of the onward march of global warming. Yet the longer we delay taking action over this then the more expensive it will be when finally we do – and the less likely to have the desired effect as we face the process at a far more advanced stage.

Whether green energy ever could replace the fossil-fuel variety entirely is still a very open question, but it deserves more than the token gestures towards its development that it is tending to receive from most governments at present – gestures that are likely to become even more token under the impact of a financial crisis. Far more of a lead needs to be given by governments to alter public attitudes, which means consciously propagating a moral agenda about our use of the environment. Relying on the good will of the private sector to change its ways is an exercise in wishful thinking, since there is always the danger of companies indulging in deception about their policies – 'greenwash' as it has been called.

We shall probably only receive such a lead, however, if pressure is consistently exerted on governments from below to show that this is what we want from our politicians, that we really do desire a new direction and a new set of standards by which to conduct our lives. We are locked into a symbiotic relationship in that regard: they will do what they think it is we want, and unless we make it clear that we are unhappy with what they are doing then they will continue doing it. This cycle has to be broken if we are ever to overcome our material progress syndrome, and that will mean tapping into what the political scientist John Keane has called 'monitory democracy' far more purposefully. Monitory democracy involves closely auditing the formal political system through a wide range of 'extra-parliamentary power-monitoring institutions', such as watchdog bodies of various kinds, think-tanks and the media, the idea being to promote 'constant public scrutiny' of our official representatives.[13] There is an echo of Lyotard's little narrative in the notion, with a diffuse, and constantly changing, set of players contesting the build-up of central power. A critical role can be played by the internet, the natural home of the little narrative, where anyone can start a campaign against authority and tout around for support (although as noted above, use of the internet does bring resource problems in its train). To avail ourselves of these resources is to 'have the effect of potentially bringing greater humility to the established model of party-led representative government', and Keane is all in favour of that as an objective.[14]

Keane is advocating an essentially negative concept of politics, basing this on the premise that,

> although citizens and representatives require institutions to govern, *no body should rule*. Democratic institutions – monitory democracy is so far the best-developed overall example – ideally dispense with *rule*, if by that is meant bossing others who have few or no means of redress. Under democratic conditions, nobody rules in the sense that those who govern others are subject constantly to the ideal of public chastening.[15]

The more positive side of the monitory process is that it can be deployed not just to check the excesses of our elected representatives (which is undeniably needed), but also to state the case for a more morally conscious government of the kind that the situation after modernity patently requires. Politicians will only cease to be obsessed with economic growth if the general public indicates that it is ready to do so too, and makes its voice heard loud and clear.

A moral agenda would certainly include debate on the principle of enough, inviting us to consider the value of moving away from the overtly consumerist culture that modernity has so aggressively promoted in the last century. We have become comprehensively addicted to consumerism and material progress, with the fast food industry providing a classic example of how this can be embedded in us as individuals at a very basic level. David A. Kessler's book *The End of Overeating* is highly instructive in this regard in revealing how the industry goes about keeping us physically hooked on its products: 'Food manufacturers, food designers, and restaurant owners may not fully understand the science behind the appeal of their foods, but they know that sugar, fat, and salt sell.'[16] As an (understandably) unnamed food industry insider confides to Kessler, '[h]igher sugar, fat, and salt make you want to eat more'.[17] He goes on to admit that these are the 'three points of the compass' as far as the industry is concerned, and as 'the manipulator of the consumers' minds and desires' it is only too happy to saturate its products with these ingredients and both feed and promote our subsequent cravings.[18]

Americans spend 50 per cent of their food budget in restaurants (often chains with identical products being offered across the country), and, as Kessler notes:

> Countless new foods have been introduced in restaurants, and most of them hit the three points of the compass. Sugar, fat, and salt are either loaded onto a core ingredient (such as meat, vegetable, potato, or bread), layered on top of it, or both. Deep-fried tortilla chips are an example of loading – the fat is contained in the chip itself. When the potato is smothered in cheese, sour cream, and sauce, that's layering.[19]

The obesity epidemic in the West bears all too obvious witness to the considerable success of the industry's manipulative skills, with fast food chains being at the forefront of the operation. Felicity Lawrence makes a similar point when she remarks that '[t]he genius of contemporary globalized capitalism . . . has been not just that it gives consumers what they want but that it is able to make them want what it has to sell', and what we want more and more of, it would seem, is 'degraded industrialized food'.[20] (I will be returning to the topic of fast food in Chapter 9, considering some of the opposition that has arisen in response to the industry's unremitting global expansion and its effect on our lifestyles.)

It could be argued, however, that the energy this addiction to consumerism generates in us to keep the system expanding is a positive trait in terms of humankind's development; that it prevents us from becoming stuck in a rut, culturally speaking, or perhaps even regressing as a species. Societies can ossify, and history provides us with numerous thought-provoking examples of this phenomenon. When European colonisation took off, it kept encountering cultures which had failed to develop past a certain point and were as a result very vulnerable to outside intrusion. Africa, Asia and South America could all be said to have suffered from having allowed themselves to become relatively static societies, thus unable to respond very effectively to changing or unforeseen circumstances (which is no excuse for colonialism of course, and is not intended to be). These are the kind of arguments that can be backed up by complexity theory, which sees physical systems, including species, as at their most efficient and creative when they are struggling to maintain themselves at the 'edge of chaos', that is, being kept under pressure to be innovative in order to prevent collapse (and we know that societal collapse is a normative experience, for one reason or another, over the course of human history). That could be said to describe the condition of modernity, which demands constant innovation to propel expansion. How can we ensure that embracing a programme of reduced materialism would not lead to cultural regression?

The first point to make in reply is that there are other ways of developing and directing human energy than in the pursuit of purely economic goals. We have become fixated on material progress to an unhealthy degree, envisaging this as the only way to underpin a society such as ours, the argument essentially being that the economic realm took precedence and that all other activities were to be considered secondary – that these were in a sense parasitic on economic success and the entrepreneurial imperative. Publicly funded arts were all well and good, but only if the economy was in rude good health and had some spare resource to expend. The same went for most welfare systems, which are so often pictured, particularly by the political right, as a drain on the economy and the development of the entrepreneurial spirit. Yet there is, as mentioned before, no lack of enterprises we could undertake to improve the human lot (combatting poverty and disease in the developing world, and environmental abuse, for starters), and that would surely count as keeping chaos at bay and exercising our faculties to the fullest. We are capable of developing that compassionate side of our natures if given some encouragement. Peter Singer for one is in no doubt that we are ethically obliged to do so, urging us all in his book *The Life You Can Save* to divert 5 per cent of our income to projects to alleviate poverty in the developing nations.[21]

Part of the problem is that we are still prone to think in narrowly national terms: striving to keep our own nation on the right side of chaos, staving it off by our collective ingenuity, while regarding any slip by our competitors as to our political benefit, a breach for us to step into to improve our GDP at their expense. Politicians openly support this kind of competition, and are quick to turn it to account for themselves and their party whenever they can as evidence of their economic competence, their practised skill at negotiating the complexities of the market. The national idyll conspires to prevent change, with the main parties colluding to maintain this practice, but internationally – and glocally, we might say – this is simply counter-productive. It is not helping in the struggle against global warming, which just cannot be left to the whims of individual nation states – which pretty much describes the real state of affairs at present once you move past the rhetoric about international cooperation. There is still a marked reluctance among the world's major powers to put the international before the national interest.

Happiness, Wellbeing and Politics

There is one nation in the world that has tried to shift the focus of politics away from the economic to a different lifestyle criterion in recent times, and that is Bhutan, which has developed what it calls a Gross National Happiness (GNH) index. Happiness is held to require a spiritual dimension as well as a material, and is now taken to be the primary objective of Bhutanese national life, with the political class considering itself to be under an obligation to gear their policies towards that end. The GNH was established by King Jigme Singye Wangchuck in 1972, and it was designed to ensure that the country's Buddhist values continued to play a criti-cal role in national life despite a drive towards modernisation of the economy. In the words of the current ruler, King Khesar, in his coro-nation speech of 2008: 'As the king of a Buddhist nation, my duty is not only to ensure your happiness today but to create the fertile ground from which you may gain the fruits of spiritual pursuit and attain good Karma.'[22]

GNH is based on a commitment to sustainable development, the preservation of cultural values and environmental conservation, and it has prompted enough interest to generate a series of international conferences exploring the geopolitical import of the concept. The Buddhist dimension certainly opens up a new perspective as regards modernity, and raises the interesting prospect of the development of a Buddhist work ethic to contest the field with the better-known Protestant variety. In a study undertaken at the University of Leicester in 2007, Bhutan came eighth out of 178 countries in terms of 'Subjective Well-Being' (SWB), outscoring many major Western nations and their considerably richer economies – notably the UK, USA and Canada, for example.[23] (Just for the record, Denmark and Switzerland came joint first, so the developed world can be successful at this game too.)

It would be easy to be critical of the Bhutanese approach, to argue that it is out of touch with the real world where tough political decisions have to be made in the face of fierce international competition for trade and resources, and where small nations can render themselves vulnerable by not playing that game as hard as they can. Lack of economic power tends to be equated with weakness in the harsh climate of globalisation, and others can be quick to take advantage of this (not least the multinationals looking for cheap sources of outsourced production, and intent on driving as hard a bargain with the local governing authorities as they can). Neither is the IMF or the World Bank going to be too impressed with happiness being deemed to take precedence over economic performance. To apply for a loan to pursue such a goal would most likely strike them as a sign of naiveté. The spiritual dimension is of no particular interest to such institutions; nor for that matter are the unique cultural values of individual nations, not if the preservation of these proves to be a barrier to the economic restructuring held to be necessary to comply with the globalisation ethic. What makes the globalisation lobby happy is homogenisation, not the maintenance of difference.

Whether GNH has been adhered to by the Bhutanese political class over the years, official statements notwithstanding, is a matter of some debate, as is whether the principle is consistent with the thrust of modernisation, which is unashamedly material-istic. Consumer goods can so easily lead both rulers and populace astray, no matter how good their original intentions may have been – we have ample experience of the process ourselves. Yet the symbolic significance of the notion of happiness is intriguing all the same. Here is a nation which is actively engaging with the issue of social value, and attempting to redefine this in a manner which runs counter to most current Western beliefs – in itself a bold thing to do in a globalised world where commerce is indis-putably king. Quality of life in the West tends to be identified with economic wellbeing, and economic wellbeing with a buoyant and expanding economy (the opposite being known, tellingly enough, as depression). Happiness, or at least content, is assumed to follow on from such a condition, although we are expected to keep striv-ing to improve our economic performance, both individually and nationally, and not to rest on our laurels and run the risk of falling behind our peers – establishing ourselves in a position to best the opposition must always remain a key goal. Free market economics demands that there be a certain edge to our lives, and insists that competition provides the most effective means to achieve this – and the more competitive the environment is the better. That is the free market version of staying on the right side of the edge of chaos. As I have been noting frequently throughout this book, however, and shall be emphasising again in the final chapter, there are a range of other activities that could achieve the same result, and none of them is precisely tied to the market. These need not have the spir-itual dimension demanded by the GNH (or the originators of the 'enough' principle), but they would certainly not be materialistically inspired either.

The development of the SWB metric does indicate there is a concern to look beyond the economic sphere in the West as well. SWB is defined as 'a field of psychology that attempts to understand peo-ple's evaluations of their lives . . . and includes variables such as life satisfaction and marital satisfaction, lack of depression and anxiety, and positive moods and emotions'.[24] While income levels can have an affect on SWB, they are by no means the whole story and, as a study pointed out in 1998, 'SWB reports have not changed at all in wealthy nations such as the U.S.A., Japan, and France as they have gained more income over the last 20 years'[25] (and that gain was considerable). Indeed, the authors emphasise 'that the correlation between income and SWB is small in most countries'[26] – although one might want to find out whether that still applies in a credit crisis such as the current one, with anxiety over the safety of one's savings, mortgages and investments kicking in, especially as the bad economic news continues to pile up. (It would be interesting to conduct an SWB survey in Iceland at the moment; one suspects it would come up with far lower ratings than in the past.) Practitioners in the field feel their findings have important political implications, however, and that SWB should be deployed by governments in any 'assessment of a nation's success', and even help to 'form a basis of political governance'.[27]

There are in fact a number of such metrics in circulation at present, such as the 'Genuine Progress Indicator' (GPI) developed by 'Redefining Progress' and the 'Happy Planet Index' (HPI) of the New Economic Foundation (NEF). These both take it as their task to challenge the most widely used metric of national life, the Gross Domestic Product (GDP), which as the name suggests focuses entirely on the factor of economic performance. Redefining Progress proceeds to raise some very awkward questions about the concept of progress itself, arguing that the GDP makes 'no distinctions between transactions that enhance wellbeing and those that diminish it'.[28] The foundation's concern instead is 'to measure sustainable economic welfare rather than economic activity alone'.[29] In other words, progress is officially being measured in purely economic terms of 'more is better', whereas Redefining Progress's emphasis is on its social aspect, the objective being to make us aware of such injustices as the fact that the 'GDP is oblivious to gross inequality', treating all expenditure as exactly the same.[30] Conspicuous consumption by the wealthy therefore serves to improve the GDP, despite signally failing to add anything of social value to the nation's life (unless you still believe in 'trickle down').

It is also pointed out that environmental pollution increases the GDP because the necessary activity of cleaning it up, which can be very expensive (think oil spills from tankers, for example, or dealing with radioactive waste), simply adds to economic activity overall. The costs of fighting crime also contribute to the GDP – and, as Douglas Rushkoff has witheringly observed, so do '[c]ancer, divorce, attention-deficit/hyperactivity disorder diagnoses, and obesity'.[31] Again, expenditure alone is what counts and, although the public does gain something by the environment being cleaned up and criminals brought to justice, it would rather that such activities were not necessary. No-one would seek an increase in pollution and crime in order to improve the economy, never mind welcome a greater incidence of cancer, divorce and obesity throughout their society. The point is that whatever is purchased, for whatever reason, pushes the GDP up, and for the majority of politicians that is all that matters – they can take refuge behind the figures. As I pointed out before, modernity revels in statistics.

GPI, in contrast, measures such things as welfare equivalent income, sustainable income and net social profit. This leads Redefining Progress to lend strong support to green projects, which manifestly do benefit the environment. In a general sense it is the benefits of economic activity in which they are more interested, and where they see social value as residing. When it comes to something like pollution, therefore, that would mean deducting clean-up costs from the income generated by the original polluting activity, giving us a very different figure to that listed in the GDP (and the same would apply with crime). The metrics diverge quite considerably on how they interpret the data of national performance, and at the very least this ought to spark debate.

The New Economics Foundation (NEF) takes a very similar line with their HPI index, which emphasises the environmental side even more than Redefining Progress does, seeking 'to combine environmental impact with human well-being to measure the environmental efficiency with which country by country, people live long and happy lives'.[32] A happy planet is an environmentally sound one, and this is the only way we shall ever achieve 'real economic wellbeing'.[33] Bhutan scores well in NEF's league table too, although falling back to 13th out of 178 this time around. Compare this to the UK and USA, however, which can only manage 108th and 150th respectively, for all their indisputably stronger economies and GDPs. Environmental soundness is something we cannot depend on the major Western powers to deliver, it would appear. The world leader this time around turns out to be the tiny South Pacific island-chain nation of Vanuatu, despite its scarce resources (what little agricultural land it has would be at risk from any significant rise in sea levels caused by global warming, for example) and rapidly growing population.

There is clearly a substantial degree of support for a move away from an economics-biased politics in contemporary culture, although also a recognition that official politics still in the main tends to define itself against economic criteria such as GDP figures. (Neither is it in the nature of politics as currently practised that there will be much interest shown in government circles for switching to indices that show one's country performing badly – especially when it is against the developing world. That would most likely be regarded as a humiliation.) GDP turns out to be the crudest of measuring schemes, with nothing to say about social value or the adverse impact that certain kinds of economic activity can have on the environment: GDP welcomes increased carbon emissions as proof of economic growth, in fact. GPI and HPI tell a very different story, and suggest the need for a very different kind of politics, one that takes redefinition seriously, and is concerned with quality as opposed to just quantity: one that would be inspired rather than humiliated by the example of such as Bhutan.

Even politicians in the UK concede that there is more to life than money, but it is noticeable how the debate tends to revert back to the economic when elections loom or financial crisis strikes. And even if there is some rhetoric expressed about the importance of enhancing personal well-being, it rarely goes to the lengths of attacking consumerism, entrepreneurialism or wealth creation. I am arguing that it should, however, and we will only really know that we have achieved a politics fit to deal with life after modernity when it starts to do so in earnest. How we might adjust our priorities accordingly is where I will take the argument in conclusion.

9
Conclusion: A Post-Progress World

The real threat in our current situation is that the political class will consider the credit crunch as constituting merely a brief hiatus in the onward march of modernity, and seek to find new sources of fossil fuel (still, unfortunately, the most reliable and best-developed source of energy we have at our disposal at present) to rebuild the economy – thus continuing the highly dangerous process of global warming. Politically seductive though the prospect may be to a society brought up on the promises of modernity, and still largely under its spell, it has to be recognised that whatever leads to overheating the economy will only succeed in its turn in overheating the planet too: in which case modernity might well be the death of us not just as a culture but as a species. This will be especially so if we do enter into an age of 'contested modernity', as Martin Jacques has claimed is imminent with China's rise. Global warming sceptics notwithstanding, we cannot go on as before once we have crossed over the threshold into after modernity: modes of living based on considerations other than material progress, and the competitive ethic lying behind that, just have to be developed.

This last chapter investigates what such an adjustment to our priorities ought to involve, and how we can respond creatively to the huge challenge this undoubtedly will pose for us. There is considerable scope for philosophers and critical theorists to make a significant contribution here, encouraging us to re-examine what we mean by concepts such as 'progress' and 'competition', not to mention 'value', and to engage in more public debate about how we can reconstruct society in the wake of modernity. The various metrics just considered in Chapter 8 give us a lead in this respect. Post-Marxism, radical democracy and cosmopolitanism all have something to say to us as well, especially in their commitment to new forms of pluralism, as well as to rethinking the character of the global political order (and, in a general sense, rethinking our ethics).

Progress, Competition and Value in a 'Post-Progress' World

What might a world 'post-progress' look like? There are already voices in the radical ecology lobby calling for a return to a pre-industrial lifestyle (EarthFirst!, for example), and, although these are unlikely to find favour with the wider public, they still have to be given serious consideration. It could be that some aspects of their programme could be adapted to a less-severe regimen than they are proposing (their call for a reduction in the Earth's population, for example, is eminently sensible, if socially and politically daunting to bring about). The notion that everything we can do technologically we *should* do, manifestly needs to be reassessed: many so-called technological innovations are of little real benefit to humanity (merely glorified toys in many cases), and often of considerable harm. What seems more sellable to the wider public is a significantly modified version of the current system that takes into account the need to eradicate the excesses of the previous order (and warnings about the dangers of losing one's sense of proportion go right back to classical Greek thought, hence the maxim 'nothing in excess').[1]

The modifications would have to include much wider powers for the government in the economic sphere. Governments have to become more involved as well with setting a moral agenda, and there is a real argument for a return to a more socialist outlook where the public good is placed above the private – rather than just assuming, as the more radical interpretations of free-market capitalism always do, that the latter will automatically lead to the former (the notion of public service, as I shall go on to discuss below, very much needs to be revisited and revived). The dubious 'trickle down' principle must surely now be consigned to oblivion: yes, it worked to some extent, but only at the expense of licensing even more greed at the top end of the economic scale, thereby widening markedly the inequality between there and the bottom end and fuelling the growth of self-interest even further. The cynicism that lies behind 'trickle down' is inimical to the development of a just society.

The hyper-individualism associated with advanced modernity has to be phased out therefore, and a more collectively oriented world-view implemented in its stead. Egalitarianism is an idea whose time has surely arrived, and with the right kind of monitory democracy we can start campaigning spiritedly for that: radical democracy, cosmopolitanism and post-Marxism all push us in that direction. There are a host of projects around the world – alleviating poverty, combatting disease, cleaning up the environment, for example – which would improve the quality of life for the majority of humanity far more than the creation of yet more private wealth in the market ever would. The argument often heard back, in a variant of the 'trickle down' notion, that greater wealth promotes greater incidence of philanthropy, enabling such problems to be tackled, also should be challenged. In the first place, the arbitrariness of philanthropy has to be acknowledged: it will not always be applied where there is the greatest social need, and neither is it publicly accountable for its policy decisions. Too often it is a rich person's plaything, with all the self-publicising connotations that this carries with it. Philanthropy is also contingent on economic success: funding can be withdrawn quite suddenly if the individual or business behind it runs into difficulty (or even, more mundanely, just loses interest), meaning that continuity, which is essential in these cases, can never really be guaranteed. The idea that governments can transfer some of their welfare functions to the private sector runs into the same difficulty: in bad economic times such schemes become very vulnerable to cutbacks. (Transferring public transport systems, such as rail, bus or subway, to the private sector has a pretty chequered history also, generally leading to higher fares and reduced services in the long run.)

Overall, philanthropy promotes a 'them' and 'us' situation that is not socially beneficial, making those of 'us' lower down the social scale feel acutely aware of our lack of power and resource. No doubt the George Soroses and Bill Gateses of the world are sincere in their desire to put something back into society, but having to be reliant on the whims of rich individuals is in the final analysis a rather demeaning condition for any society to be placed in: a step backwards in time. We do not really share in such an exercise. At a personal level, to be the recipient of charity can be damaging to one's self-respect, far more so than being given government aid. Philanthropists cannot realistically replace government when it comes to looking after the public's welfare requirements.

Whatever we do, we really must set about changing our belief that endless material progress is the most desirable of human goals: neither ethically nor environmentally is this so, and the point needs to be made vigorously and often. We have to develop a 'post-progress' mindset to chart our way through the real postmodern – and the first step in the process is to face up to the fatal contradiction that lies at the heart of our current ideological paradigm. Material progress cannot be endless, our energies need to be redirected and we have to start exploring possible ways of doing this. Going on as before is not an option, and we would be in denial to think it is.

I drew attention in Chapter 7 to *El Sistema*, the Venezuelan scheme to use musical education as a method of combatting social deprivation and alienation among the nation's youth. The main virtue of the scheme is that it gives Venezuelan youth something concrete to which to aspire, in the first instance participation in the Simón Bolivar Youth Orchestra, which now has a well-deserved international reputation and is much in demand on the Western concert circuit. In effect, musical education has become an ideological tool for the Venezuelan government, their longer-term goal being to re-educate people away from a life of drugs, crime and political apathy (another effort in this direction has been to mass-produce copies of *Don Quixote* for public consumption). Results so far have been extremely promising, and other governments around the globe are beginning to take notice of what has to be described as one of the most innovative schemes of social engineering of our time – one in which it is hard to find any flaw so far. Pilot schemes are already up and running in the UK, and no doubt others will soon follow on in other countries. It is hard to see how any country can fail to benefit from the development of such schemes.

A similar kind of project to *El Sistema* is the East-West Diwan Orchestra set up by the conductor and pianist Daniel Barenboim, which aims to inspire cooperation between youth across the Arab-Israeli political divide. This is another group to have gained considerable international acclaim on the Western concert circuit. In both instances the goals involve a reorientation of mindset, on the part of the players and their audiences too. Clearly, competition is involved, but it is channelled towards personal artistic achievement, to be expressed subsequently in the common good of the orchestra rather than in the pursuit of individual material success. The latter pursuit is invariably a socially divisive phenomenon. When it comes to the business world, for example, the goal of competition is not just to triumph over one's opponents, but to remove them from the equation if at all possible: corporations have a natural tendency towards monopoly. Business is not conducted on Olympic principles (New Olympianism is something else altogether), and its attitudes permeate our belief system. The East-West Diwan and *El Sistema* represent a welcome reorientation of the competitive instinct.

It would be very much to society's benefit if more schemes such as these were set up – many more, and across the arts in general, not just in the field of music. The point would be to challenge the notion that we can only derive value from the pursuit of material gain, or that entrepreneurialism is the character trait we should be striving to develop at the expense of almost all others. The self-development being encouraged here brings a whole new outlook on life in which the fostering of one's talent takes precedence, but a talent subsequently to be socially applied. Much the same kind of points can be made about science, which is rarely chosen as a career on financial grounds. When it comes to research in particular, the majority of scientists are motivated by intellectual considerations, although it has to be conceded that such research is then open to exploitation by the corporate sector. That is a political issue, however, and for practitioners the value of scientific enquiry lies in the practice itself, not its economic potential. Encouraging that form of creativity would be as worthwhile as doing so in the sphere of the arts. It is not sufficient to cut consumption and curb the excesses of entrepreneurialism: we must also find a new focus for the energies that went into activities such as these.

Rediscovering Public Service

One of the many victims of neoliberal economics has been the concept of public service, which has systematically been vilified by the school of Friedman as if it summed up everything that was wrong with our society: the haven of the petty bureaucrat and meddling small 'l' liberal, who created no wealth, curbed initiative and presided over a culture of spirit-sapping dependence. Margaret Thatcher was particularly noted for such attacks while she was in office, and did her level best to tarnish the reputation of the public sector – an activity the UK's right-wing press were only too happy to provide support for (many still are). I want to argue that the time has come for that reputation to be resurrected and for the virtues of public service to be rediscovered. Public service has the capacity to provide yet another means of redirecting our energies away from the purely economic and finding value, and personal fulfilment, in socially useful activity.

Neoliberalism treated public service as parasitic on the body politic, claiming that it drained it of resources and prevented the private sector from expanding its empire to the ultimate public benefit. The argument was that the commercial world would run all institutions far more efficiently, that the introduction of competition into the public realm would revolutionise its performance out of all recognition. Public service was taken to be the refuge of mediocrities who could not cut it in the private sector, and who were content to sponge on the public purse instead. As far as the neoliberals were concerned, private always meant better than public, whether in health, education, transport systems or the media; the application of market principles saw to that, rendering the institution in question not just more efficient, but cheaper as well. The proponents of small government were particularly keen on the idea, regarding 'going private' as the solution to a host of our social ills. Here again, deregulation was seen as a panacea, a means to liberate healthcare, education and broadcasting – to name some of the primary targets of the neoliberal ascendancy – from the dead hand of public bureaucracy, thus generating initiative and enterprise. (The American government went so far as to privatise many of the functions of its army in the field in Iraq, a policy which has been very controversial and a source of many ethical complications as to where responsibility for actions then lie. But it does show just how deep the belief in deregulation went in official circles: nothing could be considered sacred anymore.)

Needless to say, such a campaign had an extremely demoralising effect on those working within the public sector, who were made to feel as if they were collectively barriers to progress, little better than relics of a bygone socialist age which had misunderstood how our society really worked. The plan was to pare down the entire edifice, driving out the unproductive elements in the process: 'Populating the world with more caring people', was not, as Zygmunt Bauman observed, any part of 'the panoramas painted in the consumerist utopias'.[2] Those with real talent, so the story went, were going into the cutting-edge industries of the new technological age – including, of course, the increasingly trendy financial sector, where fortunes were waiting to be made by the enterprising. The ethos of public service, serving others for the public good and helping to improve the general quality of life thereby, suffered badly from such a change in climate; instead, being in the public sector almost became something to be apologetic about, as if it signalled a lack of personal ambition. Those who work in the public sector tend to have a strong sense of social responsibility but, as noted repeatedly throughout this book, this is not something that Friedmanite neoliberals concern themselves with overmuch. Anything that gets in the way of chasing alpha is to be avoided. Public sector workers have also traditionally put job satisfaction above financial reward in their priorities (which governments have been only too willing to exploit in a fairly cynical fashion over the years), but again, neoliberals can only see this as self-defeating – and, in their terms of reference, bad for the economy.

The public service ethos is still there under the surface of our society, however, and it can, and should, be developed and fostered again. That would be a socially valuable exercise, encouraging us to put the public good before private gain; encouraging us, also, to think beyond being mere consumers, to being instead participants in a larger social project that bonds us together as fellow citizens. Institutions such as the National Health Service and the BBC have been civilising influences in British life, and deserve continued public funding rather than, as the neoliberals would prefer, being turned over to the private sector and submitted to the dictates of the profit motive. One of the things the crisis should have taught is how much we need a vibrant, socially committed public sector looking after the public interest. It is one of the many ironies of the crisis, however, that the rescue of the banking industry by governments is likely to be paid for by cuts in the public sector over the next few years (quite a few cuts and quite a few years, if the more pessimistic accounts are to be believed). Even if this happens, the case for public service ought to be made as strongly as possible: it has to be made clear that there is life beyond self-interest, and that it would be to our benefit to promote the development of the social side of our nature wherever we can. A post-progress world is one in which the public sector can regain its sense of mission, its virtues once again recognised. We certainly cannot depend on the private sector to raise the level of social responsibility in our society, nor to nurture altruism.

Douglas Rushkoff suggests that we develop this notion of public service at an even more basic level, such as becoming more involved with voluntary activities in our everyday round:

[T]he more social we get, the more one voluntary act will encourage another one, and so on. We learn it's more fun and less time-consuming to provide real help to our local elementary school than to take on an extra corporate job to pay for that private one . . . Reciprocity is not a market phenomenon; it is a social one. And when the market is no longer functioning properly, it is a necessary life skill.[3]

Rushkoff also draws attention to a range of locally oriented non-profit organisations to attach ourselves to, all of them designed to bypass the mainstream corporate sector in the cause of the public good. Community-supported-agriculture groups (CSAs), for example, 'let typical food consumers become members of their local agricultural community', instead of relying on supermarket produce brought in from farther afield at considerable cost in terms of carbon emissions. Schemes of this nature will contribute to what Rushkoff rather engagingly calls a 'melt-up' to counteract the financial melt-down that has been visited upon us by the excesses of corporatism.[4]

Sympathetic though I am to this idea, I do not think it will be enough on its own to take us through the crisis. There will still be a need for assertive governments to protect us against an ever-inventive corporate sector eager to bring back modernity – and the profits that accrue from it. Rushkoff seems to want to bypass government where possible (that classic American response), hence his support for local currency schemes based on bartering for particular services. But if this were to take off it would most likely serve to weaken the power of central government to intervene in the market on the public's behalf. Rushkoff does none the less point the way to the kind of change of consciousness that the new situation calls for, a turn away from the private and hyperindividualism to the needs of the collective. He is also clearly making a case for the principle of enough, and his emphasis on the value of reciprocity is a welcome antidote to greed. In his pointed words, it is time to stop thinking about 'how much money we'll need to insulate ourselves from the world', and concentrate instead on 'how much we can get from and give to that world with no money at all'.[5] One can hardly get further away from the alpha mindset than that.

Conspicuous Consumption

What most demands to be challenged in a post-progress world is the culture of conspicuous consumption, a culture which has been driven on to ever greater excesses by the credit boom of the last few decades which has swept all opposition aside. I would not wish to sound overly puritanical about this: consumer goods can make life more pleasurable, and consumption as such is not a bad thing. It is the scale of consumption that needs to be addressed, the takeover of so much of our lives by the cult of conspicuous consumption that is so deeply worrying. This is exemplified above all by our addiction to shopping, as commentators such as Neal Lawson have pointed out: 'The more we rely on shopping, the more other ways of being human are diminished because there is less space for them to flourish'.[6] The consumer ethic has crept into nearly every area of our existence, and so often to destructive effect. As a case in point, higher education, which ought in the main surely to be about self-development, has in Britain (as well as many other Western countries) now been transformed into a consumer product, viewed in increasingly crude commercial terms. Students are exhorted to think of themselves primarily as consumers, which significantly alters the character of their relationship with their teachers, and of their own performance. A degree becomes a product, and the onus is put on the university and its staff to provide this, with the assumption being that any failure that occurs reflects more on them than it does on the consumer.

The introduction of often quite punitive tuition fees has intensified this sense of higher education being a predominantly commercial transaction, to be regarded above all as an investment to improve one's career prospects (which is increasingly how universities advertise their wares these days, in terms of the individual's lifetime earning potential). This has not been to the benefit of the system or its ideals. Knowledge has been turned into a mere commodity, and unless it is commercially useful it tends to find itself being marginalised in the academic scheme: esoteric subjects simply fall by the wayside as unmarketable. Value is seen in unremittingly economic terms, and that is just taken to be the way of the world. We are often reminded that we live in a knowledge economy nowadays, but the range of that knowledge is actually quite narrow, consisting only of the knowledge found to be commercially exploitable on the mass scale by the big corporations. The self-developmental side is very much secondary now, a sad comment on the degree to which we have allowed hypercommercialisation to infiltrate our consciousness.

The credit boom in general promoted conspicuous consumption, both at the corporate and individual level. Credit was being extended extremely liberally by financial institutions, against assets they did not have in far too many cases, and as long as property prices kept rising (and at times they were soaring upwards quite astonishingly) then individuals felt safe in borrowing against their personal assets, often quite heavily. Conspicuous consumption soon becomes very competitive, drawing more and more people into its orbit (all too easy to be 'swept away by the current' in this activity too), and it can turn into a way of life that individuals become addicted to very quickly. Consumption takes on a momentum of its own under those circumstances, and while the economy benefits, whether individuals in reality do past a certain point is more questionable: GDP improves, but does GNH, GPI, HPI or SWB?

A particularly interesting reaction to our aggressively consumerist society is the development of the 'Slow Food' movement, which started in Italy in the 1980s, founded by Carlo Petrini, and has since gone on to become a world-wide phenomenon. Slow Food campaigns against the colonisation of food and eating by the fast food industry, describing their philosophy as follows:

> We believe that everyone has a fundamental right to pleasure and consequently the responsibility to protect the heritage of food, tradition and culture that makes this possible. Our movement is founded upon this concept of eco-gastronomy – a recognition of the strong connections between plate and planet.[7]

The original motivation for the movement was the opening of a McDonald's restaurant close by the Spanish steps in Rome, which generated a vigorous campaign of resistance (McDonald's also aroused similar sentiments in France, another country with a proud culinary tradition). Fast food could be regarded as a microcosm of what has gone wrong in our consumer culture. It reduces consumption to its basics, and operates on the premise that it is highly desirable to speed up the process as much as possible in order to move on to yet other episodes of the same. Life is turned into an endless round of consumption, an almost machine-like consumption designed to drive up company profits and thus the GDP (not to mention the individual's body mass). As David A. Kessler has remarked:

> Understanding the nuances of our own biology casts the food industry's plans in a very different light. What did we expect to happen when this industry embarked on a highly profitable business model that made foods high in sugar, fat, and salt widely available; conditioned us to associate their products with positive emotions; and created environments that foster these positive associations?[8]

'Slow Food' challenges this style of culture by emphasising the social and aesthetic aspects of food and eating, asking us to treat these activities as more than mere commercial transactions to be hurried through as quickly as possible, insisting that '[w]e consider ourselves co-producers, not consumers, because by being informed about how our food is produced and actively supporting those who produce it, we become a part of and a partner in the production process'.[9] We are being asked to accord respect both to the products themselves and their sourcing, which is not really a concern of the fast food industry: turnover alone is what counts there – if it sells then it is good for business – no more needs to be said (or thought about). Critics may see 'degraded industrialised food', the industry just sees substantial profit.

It is an entire way of life which is being rejected by the Slow Food movement, and we are being invited to reassess the system of values that goes along with that; as their Manifesto uncompromisingly declares:

> We are enslaved by speed and have all succumbed to the same insidious virus: *Fast Life*, which disrupts our habits, pervades the privacy of our

homes and forces us to eat Fast Foods. To be worthy of the name, *Homo Sapiens* should rid himself of speed before it reduces him to a species in danger of extinction.[10]

Fast Life is very much what modernity has been about: speed, efficiency, production, consumption (speed in particular being for the theorist Paul Virilio the defining characteristic of modern culture, almost turning into our 'destiny' as a species).[11] Perhaps we could even ascribe a large part of our financial downfall to the development of 'fast credit' as an enticement to instant consumption? Slow Food represents a significant step away from a consumption-driven existence, therefore, and the fact that it is spreading around the world (branches can now be found in over 120 countries) and gaining increasing attention from the media indicates it has struck a chord. This is a message many want to hear and are keen to put into practice – monitory democracy in action, we might say. Its American branch publishes a journal by the name of *The Snail*, indicating that even the most consumerist nation on Earth can harbour grave doubts about the direction in which it is heading – and the speed at which it is trying to do so.

More is simply better from the production-oriented perspective, however, and it is in effect seen by its defenders as our duty to ensure that there always is more coming on stream incessantly: modernity countenances no end on this score, which is why we push ourselves to be as busy as we can for as long as we can. Being slow is identified with inefficiency, one of the cardinal sins of modernity, motivated as it is by such a powerful sense of goal-directedness. Slow Food constitutes a rebellion against modernity therefore, promoting social values over commercial, reflection over production. I would claim they have succeeded in developing a genuinely 'post-progress' attitude that prizes quality above quantity, and they are to be commended for it. We could say much the same thing about the Bhutanese GNH index; that it is focused on the quality of life above all, and does not conceive of this as being at all contingent on the quantity of consumer goods we have amassed – or desire to go on amassing almost by reflex into the indefinite future.

Taking Slow Food as the inspiration, there have been various other schemes devised to slow down our lifestyle, with much the same object in view: to make us think about the validity of our intensely consumer-driven culture. Cittaslow (Slow City) was founded in Italy in 1999, and has since gone international too. To become a Slow City is to agree to ban traffic in historic city centres, to encourage walking and cycling over car or bus use, and to promote green policies (energy, recycling, etc.) wherever possible. The movement has an inspectorate which checks applications to join (one criterion being that the population must be under 50,000, which unfortunately does restrict the impact the movement can have), and dozens of places around the globe have successfully done so.

The upshot is that there is now a more general 'Go Slow' movement in operation, which extends over various other areas of our lives – travel, education and books, for example.[12] It has led to such events as the 'Slow Down London Festival' in April-May 2009, which was supported by several of the city's major cultural institutions such as the British Museum. There are plans to extend this to other British cities in coming years. The overall recommendation is that we slow down in our daily activities in general, taking more notice of the world around us rather than rushing through it from one activity or appointment to another, continually fighting the clock and largely oblivious of our surroundings: goal-directed up to the hilt. Again, this calls for a reassessment of our system of values, which puts such a premium on efficiency and multiple tasking[13] – the busier we are, the more productive we are assumed to be. 'Slow' is simply not part of the agenda from this outlook. In similar vein, Neal Lawson puts the case for downshifting, whereby 'there is less work and more life', and strongly recommends that we spend a significant amount of the time freed up from working in practising 'idleness'.[14] (John Naish even suggests, somewhat more humorously, that we try 'sideshifting' – doing just enough to pass muster in our current job, but not enough to merit promotion – as a way of keeping our worklife balance under control; although it has to be said that it sounds a potentially fraught activity.)[15] While this will be a step too far for anyone afflicted with the Protestant work ethic, the overall aim of reducing the pace of our life is certainly defensible. Idleness constitutes a welcome antidote to the frantic world of financial innovation.

We are in fact obsessed, as the postmodern theorist Jean Baudrillard pointed out, with the phenomenon of production in our culture, regarding this as a good in its own right and always concerned to increase it from previous levels: onward and upward as the only acceptable mode of existence. For Baudrillard, this is one of the most pernicious legacies of modernity, and it has come to rule our lives. In his view it was one of the main flaws of the communist system, which as noted before was at least as much captivated by the concept of modernity as the capitalist world ever was: 'The liberation of productive forces is confused with the liberation of man' by communists, and Baudrillard is scathing of such an overt idealisation of production which, in his view, contra-Marx, traps rather than frees us.[16] Conspicuous production is as suspect a notion as conspicuous consumption; neither does much for our sense of humanity nor improves social relations. To go slow is to attempt to recover some of that sense by reconnecting with our environment, and it has to be seen as an entirely laudable aim, a philosophy worth applying even more widely. Life has to be about more than production, but that seems to be what late modernity, under the guiding hand of neoliberal economics, tried its very best to narrow it down to. And there seems to be no escaping its reach: we know only too well where the production line of financial innovations has landed us.

Adding a further strand to this argument is Andrew Price, who in his book *Slow-Tech* puts the case for a more old-fashioned approach to technology that puts robustness ahead of efficiency. Engineering projects often fail to do their job (as in the notorious case of the storm defences in New Orleans that were overwhelmed by Hurricane Katrina) because they were designed at speed, 'under the spell of a here-and-now mindset' for which 'efficiency at all costs is all that counts'.[17] This is yet another area, the author feels, in which we need to slow down and show more respect for our environment rather than being concerned to produce the quickest possible result. 'Modernity', Price argues, 'needs a fresh and radically different way of assessing performance.'[18] I would agree, but it would not be modernity as we have known it any longer – which would be a good thing.

From the Postmodern to the Real Postmodern

Postmodernism has given us a lead on how to attack grand narratives and, particularly in the arts in relation to modernism, how to undermine them. Moving to a post-progress, or 'real postmodern' in my terms, world means moving away from many of the principles of postmodernism, however, and it is a good idea to summarise what these are now. First of all, grand narratives, in the form of socially conscious nation states and regional political groupings (such as the EU), have to come back into the picture to some extent in order to protect their vulnerable citizens from the market, both in terms of its propensity to generate devastating bubbles and to inspire increased incidence of carbon emissions. The grand narrative of the financial sector may have collapsed, but something has to replace it to coordinate how the global economy is run: it cannot be left to the whim of the deregulation crowd and their bonus-happy culture. We have seen the havoc the schemes of the New Olympians have wreaked; now we need some kind of strong central authority to clear up the mess left behind by them, as well as to establish a meaningful response to global warming while there is still time to prevent it running completely out of our control. For postmodernists, grand narratives are by definition bad and therefore just asking to be dismantled as power bases, but we shall need to reconstruct them in a socially responsible form if we are to have any success in adapting to the conditions that apply after modernity. This will go against the grain for many, especially as politicians' status is anything but high at the moment, given their collusion in the creation of the credit bubble (and, in the UK, their part in the somewhat sordid parliamentary expenses scandal of 2009); but it would be folly to believe we would be better off without something larger to come to our aid when misfortune strikes – and there is no shortage of sources for misfortune in our lives at present.

The little narrative idea is still worth preserving, but it cannot be seen as a viable basis for politics all on its own. In fairness, postmodern thinkers like Lyotard have always conceived of little narratives in essentially tactical terms, as methods of confronting particular abuses perpetrated by the dominant powers in our culture – the multinationals, overbearing governments and official institutions, etc. But they have little else to offer as focal points for political action, and, being somewhat ephemeral (as Lyotard conceived of them), in the current climate they will not be anything like adequate enough to deal with the problems set by bankrupt nations, a corrupt and failing financial industry and rapidly accelerating climate change. Little narratives will still have a relevant role to play, but mainly as techniques of scrutiny against the reconstructed grand narratives that the new situation demands, part of the campaign to keep those in power honest and acting for the public good rather than creating their own empires. Postmodernism was right to be worried about the authoritarianism that has been so prevalent in our society, and to want to eradicate it. But we cannot dispense with the entire notion of authority; something has to stand between us and the anarchy of the market: the real postmodern requires such safeguards to be in place to protect us against greed. If there had been a stronger regulating authority in operation, properly respected by everyone, we would not be in the position we are now.

A Politics of Enough: An Economics of Enough

So there is a strong case to be made for a politics of enough and an economics of enough. In the world after modernity those have to be the sources of our principles, replacing alpha and the excesses committed in its name. To call for limitations in this way is to run counter to everything modernity stood for (growth, growth and more growth), and it will take a considerable amount of adjustment on our part to absorb it; alpha will continue to have its supporters, the current financial catastrophe notwithstanding. Yet it is a possible target all the same, and not just possible but highly desirable given the state in which the cult of progress has landed us – socially, politically and environmentally. Even to circumscribe growth more widely does not mean that the problems created by progress will disappear entirely. The environmental damage already done, and inescapably in train because of past and present energy practices, dictates that we shall have to cope with a significant amount of global warming – 2 °C would seem to be the agreed minimum, and that undoubtedly will tax us very severely. The point of abiding by enough is to ensure we stay somewhere within the low end of such projections (which go far higher, apocalyptically so in some cases as far as humanity's survival prospects are concerned), therefore we need to be realistic about what it can achieve; but to ignore the principle altogether would be to expose ourselves to disaster on the large scale.

Of necessity, we must reorder our cultural priorities and set about generating more socially conscious narratives than have been the rule of late. Postmodern thought has always emphasised the importance of recognising the existence of limits to human capabilities, and that should apply to our productive and consuming behaviour as well. We have lost our sense of proportion about the role that production and consumption play in our lives, allowing them to dominate to a very unhealthy, as well as socially divisive, degree. Or perhaps I should say that we have actively been encouraged to lose our sense of proportion in the name of the cult of progress – but it is in our hands to alter the process and institute a new outlook, where human beings are more than just mere links in a seemingly endless production chain.

It may well be that green technology does come into its own at some future point, and that progress may come to seem an objective to be resurrected using that route, a range of renewables rendering it feasible. But that day is not with us yet, and it would have to be certain that the new technology really was absolutely clean and would not simply start a new cycle of environmental problems. At the moment, opinion is divided on just how clean many renewables, such as ethanol as a petrol substitute, actually are once all the other factors in their production (transport, deforestation, etc.) are taken into account. It would also have to be hoped a lesson had been learnt from the last progress-obsessed project, and that a new cycle of greed was not allowed to begin either, because we have seen from the experience of late modernity how badly that can distort the development of our culture. Clean entrepreneurialism is no less socially desirable a phenomenon than clean energy (and unfortunately it is proving to be just as elusive at present). There is an educational task waiting to be performed on the basis of the 'Redefining Progress' approach, insisting that entrepreneurs be required to deduct the negative impacts of their activities from the profits. Perhaps a tax should even be levied on such impacts? That would seem to me to be entirely consistent with social justice.

It may well be, too, that the economy recovers enough – or appears to recover enough – to imply we can resume the process of growth. Politicians will seize on any such indicators that emerge – a slight rise in house prices, consumer spending, or industrial output, etc. – and do their best to convince us that normal service has returned. No doubt they will also claim the credit for having sparked the upturn through their prudent policies in response to the crisis:'it's the economy, stupid' in action all over again. But I would argue that would constitute a state of denial, a refusal to acknowledge that we cannot go on playing 'pass the parcel' for ever (especially since, as those of us getting older will have realised to our alarm, pension funds are part of that chain). It would be an example of false consciousness to believe that modernity can go on unfolding indefinitely into the future: we ignore the existence of the economic sublime at our peril. The cult of progress as we have understood it is simply unsustainable, as is the hyper-consumerist culture it has spawned, and we cannot delay for much longer dealing with the accumulating consequences, such as global warming.

With regard to global warming, it is distinctly worrying that several potential new sources of oil have been identified recently, under the Arctic Ocean as a case in point, and that the prospect of being rescued from peak oil has meant that the environmental consequences of exploiting these has been sidelined in most public discussion so far. It is also worrying that the more new oilfields that are brought on stream then the lower the price of oil is likely to be, which can only encourage reckless consumption. While the oil companies would be only too happy to oblige us with the product to do so (and it might well help to revive a beleaguered automotive industry too, which politicians with an eye on their GDP would be happy to see), the effect would simply be to shorten our journey to the next set of critical tipping points. We might also want to reflect on proposals to develop techniques to extract the methane gas from methane clathrates as an energy source, on the grounds that its carbon emissions are lower than those of coal (by about a half). The gas is trapped in ice and is found in permafrost and beneath the continental shelves in copious quantities, but the side-effects of extraction are potentially catastrophic, particularly from the seabed, as the science writer Fred Pearce warns: 'The result could be an uncontrollable chain reaction – a "methane burp" that could cascade through undersea reserves, triggering landslips and even tsunamis.'[19] To insist that we maintain a high energy using culture is to keep forcing such uncomfortable dilemmas upon us.

Neither can we assume that we have finally overcome the problem of credit bubbles, or successfully shackled the greed that insistently fuels their growth. If the market is ever given its head again as it has been since the deregulation mania started in earnest back in the 1980s (one can only too easily imagine the arguments being put forward that they have learned their lesson this time around, just as they said after the Depression), then we shall find ourselves sinking into the Slough of Economic Despond once more. Paul Mason may believe that the crash signals 'the end of the age of greed', but that trait will not disappear altogether, more likely remain latent, and we must be on guard to ensure it is given no room for further development.[20] It would be wise always to keep Japanese Knotweed firmly in mind, especially since, at the annual conference of the British Banking Association in the summer of 2009, a senior figure in the financial industry boasted that '[f]inancial innovation continues to grow, transaction and risk are getting more complex'.[21] We have been well and truly warned as to the scale of the task before us. Ideology abhors a vacuum just as much as nature does: we must be extra careful not to let the discredited one of what Philip Augar has labelled the 'greed merchants' slide back into place by default.[22]

Conclusion: a post-progress world

A post-progress world will not be to everyone's taste, therefore, and the adoption of an economics and politics of enough will no doubt invoke some resistance, especially from the business community and the commercial world, who are hardly attuned to this after centuries of modernity (never mind the modernity in overdrive which has been our recent lot). Yet we would continue to chase after the goals of modernity at our considerable collective cost. Global warming is no freak accident: it is a direct product of the modernist imperative being allowed to run riot – modernity in overdrive means warming in overdrive too. Enough in this domain is not a metaphysical notion; it is the key to ensuring the planet remains habitable in something like its current form. We should have the courage both to say it and to work towards it.

To end, a plea that we reconsider socialism as a source of cultural ideals. The term has become jaded because of its association with communism and its failures, as well as the adoption of pro-free market policies by many erstwhile socialist parties over the last few decades: to have socialism or any of its equivalents in your name does not always mean very much now, it has to be conceded. But its virtues need to be restated, particularly its commitment to egalitarianism. We have lost sight of that commitment during the years of modernity in overdrive, and it is imperative we recover it as we head into the problematical condition that is life after modernity. Unless we have a greater measure of egalitarianism as regards wages and access to resources, then we shall continue to be at the mercy of our worst instincts, such as greed. Giving greed free rein has suppressed our sense of social justice, but it can be resurrected and a new attitude towards public life constructed. To continue with the hyperindividualistic culture so actively fostered in recent decades is to be in a state of denial as to its role in the current crisis. That form of self-interest is not in the public interest, and the sooner it is circumscribed then the better our chances of facing up to our current plight: in essence, that is the intellectual challenge now awaiting us in the world of the real postmodern.

Notes

Preface

1 Francis Fukuyama, 'The end of history?', *National Interest*, 16 (Summer 1989), pp. 3–18; the article was subsequently worked up into the book *The End of History and the Last Man*, London: Hamish Hamilton, 1992.

2 See, for example: Martin Jacques, *When China Rules the World: The Rise of the Middle Kingdom and the End of the Western World*, London: Allen Lane, 2009; and also Fareed Zakaria, *The Post-American World*, London: Allen Lane, 2008.

3 George Soros, *The Crash of 2008 and What It Means: The New Paradigm for Financial Markets*, New York: PublicAffairs, 2009, p. 144.

4 See, for example, the following studies: Bill McKibben, *The End of Nature: Humanity, Climate Change and the Natural World*, 2nd edn, London: Bloomsbury, 2003; James Lovelock, *The Revenge of Gaia: Earth's Climate Crisis and the Fate of Humanity*, London: Allen Lane, 2006; Fred Pearce, *The Last Generation: How Nature Will Take Its Revenge for Climate Change*, London: Eden Project, 2006; George Monbiot, *Heat: How We Can Stop the Planet Burning*, 2nd edn, London: Penguin, 2007.

5 Neal Lawson, *All Consuming: How Shopping Got Us into This Mess and How We Can Find Our Way Out*, London: Penguin, 2009, p. 2.

6 See, for example: Al Gore, *An Inconvenient Truth: The Movie*, Paramount DVD, 2006; and Nicholas Stern, *The Economics of Climate Change: The Stern Review*, Cambridge: Cambridge University Press, 2007.

7 Stuart Sim, *Fundamentalist World: The New Dark Age of Dogma*, Cambridge: Icon Press, 2004. See also my *Empires of Belief: Why We Need More Doubt and Scepticism in the Twenty-First Century*, Edinburgh: Edinburgh University Press, 2006.

8 Some of the more radical groups in the ecology movement have argued for a return to a pre-industrial lifestyle, based on a much lower population model; others have resorted to violence to protest against environmental abuse (EarthFirst! in America, for example).

1 Introduction: The End of Modernity

1 Charles Jencks, *The Language of Post-Modern Architecture*, 6th edn, London: Academy Editions, 1991, p. 23.

2 Le Corbusier, *Towards a New Architecture*, trans. Frederick Etchells, London: Architectural Press, [1923] 1946, pp. 56, 61.

3 See, for example, the various reports of the International Panel on Climate Change (IPCC).

4 See, for example: Jared Diamond, *Collapse: How Societies Choose to Fail or Survive*, London: Allen Lane, 2005; and Joseph A. Tainter, *The Collapse of Complex Societies*, Cambridge: Cambridge University Press, 1988.

5 Douglas Rushkoff, *Life Inc.: How the World Became a Corporation and How to Take It Back*, London: Bodley Head, 2009, pp. 3, 226.

6 Ibid. p. 70.

7 T. S. Eliot, *The Waste Land* [1922], line 1, in T. S. Eliot, *The Complete Poems and Plays of T. S. Eliot*, London: Faber and Faber, 1969.

8 Paul Mason, *Meltdown: The End of the Age of Greed*, London and New York: Verso, 2009, p. 17.

9 For an analysis of Japan's problems in this period, see Chapters 7 and 8 of Graham Turner, *The Credit Crunch: Housing Bubbles, Globalisation and the Worldwide Economic Crisis*, London: Pluto Press, 2008.

10 George W. Bush, 'The surest path back to prosperity', *Wall Street Journal* (Opinion Journal), 15 November 2008, <online.wsj.com/article/SB122670648178429695.html> (accessed 31 July 2009).

11 See John Bunyan, *The Pilgrim's Progress*, Part I, ed. J. B. Wharey, rev. Roger Sharrock, Oxford: Clarendon Press, 1960, pp. 14–15.

12 See Ulrich Beck, 'This crisis cries out to be transformed into the founding of a new Europe', *The Guardian*, 13 April 2009, p. 25.

13 Ibid. p. 25.

14 Ibid. p. 25.

15 Ulrich Beck, *World Risk Society*, Cambridge and Malden, MA: Polity Press, 1999, p. 15.

16 I discuss the arguments put forward by both sides in this debate in Stuart Sim, *The Carbon Footprint Wars: What Might Happen if We Retreat from Globalization?*, Edinburgh: Edinburgh University Press, 2009.

17 For a thought-provoking study of what the effects would be as the average global temperature climbs a degree C at a time, see Mark Lynas, *Six Degrees: Our Future on a Hotter Planet*, London: HarperCollins, 2007.

18 Felicity Lawrence, 'The pig's revenge', *The Guardian*, 2 May 2009, pp. 30–1. For more on the risks arising from the industrial farming system that has been developed to service Western consumers, see the same author's *Eat Your Heart Out: Why the Food Business Is Bad for the Planet and Your Health*, London: Penguin, 2008, particularly Chapter 4, 'Pigs'.

19 Lawrence, 'Pig's revenge', p. 30.

20 On this, see Tom Quinn, *Flu: A Social History of Influenza*, London: New Holland, 2008, particularly Chapters 5 and 6.

21 Lawrence, 'Pig's revenge', p. 31.

22 The political implications of the impact of accelerating climate change on the developing world is discussed in Dan Smith and Janani Vivekananda, *A Climate of Conflict: The Links between Climate Change, Peace and War*, London: International Alert, 2007.

23 This was one of the recommendations offered in the 2009 BBC Reith Lectures by the American academic Michael Sandel; <see www.bbc.co.uk/programmes/b00729d9> (accessed 29 July 2009).

24 This is the line of argument pursued by Ernest Gellner in *Postmodernism, Reason and Religion*, London and New York: Routledge, 1992: 'Muslim fundamentalism is an enormously simple, powerful, earthy, sometimes cruel, absorbing, socially fortifying movement, which gives a sense of direction and orientation to millions of men and women, many of whom live lives of bitter poverty and are subject to harsh oppression' (p. 72).

25 See James Lovelock, *The Revenge of Gaia: Earth's Climate Crisis and the Fate of Humanity*, London: Allen Lane, 2006, and 'The Earth is about to catch

a morbid fever that may last as long as 100,000 years', *The Independent*, 16 January 2006, <http://www.independent.co.uk/opinion/commen tators/james-lovelock-the-earth-is-about-to-catch-a-morbid-fever-that-may-last-as-long-as-100000-years-523161.html> (accessed 17 September 2008).

26 By the scientist James Hansen, quoted in Ed Pilkington, 'Climate target is guaranteed catastrophe', *The Guardian*, 7 April 2008, p. 1.

27 Richard Wilkinson and Kate Pickett, *The Spirit Level: Why More Equal Societies Almost Always Do Better*, London: Allen Lane, 2009, p. 53.

28 See graph in ibid. p. 17.

29 See graphs in ibid. pp. 23, 24.

30 Ibid. p. 265.

31 Michael Schut, 'Overview', in Michael Schut, ed., *Simpler Living: Compassionate Life. A Christian Perspective*, Denver, CO: Church Publishing, 1999, pp. 11–17 (p. 14).

32 Schut, 'Overview', p. 11. For more on the concept of simplicity in this context, see Jerome M. Segal, *Graceful Simplicity: Towards a Philosophy and Politics of Simple Living*, New York: Henry Holt, 1999.

33 John Naish, *Enough: Breaking Free from the World of Excess*, London: Hodder and Stoughton, 2009, p. 2.

2 Modernity: Promise and Reality

1 For an investigation into what those disparities are and how they come to arise, see Fred Pearce, *Confessions of an Eco-Sinner: Travels to Find Where My Stuff Comes From*, London: Eden Project, 2008.

2 Two recent best-sellers in this area, both having chosen the same title revealingly enough, sum up the attitude encouraged towards entrepreneurialism in our society particularly well: Sahar Hashemi and Bobby Hashemi, *Anyone Can Do It: Building Coffee Republic from Our Kitchen Table – 57 Real-Life Laws on Entrepreneurship*, 2nd edn, Chichester: Capstone, 2004; and Duncan Bannatyne, *Anyone Can Do It: My Story*, London: Orion, 2006.

3 Douglas Rushkoff, *Life Inc.: How the World Became a Corporation and How to Take It Back*, London: Bodley Head, 2009, p. 240.

4 See the criticisms offered by Terry Macalister, for example, who speaks

of a frequent 'greenwash' when it comes to environmental issues: 'A change in the climate: credit crunch makes the bottom line the top issue', *The Guardian*, 6 March 2008, p. 28.

5 John Naish, *Enough: Breaking Free from the World of More*, London: Hodder & Stoughton, 2009, p. 34.
6 Theodor W. Adorno and Max Horkheimer, *Dialectic of Enlightenment*, trans. John Cumming, London and New York: Verso, [1944] 1979, p. 3.
7 Ibid. p. 204.
8 See, for example, Samuel P. Huntington, *The Clash of Civilizations and the Remaking of World Order*, New York: Simon and Schuster, 1996. Huntington posits 'seven or eight major civilizations' around the globe with the potential for significant clashes; the greatest challenge to the West coming from Asia and Islam, 'the dynamic civilizations of the last quarter of the twentieth century' (pp. 29, 102).
9 Adorno and Horkheimer, *Dialectic*, pp. 204–5.
10 Ibid. p. 205.
11 Jürgen Habermas, *The Philosophical Discourse of Modernity: Twelve Lectures*, trans. Frederick Lawrence, Cambridge: Polity Press, 1987, pp. 106, 129.
12 Jürgen Habermas, 'Modernity: an unfinished project', trans. Nicholas Walker, in Maurizio Passerin d'Entrèves and Seyla Benhabib, eds, *Habermas and the Unfinished Project of Modernity: Critical Essays on 'The Philosophical Discourse of Modernity'*, Cambridge and Oxford: Polity Press and Blackwell, 1996, pp. 38–55.
13 Jürgen Habermas, 'Modernity versus postmodernity', *New German Critique*, 22 (1981), pp. 3–14 (p. 13).
14 Habermas, *Philosophical Discourse*, p. 5.
15 Habermas, 'Modernity versus postmodernity', p. 9.
16 Jürgen Habermas, *The New Conservatism: Cultural Criticism and the Historians' Debate*, ed. and trans. Shierry Weber Nicholsen, Cambridge and Oxford: Polity Press and Blackwell, 1989, p. 39.

3 Beyond Postmodernity

1 For a survey of the term's historical development, see Chapter 1, 'The emergence of the postmodern', in Stuart Sim, *Irony and Crisis: A Critical History of Postmodern Culture*, Cambridge: Icon Press, 2002, pp. 15–25.

2 Critical though he is of Le Corbusier's influence on the development of the International Style, Jencks nevertheless feels that he remains an interesting figure, and one of greater range than his peers tended to notice. In his biography of him, Jencks even argues that, in later career, 'Le Corbusier becomes a Post-Modernist before the fact, a nascent eco-hippy, building regional and contextual objects that are poems to nature-worship', which is certainly not what his legacy has been (Charles Jencks, *Le Corbusier and the Continual Revolution in Architecture*, New York: Monacelli Press, 2000, p. 189).

3 That homogenisation became a hallmark of all the public spaces constructed under modernist principles, creating the strange, but highly characteristic, 'non-places' dealt with by Marc Auge in his *Non-Places: Introduction to an Anthropology of Supermodernity*, trans. John Howe, London and New York: Verso, [1992] 1995.

4 Charles Jencks, *The Language of Post-Modern Architecture*, 6th edn, London: Academy Editions, 1991, p. 24.

5 Ibid. p. 12.

6 Ibid. p. 13.

7 Donald Kuspit, 'The contradictory character of postmodernism', in Hugh J. Silverman, ed., *Postmodernism – Philosophy and the Arts*, New York and London: Routledge, 1990, pp. 53–68 (p. 67).

8 Robert Venturi, Denise Scott Brown and Steven Izenour, *Learning from Las Vegas: The Forgotten Symbolism of Architectural Form*, 2nd edn, Cambridge, MA, and London: MIT Press, 1977, p. 3.

9 See Ezra Pound, *Make It New*, London: Faber and Faber, 1934.

10 Jean-François Lyotard, *The Postmodern Condition: A Report on Knowledge*, trans. Geoff Bennington and Brian Massumi, Manchester: Manchester University Press, [1979] 1984, p. 71.

11 Owen Hatherley, *Militant Modernism*, Winchester and Washington: Zero Books, 2008, p. 7.

12 Ibid. p. 42.

13 Agnes Heller and Ferenc Fehér, *The Postmodern Political Condition*, Cambridge and Oxford: Polity Press and Blackwell, 1988, p. 4.

14 Edward W. Soja, *Postmodern Geographies: The Reassertion of Space in Critical Social Theory*, London: Verso, 1989, pp. 60–1.

15 For an analysis of post-Marxism as a movement, see: Stuart Sim,

Post-Marxism: An Intellectual History, London and New York: Routledge, 2000; and also Goran Therborn, *From Marxism to Post-Marxism*, London: Verso, 2008.

16 Terrell Carver, *The Postmodern Marx*, Manchester: Manchester University Press, 1998, p. 5.

17 Ibid.

18 See Ernesto Laclau and Chantal Mouffe, *Hegemony and Socialist Strategy: Towards a Radical Democratic Politics*, London: Verso, 1985. For more recent work on radical democracy, see: Lars Tonder and Lasse Thomassen, eds, *Radical Democracy: Politics Between Abundance and Lack*, Manchester and New York: Manchester University Press, 2005; and Adrian Little and Moya Lloyd, eds, *The Politics of Radical Democracy*, Edinburgh: Edinburgh University Press, 2009.

19 Chantal Mouffe, *The Democratic Paradox*, London and New York: Verso, 2000, p. 96.

20 Lyotard, *Postmodern Condition*, p. 82.

21 Jean-François Lyotard, *Political Writings*, trans. Bill Readings and Kevin Paul Geiman, London: UCL Press, 1993, p. 302.

22 Jean-François Lyotard, *Libidinal Economy*, trans. Iain Hamilton Grant, London: Athlone Press, [1974] 1993, pp. 97–8.

23 See Karl Marx, *Capital*, I-III, trans. Ben Fowkes, Harmondsworth: Penguin, [1867, 1885, 1894] 1976, 1978, 1981.

24 André Gorz, *Farewell to the Working Class: An Essay on Post-Industrial Socialism*, trans. Mike Sonenscher, London: Pluto Press, 1982, p. 69.

25 Pamela Sue Anderson, 'Postmodernism and religion', in Stuart Sim, ed., *The Routledge Companion to Postmodernism*, 2nd edn, London and New York: Routledge, 2005, pp. 45–50 (p. 45).

26 See, for example, John Millbank, Catherine Pickstock and Graham Ward, eds, *Radical Orthodoxy: A New Theology*, London: Routledge, 1999.

27 The neoclassical style in music was in vogue from the 1910s through the 1940s, and involved the appropriation of earlier works. Igor Stravinsky was one of its major exponents, as can be seen in works like *Pulcinella* (1920), based on material taken from the eighteenth-century Italian composer Giovanni Pergolesi. Neoclassicism became popular enough to draw in several other high-profile composers of the post-First World War period and there is a definite suggestion of double-coding at work

in such compositions, even if the notion as such had not yet been formulated. Modernism continued simultaneously in its more militant form in the twelve-tone, serial style of Arnold Schoenberg and the Second Viennese school of composers, who definitely were concerned to 'make it new' in their dense and uncompromising compositions, which the public has found difficult to assimilate right through to our own day. It is fair to say that neoclassicism did not have much impact outside the musical field, however, and cannot be considered as mainstream to modernism as an artistic movement. Stravinsky himself went on to adopt the serial style in later life.

4 Marx was Right, But . . .

1 Slavoj Žižek, *The Sublime Object of Ideology*, London and New York: Verso, 1989, p. 33. Žižek develops this idea out of the work of the philosopher Peter Sloterdijk and his notion that ideology is built on cynicism; see Peter Sloterdijk, *Critique of Cynical Reason*, trans. Michael Eldred, London: Verso, 1988.
2 Jeanette Winterson, *The Stone Gods*, London: Penguin, 2008, p. 164.
3 Frederick Engels, *The Condition of the Working Class in England*, ed. David McLellan, Oxford: Oxford University Press, [1845] 1993, p. 75.
4 Karl Marx, *The Communist Manifesto*, ed. Frederic L. Bender, New York and London: W. W. Norton, [1848] 1988, p. 86.
5 Karl Marx, *Economic and Philosophic Manuscripts of 1844*, Moscow: Progress Publishers, 1974, p. 24.
6 Marx, *Communist Manifesto*, p. 58.
7 Even though this notion led to China's disastrous 'Cultural Revolution' of the 1960s, its insistence on the need to keep breaking with the past as a matter of principle could be regarded as an example of modernism being taken to its extreme. Politics was to be made anew each and every day.
8 Francis Wheen, *Karl Marx*, London: Fourth Estate, 1999, p. 5.
9 Žižek, *Sublime Object*, p. 43.
10 Antonio Gramsci, *The Modern Prince and Other Writings*, trans. Louis Marks, New York: International Publishers, 1957, p. 187.
11 'The Repressive State Apparatus functions "by violence", whereas the Ideological State Apparatuses *function by ideology*' (Louis Althusser,

Lenin and Philosophy and Other Essays, trans. Ben Brewster, London: NLB, 1971, p. 138).

12 Althusser, *Lenin and Philosophy*, p. 152. For an analysis of how Althusser's notion of ideology as a distorted representation of the real was perceived to work in areas of the arts like literature, see the work of his disciple, Pierre Macherey, such as *A Theory of Literary Production*, trans. Geoffrey Wall, London, Henley and Boston: Routledge and Kegan Paul, [1966] 1978.

13 Althusser, *Lenin and Philosophy*, p. 138.

14 Gilles Deleuze and Felix Guattari, *Anti-Oedipus: Capitalism and Schizophrenia*, trans. Robert Hurley, Mark Seem and Helen R. Lane, London: Athlone Press, [1972] 1983, p. 140.

15 Ernesto Laclau and Chantal Mouffe, *Hegemony and Socialist Strategy: Towards a Radical Democratic Politics*, London: Verso, 1985.

16 Barry Hindess and Paul Q. Hirst, *Pre-Capitalist Modes of Production*, London, Henley and Boston: Routledge and Kegan Paul, 1975, p. 308.

17 Jean-François Lyotard, *Political Writings*, trans. Bill Readings and Kevin Paul Geiman, London: UCL Press, 1993, p. 67.

18 Ernesto Laclau and Chantal Mouffe, 'Post-Marxism without apologies', *New Left Review*, 166 (1987), pp. 79–106 (p. 80).

19 Michel Foucault, *The Order of Things: An Archaeology of the Human Sciences*, trans. Alan Sheridan-Smith, London and New York: Routledge, [1966] 1989, p. 261.

20 Lyotard, *Political Writings*, p. 64.

21 Žižek, *Sublime Object*, p. 147.

22 Ibid. p. 33.

23 Ibid. p. 29.

24 Simon Tilford, 'Economic liberalism in retreat', *International Herald Tribune*, 17 July 2009, p. 6.

5 Diagnosing the Market: Fundamentalism as Cure, Fundamentalism as Disease

1 Adam Smith, *An Inquiry into the Nature and Causes of the Wealth of Nations*, I-II, eds R. H. Campbell, A. S. Skinner and W. B. Todd, Oxford: Oxford University Press, [1776] 1976, I, p. 456.

Notes

2 John Maynard Keynes, *The General Theory of Employment, Interest and Money* [1936], in John Maynard Keynes, *The Collected Writings of John Maynard Keynes*, vol. VII, London and Basingstoke: Macmillan, 1973, p. 144.

3 See Martin Wolf, *Fixing Global Finance: How to Curb Financial Crises in the 21st Century*, New Haven and London: Yale University Press, 2009.

4 Andrew W. Lo, *Hedge Funds: An Analytic Perspective*, Princeton, NJ, and London: Princeton University Press, 2008, p. 3.

5 Ibid., p. 302.

6 'FSA proposes greater disclosure re short selling', <http://www.fsa.gov.uk/Pages/Library/Communication/PR/2002/078.shtml> (accessed 1 August 2009).

7 Paul Krugman, *The Return of Depression Economics and the Crisis of 2008*, London: Penguin, 2008, p. 5.

8 Ibid. p. 180.

9 Ibid. p. 184.

10 Ibid. p. 191.

11 Ibid. p. 191.

12 Gillian Tett, *Fool's Gold: How Unrestrained Greed Corrupted a Dream, Shattered Global Markets and Unleashed a Catastrophe*, London: Little, Brown, 2009, p. 299.

13 Ibid. p. ix.

14 Ibid. p. x.

15 Ibid. pp. xi. Those with an urge to delve deeper into such esoteric practices might try consulting Janet M. Tavakoli, *Credit Derivatives and Synthetic Structures: A Guide to Instruments and Applications*, 2nd edn, New York: John Wiley and Sons, 2001.

16 Tett, *Fool's Gold*, p. 14.

17 Ibid. p. 47.

18 Ron den Braber, a one-time employee in the Collateral Debt Obligations department of the Royal Bank of Scotland (quoted in Tett, *Fool's Gold*, p. 161).

19 Quoted in Philip Augar, *Chasing Alpha: How Reckless Growth and Unchecked Ambition Ruined the City's Golden Decade*, London: Bodley Head, 2009, p. 14.

20 Bill Demchak of the J. P. Morgan banking house (quoted in Tett, *Fool's*

Gold, p. 58). Demchak was one of the pioneers of the current credit derivatives system.

21 Tett, *Fool's Gold*, p. 286.

22 Ibid. p. 300.

23 Augar, *Chasing Alpha*, p. ix.

24 Ibid. p. 14.

25 Ibid. p. 199.

26 Philip Augar, *The Death of Gentlemanly Capitalism: The Rise and Fall of London's Investment Banks*, London: Penguin, 2000, p. 331.

27 Paul Mason, *Meltdown: The End of the Age of Greed*, London and New York: Verso, 2009, p. viii.

28 Ibid. p. x.

29 Ibid. p. 1.

30 Ibid. p. 13.

31 Ibid. pp. ix, 1.

32 Ibid. p. 163. For Minsky's theories, see Hyman P. Minsky, *Stabilizing an Unstable Economy*, 2nd edition, New York: McGraw Hill, 2008. The original edition came out in 1986, and was indeed as the Foreword to the new edition has it, 'ahead of its time' (p. vii) in its recognition of the fundamental instability of the free market and the need for greater government involvement in its running.

33 Larry Elliott and Dan Atkinson, *The Gods That Failed: How Blind Faith in Markets Has Cost Us Our Future*, London: Bodley Head, 2009, p. 4.

34 Ibid. p. 4.

35 Ibid. p. 310.

36 Ibid. p. 8.

37 Ibid. p. 289.

38 Ibid. pp. 298, 299.

39 Graham Turner, *The Credit Crunch: Housing Bubbles, Globalisation and the Worldwide Economic Crisis*, London: Pluto Press, 2008, p. 9.

40 Ibid. p. 83.

41 George Soros, *The Crash of 2008 and What It Means: The New Paradigm for Financial Markets*, New York: PublicAffairs, 2009, p. vii.

42. Ibid. p. xxiv.

43 Ibid. p. xxiv.

44 Ibid. p. xxi.

45 George Soros, *The New Paradigm for Financial Markets*, New York: PublicAffairs, 2008.

46 See David Hume, *A Treatise of Human Nature*, eds David Fate Norton and Mary J. Norton, Oxford: Oxford University Press [1739, 1740], 2001. Hume's point is that the future is always a matter of probability rather than certainty.

47 Soros, *Crash*, p. 6.

48 Ibid. p. x.

49 Ibid. p. ix.

50 Wolf, *Fixing Global Finance*, p. 2.

51 Another to emphasise the constitutional instability of the markets has been Robert J. Shiller; see his *Irrational Exuberance*, 2nd edn, Princeton, NJ: Princeton University Press, 2005.

52 Soros, *Crash*, p. 30.

53 Ibid. pp. 44, 45.

54 Ibid. p. 51.

55 See, for example, Jean-François Lyotard and Jean-Loup Thébaud, *Just Gaming*, trans. Wlad Godzich, Manchester: Manchester University Press, [1979] 1985.

56 Soros, *Crash*, p. 72.

57 Tett, *Fool's Gold*, p. 264.

58 Soros, *Crash*, p. 77.

59 Augar, *Chasing Alpha*, p. 74.

60 William D. Cohan, *House of Cards: How Wall Street's Gamblers Broke Capitalism*, London: Allen Lane, 2009.

61 Gordon Brown, quoted in Augar, *Chasing Alpha*, p. 142.

62 For a detailed analysis of the Northern Rock collapse, see Alex Brummer, *The Crunch: The Scandal of Northern Rock and the Escalating Credit Crisis*, London: Random House Business Books, 2008.

63 Thomas Hardy, 'The Convergence of the Twain', stanzas IX-XI, in Thomas Hardy, *Selected Shorter Poems of Thomas Hardy*, ed. John Wain, rev. edn, London and Basingstoke: Macmillan, 1975, pp. 45–6.

64 Brummer, *Crunch*, p. 15.

65 For a judgement of the main participants' responses, see Chapter 7, 'Central bankers: who got it right, who got it wrong', of Brummer, *Crunch*, pp. 116–41.

66 From King's Mansion House speech in 2007, quoted in Augar, *Chasing Alpha*, p. 145. Predictably enough, it was Gordon Brown's upbeat speech that got the headlines.
67 See Mason, *Meltdown*, p. 15.
68 Turner, *Credit Crunch*, p. 3.
69 See Augar, *Chasing Alpha*, p. 227. As late as 2000 bank assets and debts were in balance in the UK.
70 Mason, *Meltdown*, p. 78.
71 See ibid. p. 111.
72 Elliott and Atkinson, *Gods That Failed*, p. 288.

6 Forget Friedman

1 Milton Friedman, *Capitalism and Freedom*, 2nd edn, Chicago and London: University of Chicago Press, [1962] 1982, p. 25.
2 Ibid. p. 3.
3 Ibid. p. 3.
4 Ibid. p. 4.
5 For details on this, see particularly: Joseph Stiglitz, *Globalization and Its Discontents*, London: Penguin; 2002; and Naomi Klein, *The Shock Doctrine: The Rise of Disaster Capitalism*, London: Allen Lane, 2007.
6 Friedman, *Capitalism*, p. 9.
7 Ibid. p. 8.
8 Jean-François Lyotard, *Lessons on the Analytic of the Sublime*, trans. Elizabeth Rottenberg, Stanford, CA: Stanford University Press, [1991] 1994, p. 234. For the differend, see Jean-François Lyotard, *The Differend: Phrases in Dispute*, trans. Georges van den Abbeele, Manchester: Manchester University Press, [1983] 1988.
9 For Kant on the sublime, see Immanuel Kant, *Critique of Judgment*, trans. James Creed Meredith, Oxford: Clarendon Press, [1790] 1952.
10 Lyotard, *Lessons*, p. 162.
11 Paul Mason, *Meltdown: The End of the Age of Greed*, London and New York: Verso, 2009, p. 79.
12 George A. Akerlof and Robert J. Shiller, *Animal Spirits: How Human Psychology Drives the Economy and Why It Matters for Global Capitalism*, Princeton, NJ, and London: Princeton University Press, 2009, p. 3.

Keynes had earlier made reference to the role played by the 'animal spirits' in investors' decisions (defining these as 'a spontaneous urge to action rather than inaction, and not as the outcome of a weighted average of quantitative benefits multiplied by quantitative probabilities') in John Maynard Keynes, *The General Theory of Employment, Interest and Money* [1936], in John Maynard Keynes, *The Collected Writings of John Maynard Keynes*, vol. VII, London and Basingstoke: Macmillan, 1973, p. 161.

13 Akerlof and Shiller, *Animal Spirits*, p. 4.

14 A recent revisionist account of this episode has argued that, although there was a bubble, it was nowhere near as chronic in its effect as popular legend has had it; see Anne Goldgar, *Tulipmania: Money, Honor, and Knowledge in the Dutch Golden Age*, Chicago and London: University of Chicago Press, 2007.

15 Charles P. Kindleberger, *Manias, Panics and Crashes: A History of Financial Crises*, London and Basingstoke: Macmillan, 1978, p. 26.

16 Alan Greenspan, *The Age of Turbulence: Adventures in a New World*, 2nd edn, London: Penguin, 2008, p. 466. Greenspan went on to say that 'the key question remains, as I summarized it in a 1996 reflection I shall never live down, "How do we know when irrational exuberance has unduly escalated asset values, which then become subject to unexpected and prolonged contractions?"' (ibid. p. 466).

17 Ibid. p. 174.

18 Take, for example, boo.com, trading in designer fashion, which ran through $135 million of investors' money in 18 months, only to go into liquidation. Then there was the case of the booking agency lastminute. com. Floated on the stock market in March 2000 after being extensively hyped in the British national press, it was valued at an astonishing £832 million after the first day of trading, only for its shares to collapse dramatically the following month. Unlike so many others, the company did survive for a few years, but without ever living up to its initial promise. When it was sold to a US buyer in 2005 for £577 million, its shares were worth less than a third of their high point after the debut.

19 Philip Augar, *Chasing Alpha: How Reckless Growth and Unchecked Ambition Ruined the City's Golden Decade*, London: Bodley Head, 2009, p. 166.

20 Alex Brummer, *The Crunch: The Scandal of Northern Rock and the*

Escalating Credit Crisis, London: Random House Business Books, 2008, p. 16.

21 Michael Lewis, *Liar's Poker: Rising through the Wreckage of Wall Street*, London: Hodder and Stoughton, 1989, p. 292.

22 Brummer, *Crunch*, p. 35.

23 Robert H. Frank, *The Economic Naturalist: Why Economics Explains Almost Everything*, London: Virgin, 2008, p. 217.

24 'Why cocky pundits prosper, and why we love them', *New Scientist*, 6 June 2009, p. 15. The study, by Don A. Moore, was presented as a paper at the American Association for Psychological Science Annual Convention in 2009 ('Competing to be certain (but wrong): social pressure and overprecision in judgement').

25 The gambling culture and mentality that is rife among market traders is amusingly portrayed in Michael Lewis's *Liar's Poker*. The author was himself a trader in New York in the 1980s. For an even more lurid account of life in the trading community, see Seth Freedman, *Binge Trading: The Real Inside Story of Cash, Cocaine and Corruption in the City*, London: Penguin, 2009: 'I was caught in an endless loop, one which could ultimately lead to my downfall – whether from an obsession with the market at the expense of all else, or via off-market self-destruction. I went to work, made money, spent it on drink, drugs and other pursuits, struggled into work again the next day' (pp. 24–5).

26 Tracy McVeigh, 'The party's over for Iceland, the island that tried to buy the world', *The Observer*, 5 October 2008, <http://www.guardian.co.uk/world/2008/oct/05/iceland.creditcrunch> (accessed 1 August 2009). Among the purchases were the prestigious House of Fraser department chain in the UK and West Ham United Football Club.

27 Vince Cable, *The Storm: The World Economic Crisis and What It Means*, London: Atlantic, 2009, p. 155.

28 'Emigration from Iceland doubles from year to year', *Iceland Review*, 20 May 2009.

29 Richard Bronk, *The Romantic Economist: Imagination in Economics*, Cambridge: Cambridge University Press, 2009, p. xi.

30 Ibid. pp. xi-xii.

31 Ibid. p. 231.

32 Ibid. p. 225.

33 Peter A. Hall and David Soskice, eds, *Varieties of Capitalism: The Institutional Foundations of Comparative Advantage*, Oxford: Oxford University Press, 2001, p. 4.

34 Isabel Mares, 'Firms and the welfare state: when, why, and how does social policy matter to employers?', in Peter A. Hall and David Soskice, eds, *Varieties of Capitalism: The Institutional Foundations of Comparative Advantage*, Oxford: Oxford University Press, 2001, pp. 184–212 (pp. 211, 212).

35 See William K. Tabb, *Reconstructing Political Economy: The Great Divide in Economic Thought*, London and New York: Routledge, 1999.

36 Kenneth Hopper and William Hopper, *The Puritan Gift: Reclaiming the American Dream amidst Global Financial Chaos*, 2nd edn, London and New York: I. B. Tauris, 2009, p. xxiii.

7 Learning from the Arts: Life After Modernism

1 'Modernism is far easier to exemplify than to define. This intriguing situation is in itself a tribute to its diverse riches . . . Not surprisingly, then, cultural historians intimidated by the chaotic, steadily evolving panorama they are trying in retrospect to reduce to order have sought refuge in a prudential plural: "modernisms"' (Peter Gay, *Modernism: The Lure of Heresy from Baudelaire to Beckett and Beyond*, London: Heinemann, 2007, p. 1). Nevertheless, Gay feels there are certain 'defining attributes' that link 'modernists of all stripes', and that commentators are justified in using as a basis for analysis (p. 3).

2 Ibid. p. 4.

3 John Barth, 'The literature of exhaustion', in Malcolm Bradbury, ed., *The Novel Today: Writers on Modern Fiction*, Manchester: Manchester University Press, 1977, pp. 70–83, and 'The literature of replenishment: postmodernist fiction', *Atlantic Monthly*, 245 (1980), pp. 65–71.

4 Barth, 'Literature of exhaustion', p. 70.

5 See Samuel Beckett, *The Complete Dramatic Works*, London and Boston: Faber and Faber, 1986.

6 Barth, 'Literature of exhaustion', p. 73.

7 Ibid. p. 74.

8 Umberto Eco, *The Name of the Rose*, trans. William Weaver, London: Martin Secker and Warburg, [1980] 1983.

9 Gilbert Adair, *The Postmodernist Always Rings Twice: Reflections on Culture in the 90s*, London: Fourth Estate, 1992, p. 17.

10 Arthur Danto, *Beyond the Brillo Box: The Visual Arts in Post-Historical Perspective*, Berkeley, Los Angeles and London: University of California Press, 1992, pp. 9, 10.

11 Ibid. p. 10.

12 Jean-François Lyotard, *The Postmodern Condition: A Report on Knowledge*, trans. Geoff Bennington and Brian Massumi, Manchester: Manchester University Press, [1979] 1984, p. 81.

13 The last line of *The Hollow Men* [1925], in T. S. Eliot, *The Complete Poems and Plays of T. S. Eliot*, London: Faber and Faber, 1969.

14 Nicolas Bourriaud, 'Altermodern', in Nicolas Bourriaud, ed., *Altermodern: Tate Triennial*, London: Tate Publishing, 2009, pp. 11–24 (p. 12).

15 Ibid. pp. 12–13.

16 Ibid. p. 13.

17 Ibid. For Deleuze and Guattari on the concept of nomadism, see Gilles Deleuze and Felix Guattari, *A Thousand Plateaus: Capitalism and Schizophrenia*, trans. Brian Massumi, London: Athlone Press, [1980] 1988.

18 See Nicholas Bourriaud, *Relational Aesthetics*, trans. Simon Pleasance and Fronza Woods, Dijon: Les Presses Du Reel, [1998] 2002, which gives a fuller account of his aesthetic theories.

19 As Lyotard said of art, 'A work can become modern only if it is first postmodern. Postmodernism thus understood is not modernism at its end but in the nascent state, and this state is constant' (*Postmodern Condition*, p. 79).

20 Gay, *Modernism*, pp. 3, 4.

21 See Marc Auge, *Non-Places: Introduction to an Anthropology of Supermodernity*, trans. John Howe, London and New York: Verso, [1992] 1995.

22 Okwui Enwezor, 'Modernity and postcolonial ambivalence', in Nicolas Bourriaud, ed., *Altermodern: Tate Triennial*, London: Tate Publishing, 2009, pp. 25–40 (p. 37).

23 Ibid. p. 40.

24 Ibid.

25 Kenneth Frampton, *Modern Architecture: A Critical History*, 3rd edn, London: Thames and Hudson, 1992, pp. 306–7.

26 Deleuze and Guattari, *Thousand Plateaus*, p. 380.

27 Ibid. p. 9.

28 Le Corbusier, *Towards a New Architecture*, trans Frederick Etchells, London: Architectural Press, [1923] 1946, p. 9.

29 See, for example: Donald Barthelme's *The King*, London: Martin Secker and Warburg, 1991; or Robert Coover's *Gerald's Party*, London: William Heinemann, 1986. What one can say, however, is that there really is a consistently playful quality to their work that can be very engaging: modernist seriousness is very much missing.

30 It is worth noting, however, that *Twin Peaks* has not been short of intellectual attention since its broadcast in 1990–1. For many commentators, it is still one of the very best examples of postmodern narrative on television.

8 Politics After Modernity

1 For a study of this in the Soviet Union, see Timothy Dunmore, *The Stalinist Command Economy: Soviet State Apparatus and Economic Policy, 1945–53*, London and Basingstoke: Macmillan, 1980.

2 Dunmore insists that 'the basis of the command economy was *not* an automatic or an unquestioning obedience to commands', and that ministries did clash with each other over responsibilities (ibid. p. 143).

3 See Eric A. Schutz, *Markets and Power: The 21st Century Command Economy*, Armonk, NY: M. E. Sharpe, 2001.

4 Alan Greenspan, *The Age of Turbulence: Adventures in a New World*, 2nd edn, London: Penguin, 2008, p. 531.

5 Martin, Jacques, *When China Rules the World: The Rise of the Middle Kingdom and the End of the Western World*, London: Allen Lane, 2009, p. 11.

6 Ibid. pp. 144, 145. For a less-optimistic view of China's prospects, see Will Hutton, *The Writing on the Wall: China and the West in the 21st Century*, 2nd edn, London: Abacus, 2008. Hutton feels that China's capacity for growth has been overestimated, and that domination 'is

Notes

not possible with the current economic structure. The model that has taken China thus far will have to be transformed' (p. 32).

7 Fareed Zakaria, *The Post-American World*, London: Allen Lane, 2009, p. 1.
8 Okwui Enwezor, 'Modernity and postcolonial ambivalence', in Nicolas Bourriaud, ed., *Altermodern: Tate Triennial*, London: Tate Publishing, 2009, pp. 25–40 (p. 27).
9 Announced by the vice-chairman of the country's national development commission, Zhang Xiaoqiang; see Julian Borger and Jonathan Watts, 'China launches green power revolution to catch up on west', *The Guardian*, 10 June 2009, p. 1.
10 See, for example, Hutton, *Writing on the Wall*.
11 Zakaria, *Post-American World*, p. 134.
12 The Indian coal mining industry is notorious for its environmental insensitivity, the argument being that Indian industry in general is so heavily dependent on such fossil fuels that it would hamper the country's economic expansion were these to be cut back on significantly. The industry was the subject of a particularly shocking journalistic exposé, *Unreported World: Children of the Inferno*, on the UK's Channel 4, 24 April 2009.
13 John Keane, *The Life and Death of Democracy*, London: Simon and Schuster, 2009, pp. xxvii, 738.
14 Ibid. p. xxviii.
15 Ibid. p. 856.
16 David A. Kessler, *The End of Overeating: Taking Control of the Insatiable American Appetite*, New York: Rodale, 2009, p. xiv.
17 Ibid. p. 18.
18 Ibid. pp. 18, 21.
19 Ibid. p. 19.
20 Felicity Lawrence, *Eat Your Heart Out: Why the Food Business Is Bad for the Planet and Your Health*, London: Penguin, 2008, pp. 178, p. x.
21 Peter Singer, *The Life You Can Save: Acting Now to End World Poverty*, London: Picador, 2009.
22 Gross National Happiness, The Centre for Bhutan Studies, 'Coronation address of His Majesty King Khesar, The 5th Druk Gyalpo of Bhutan, 7th November 2008', <http://grossnational happiness.com/> (accessed 4 June 2009).
23 See Adrian G. White, 'A global projection of Subjective Well-Being: a

challenge to positive psychology', *Psychtalk*, 56 (2007), pp. 17–20, for a 'Map of world happiness' based on this SWB study.

24 Ed Diener, Eunkook Suh, and Shigehiro Oishi, 'Recent findings on Subjective Well-Being', *Indian Journal of Clinical Psychology*, 24:1 (1997), pp. 25–41 (accessed online at <www.psych.uiuc.edu/~ediener/hot-topic/paper1.html>, 29 July 2009).

25 Ibid.

26 Ibid.

27 White, 'Global projection', p. 17.

28 John Talbert, Clifford Cobb and Noah Slattery, 'The Genuine Progress Indicator 2006: a tool for sustainable development', *Redefining Progress*, <www.rprogress.org> (accessed 3 June 2009), p. 2.

29 Ibid. p. 2.

30 Ibid. p. 3.

31 Douglas Rushkoff, *Life Inc.: How the World Became a Corporation and How to Take It Back*, London: Bodley Head, 2009, p. 188.

32 *The Happy Planet Index*, <http://www.happyplanetindex.org/> (accessed 5 June 2009).

33 New Economics Foundation, <http://www.neweconomics.org/gen/m1_i1_aboutushome.aspx> (accessed 5 June 2009).

9 Conclusion: A Post-Progress World

1 *Meden agan*; allegedly inscribed in the Temple of Delphi.

2 Zygmunt Bauman, *Consuming Life*, Cambridge and Malden, MA: Polity Press, 2007, p. 50.

3 Douglas Rushkoff, *Life Inc.: How the World Became a Corporation and How to Take It Back*, London: Bodley Head, 2009, p. 240.

4 Ibid. p. 227.

5 Ibid. p. 240.

6 Neal Lawson, *All Consuming: How Shopping Got Us into This Mess and How We Can Find Our Way Out*, London: Penguin, 2009, pp. 9–10.

7 Slow Food, 'Our philosophy', <http://www.slowfood.com/about_us/eng/philosophy.lasso> (accessed 30 June 2009).

8 David A. Kessler, *The End of Overeating: Taking Control of the Insatiable American Appetite*, New York: Rodale, 2009, p. 251.

9 Slow Food, 'Our philosophy'.

10 Slow Food, 'The Slow Food manifesto', <http://www.slowfood.com/about_us/eng/manifesto.lasso> (accessed 30 June 2009).

11 'The reduction of distances has become a strategic reality bearing incalculable economic and political consequences, since it corresponds to the negation of space . . . The loss of material space leads to the government of nothing but time . . . In this precarious fiction speed would suddenly become a destiny, a form of progress' (Paul Virilio, *Speed and Politics: An Essay on Dromology*, trans. Mark Polizzoti, New York: Semiotext(e), [1977] 1986, pp. 133, 141).

12 On travel and tourism, see, for example, Alastair Sawday, *Go Slow England*, Bristol: Alastair Sawday Publishing, 2008. On the cover blurb the author proudly proclaims his company to be 'a pioneering "Slow" business'.

13 A point made humorously by the journalist Jess Cartner-Morley when her editor asked her to try a 'Go Slow' day. She found it impossible to square the principle with her daily commitments: 'Slow living is a lovely idea. I just wish there were more hours in the day' ('Life at a snails's pace', *The Guardian*, 15 April 2009, <http://www.guardian.co.uk/lifeandstyle/2009/apr/15/go-slow-movement-health-wellbeing> (accessed 1 August 2009).

14 Lawson, *All Consuming*, p. 170.

15 John Naish, *Enough: Breaking Free from the World of More*, London: Hodder & Stoughton, 2009, pp. 135–7.

16 Jean Baudrillard, *The Mirror of Production*, trans. Mark Poster, St. Louis, MO: Telos Press, [1973] 1975, p. 21.

17 Andrew Price, *Slow-Tech: Manifesto for an Overwound World*, London: Atlantic, 2009, p. 247.

18 Ibid. p. 252.

19 See Fred Pearce, 'Ice on fire', *New Scientist*, 27 June 2009, pp. 30–3 (p. 33). Methane's potentially lethal qualities can be gauged from the fact that one such burp from the seas around 55 million years ago is estimated to have destroyed around two-thirds of the species in the ocean (see Chapter 6, 'The Wind of Change', in Fred Pearce, *The Last Generation: How Nature Will Take Her Revenge for Climate Change*, London: Eden Project, 2006).

20 Paul Mason. *Meltdown: The End of the Age of Greed*, London and New York: Verso, 2009.
21 Bill Michael of KPMG, quoted in David Teather, 'Masters of the universe: shaken but not stirred', *The Guardian*, 1 July 2009, p. 23.
22 Philip Augar, *The Greed Merchants: How the Investment Banks Played the Free Market Game*, London: Penguin, 2006.

Bibliography

Adair, Gilbert, *The Postmodernist Always Rings Twice: Reflections on Culture in the 90s*, London: Fourth Estate, 1992.

Adorno, Theodor W., and Max Horkheimer, *Dialectic of Enlightenment*, trans. John Cumming, London and New York: Verso, [1944] 1979.

Akerlof, George A., and Robert J. Shiller, *Animal Spirits: How Human Psychology Drives the Economy and Why It Matters for Global Capitalism*, Princeton, NJ, and London: Princeton University Press, 2009.

Althusser, Louis, *Lenin and Philosophy and Other Essays*, trans. Ben Brewster, London: NLB, 1971.

Anderson, Pamela Sue, 'Postmodernism and religion', in Stuart Sim, ed., *The Routledge Companion to Postmodernism*, 2nd edn, London and New York: Routledge, 2005, pp. 45–50.

Augar, Philip, *Chasing Alpha: How Reckless Growth and Unchecked Ambition Ruined the City's Golden Decade*, London: Bodley Head, 2009.

Augar, Philip, *The Death of Gentlemanly Capitalism: The Rise and Fall of London's Investment Banks*, London: Penguin, 2000.

Augar, Philip, *The Greed Merchants: How the Investment Banks Played the Free Market Game*, London: Penguin, 2006.

Auge, Marc, *Non-Places: Introduction to an Anthropology of Supermodernity*, trans. John Howe, London and New York: Verso, [1992] 1995.

Bannatyne, Duncan, *Anyone Can Do It: My Story*, London: Orion, 2006.

Barth, John, 'The literature of exhaustion', in Malcolm Bradbury, ed.,

Bibliography

The Novel Today: Writers on Modern Fiction, Manchester: Manchester University Press, 1977, pp. 70–83.

Barth, John, 'The literature of replenishment: postmodernist fiction', *Atlantic Monthly*, 245 (1980), pp. 65–71.

Barthelme, Donald, *The King*, London: Martin Secker and Warburg, 1991.

Baudrillard, Jean, *The Mirror of Production*, trans. Mark Poster, St. Louis, MO: Telos Press, [1973] 1975.

Bauman, Zygmunt, *Consuming Life*, Cambridge and Malden, MA: Polity Press, 2007.

Beck, Ulrich, 'This crisis cries out to be transformed into the founding of a new Europe', *The Guardian*, 13 April 2009, p. 25.

Beck, Ulrich, *World Risk Society*, Cambridge and Malden, MA: Polity Press, 1999.

Beckett, Samuel, *The Complete Dramatic Works*, London and Boston: Faber and Faber, 1986.

Borger, Julian, and Jonathan Watts, 'China launches green power revolution to catch up on west', *The Guardian*, 10 June 2009, p. 1

Bourriaud, Nicolas, 'Altermodern', in Nicolas Bourriaud, ed., *Altermodern: Tate Triennial*, London: Tate Publishing, 2009, pp. 11–24.

Bourriaud, Nicolas, *Relational Aesthetics*, trans. Simon Pleasance and Fronza Woods, Dijon: Les Presses Du Reel, [1998] 2002.

Bourriaud, Nicolas, ed., *Altermodern: Tate Triennial*, London: Tate Publishing, 2009.

Bradbury, Malcolm, ed., *The Novel Today: Writers on Modern Fiction*, Manchester: Manchester University Press, 1977.

Bronk, Richard, *The Romantic Economist: Imagination in Economics*, Cambridge: Cambridge University Press, 2009.

Brummer, Alex, *The Crunch: The Scandal of Northern Rock and the Escalating Credit Crisis*, London: Random House Business Books, 2008.

Bunyan, John, *The Pilgrim's Progress*, Part I, ed. J. B. Wharey, rev. Roger Sharrock, Oxford: Clarendon Press, 1960.

Bush, George W., 'The surest path back to prosperity', *Wall Street Journal* (Opinion Journal), 15 November 2008, <online.wsj.com/article/SB122 670648178429695.html> (accessed 31 July 2009).

Cable, Vince, *The Storm: The World Economic Crisis and What It Means*, London: Atlantic, 2009.

Cartner-Morley, Jess, 'Life at a snails's pace', *The Guardian*, 15 April 2009, <http://www.guardian.co.uk/lifeandstyle/2009/apr/15/go-slow-movement-health-wellbeing> (accessed 1 August 2009).

Carver, Terrell, *The Postmodern Marx*, Manchester: Manchester University Press, 1998.

Cohan, William D., *House of Cards: How Wall Street's Gamblers Broke Capitalism*, London: Allen Lane, 2009.

Coover, Robert, *Gerald's Party*, London: William Heinemann, 1986.

Danto, Arthur, *Beyond the Brillo Box: The Visual Arts in Post-Historical Perspective*, Berkeley, Los Angeles, and London: University of California Press, 1992.

Deleuze, Gilles, and Felix Guattari, *Anti-Oedipus: Capitalism and Schizophrenia*, trans. Robert Hurley, Mark Seem and Helen R. Lane, London: Athlone Press, [1972] 1983.

Deleuze, Gilles, and Felix Guattari, *A Thousand Plateaus: Capitalism and Schizophrenia*, trans. Brian Massumi, London: Athlone Press, [1980] 1988.

Diamond, Jared, *Collapse: How Societies Choose to Fail or Survive*, London: Allen Lane, 2005.

Diener, Ed, Eunkook Suh and Shigehiro Oishi, 'Recent findings on Subjective Well-Being', *Indian Journal of Clinical Psychology*, 24:1 (1997), pp. 25–41 (accessed online at <www.psych.uiuc.edu/~ediener/hot topic/paper1.html>, 29 July 2009).

Dunmore, Timothy, *The Stalinist Command Economy: Soviet State Apparatus and Economic Policy, 1945–53*, London and Basingstoke: Macmillan, 1980.

Eco, Umberto, *The Name of the Rose*, trans. William Weaver, London: Martin Secker and Warburg, [1980] 1983.

Eliot, T. S., *The Complete Poems and Plays of T. S. Eliot*, London: Faber and Faber, 1969.

Elliott, Larry, and Dan Atkinson, *The Gods That Failed: How Blind Faith in Markets Has Cost Us Our Future*, London: Bodley Head, 2009.

'Emigration from Iceland doubles from year to year', *Iceland Review*, 20 May 2009.

Engels, Frederick, *The Condition of the Working Class in England*, ed. David McLellan, Oxford: Oxford University Press, [1845] 1993.

Enwezor, Okwui, 'Modernity and postcolonial ambivalence', in Nicolas

Bourriaud, ed., *Altermodern: Tate Triennial*, London: Tate Publishing, 2009, pp. 25–40.

Foucault, Michel, *The Order of Things: An Archaeology of the Human Sciences*, trans. Alan Sheridan-Smith, London and New York: Routledge, [1966] 1989.

Frampton, Kenneth, *Modern Architecture: A Critical History*, 3rd edn, London: Thames and Hudson, 1992.

Frank, Robert H., *The Economic Naturalist: Why Economics Explains Almost Everything*, London: Virgin, 2008.

Freedman, Seth, *Binge Trading: The Real Inside Story of Cash, Cocaine and Corruption in the City*, London: Penguin, 2009.

Friedman, Milton, *Capitalism and Freedom*, 2nd edn, Chicago and London: University of Chicago Press, 1982.

'FSA proposes greater disclosure re short selling', <http://www.fsa.gov.uk/Pages/Library/Communication/PR/2002/078.shtml> (accessed 1 August 2009).

Fukuyama, Francis, 'The end of history?, *The National Interest*, 16 (Summer 1989), pp. 3–18.

Fukuyama, Francis, *The End of History and the Last Man*, London: Hamish Hamilton, 1992.

Gay, Peter, *Modernism: The Lure of Heresy from Baudelaire to Beckett and Beyond*, London: Heinemann, 2007.

Gellner, Ernest, *Postmodernism, Reason and Religion*, London and New York: Routledge, 1992.

Goldgar, Anne, *Tulipmania: Money, Honor, and Knowledge in the Dutch Golden Age*, Chicago and London: University of Chicago Press, 2007.

Gore, Al, *An Inconvenient Truth: The Movie*, Paramount DVD, 2006.

Gorz, André, *Farewell to the Working Class: An Essay on Post-Industrial Socialism*, trans. Mike Sonenscher, London: Pluto Press, [1980] 1982.

Gramsci, Antonio, *The Modern Prince and Other Writings*, trans. Louis Marks, New York: International Publishers, 1957.

Gray, John, *False Dawn: The Delusions of Global Capitalism*, 2nd edn, London: Granta, 1999.

Greenspan, Alan, *The Age of Turbulence: Adventures in a New World*, 2nd edn, London: Penguin, 2008.

Gross National Happiness, The Centre for Bhutan Studies, 'Coronation address of His Majesty King Khesar, The 5th Druk Gyalpo of Bhutan, 7th November 2008', <http://grossnational happiness.com/> (accessed 4 June 2009).

Habermas, Jürgen, 'Modernity: an unfinished project', trans. Nicholas Walker, in Passerin Maurizio d'Entrèves and Seyla Benhabib, eds, *Habermas and the Unfinished Project of Modernity: Critical Essays on 'The Philosophical Discourse of Modernity'*, Cambridge and Oxford: Polity Press and Blackwell, 1996, pp. 38–55.

Habermas, Jürgen, 'Modernity versus postmodernity', *New German Critique*, 22 (1981), pp. 3–14.

Habermas, Jürgen, *The New Conservatism: Cultural Criticism and the Historians' Debate*, ed. and trans. Shierry Weber Nicholsen, Cambridge and Oxford: Polity Press and Blackwell, 1989.

Habermas, Jürgen, *The Philosophical Discourse of Modernity: Twelve Lectures*, trans. Frederick Lawrence, Cambridge: Polity Press, 1987.

Hall, Peter A., and David Soskice, eds, *Varieties of Capitalism: The Institutional Foundations of Comparative Advantage*, Oxford: Oxford University Press, 2001.

The Happy Planet Index, <http://www.happyplanetindex.org/> (accessed 5 June 2009).

Hardy, Thomas, *Selected Shorter Poems of Thomas Hardy*, ed. John Wain, rev. edn, London and Basingstoke: Macmillan, 1975.

Hashemi, Sahar and Bobby Sahar, *Anyone Can Do It: Building Coffee Republic from Our Kitchen Table – 57 Real-Life Laws on Entrepreneurship*, 2nd edn, Chichester: Capstone, 2004.

Hatherley, Owen, *Militant Modernism*, Winchester and Washington: Zero Books, 2008.

Heller, Agnes, and Ferenc Fehér, *The Postmodern Political Condition*, Cambridge and Oxford: Polity Press and Blackwell, 1988.

Hindess, Barry, and Paul Q. Hirst, *Pre-Capitalist Modes of Production*, London, Henley and Boston: Routledge and Kegan Paul, 1975.

Hopper, Kenneth and William Hopper, *The Puritan Gift: Reclaiming the American Dream Amidst Global Financial Chaos*, London and New York: I. B. Tauris, 2nd edn, 2009.

Hume, David, *A Treatise of Human Nature*, eds David Fate Norton and Mary J. Norton, Oxford: Oxford University Press, [1739, 1740] 2001.

Huntington, Samuel P., *The Clash of Civilizations and the Remaking of World Order*, New York: Simon and Schuster, 1996.

Hutton, Will, *The Writing on the Wall: China and the West in the 21st Century*, 2nd edn, London: Abacus, 2008.

Jacques, Martin, *When China Rules the World: The Rise of the Middle Kingdom and the End of the Western World*, London: Allen Lane, 2009.

Jencks, Charles, *The Language of Post-Modern Architecture*, 6th edn, London: Academy Editions, 1991.

Jencks, Charles, *Le Corbusier and the Continual Revolution in Architecture*, New York: Monacelli Press, 2000.

Kant, Immanuel, *Critique of Judgment*, trans. James Creed Meredith, Oxford: Clarendon Press, [1790] 1952.

Keane, John, *The Life and Death of Democracy*, London: Simon and Schuster, 2009.

Kessler, David A., *The End of Overeating: Taking Control of the Insatiable American Appetite*, New York: Rodale, 2009.

Keynes, John Maynard, *The General Theory of Employment, Interest and Money* [1936], in *The Collected Writings of John Maynard Keynes*, vol. VII, London and Basingstoke: Macmillan, 1973.

Kindleberger, Charles B., *Manias, Panics, and Crashes: A History of Financial Crises*, London and Basingstoke: Macmillan, 1978.

Klein, Naomi, *The Shock Doctrine: The Rise of Disaster Capitalism*, London: Allen Lane, 2007.

Krugman, Paul, *The Return of Depression: Economics and the Crisis of 2008*, London: Penguin, 2008.

Krugman, Paul, *The Return of Depression Economics*, New York: W. W. Norton, 1999.

Kuspit, Donald, 'The contradictory character of postmodernism', in Hugh J. Silverman, ed., *Postmodernism – Philosophy and the Arts*, New York and London: Routledge, 1990, pp. 53–68.

Laclau, Ernesto, and Chantal Mouffe, *Hegemony and Socialist Strategy: Towards a Radical Democratic Politics*, London: Verso, 1985.

Laclau, Ernesto, and Chantal Mouffe, 'Post-Marxism without apologies', *New Left Review*, 166 (1987), pp. 79–106.

Lawrence, Felicity, *Eat Your Heart Out: Why the Food Business Is Bad for the Planet and Your Health*, London: Penguin, 2008.

Lawrence, Felicity, 'The pig's revenge', *The Guardian*, 2 May 2009, pp. 30–1.

Lawson, Neal, *All Consuming: How Shopping Got Us Into This Mess and How We Can Find Our Way Out*, London: Penguin, 2009.

Le Corbusier, *Towards a New Architecture*, trans Frederick Etchells, London: Architectural Press, [1923] 1946.

Lewis, Michael, *Liar's Poker: Rising through the Wreckage of Wall Street*, London: Hodder and Stoughton, 1989.

Little, Adrian, and Moya Lloyd, eds, *The Politics of Radical Democracy*, Edinburgh: Edinburgh University Press, 2009.

Lo, Andrew W., *Hedge Funds: An Analytic Perspective*, Princeton, NJ, and London: Princeton University Press, 2008.

Lovelock, James, 'The Earth is about to catch a morbid fever that may last as long as 100,000 years', *The Independent*, 16 January 2006, <http://www.independent.co.uk/opinion/commentators/james-lovelock-the-earth-is-about-to-catch-a-morbid-fever-that-may-last-as-long-as-100,000-years-523161.html> (accessed 17 September 2008).

Lovelock, James, *The Revenge of Gaia: Earth's Climate Crisis and the Fate of Humanity*, London: Allen Lane, 2006.

Lynas, Mark, *Six Degrees: Our Future on a Hotter Planet*, London: HarperCollins, 2007.

Lyotard, Jean-François, *The Differend: Phrases in Dispute*, trans. Georges van den Abbeele, Manchester: Manchester University Press, [1983] 1988.

Lyotard, Jean-François, *Lessons on the Analytic of the Sublime*, trans. Elizabeth Rottenberg, Stanford, CA: Stanford University Press, [1991] 1994.

Lyotard, Jean-François, *Libidinal Economy*, trans. Iain Hamilton Grant, London: Athlone Press, [1974] 1993,

Lyotard, Jean-François, *Political Writings*, trans. Bill Readings and Kevin Paul Geiman, London: UCL Press, 1993

Lyotard, Jean-François, *The Postmodern Condition: A Report on Knowledge*, trans. Geoff Bennington and Brian Massumi, Manchester: Manchester University Press, [1979] 1984.

Lyotard, Jean-François, and Jean-Loup Thébaud, *Just Gaming*, trans. Wlad Godzich, Manchester: Manchester University Press, [1979] 1985.

Macalister, Terry, 'A change in the climate: credit crunch makes the bottom line the top issue', *The Guardian*, 6 March 2008, p. 28.

Bibliography

Macherey, Pierre, *A Theory of Literary Production*, trans. Geoffrey Wall, London, Henley and Boston: Routledge and Kegan Paul, [1966] 1978.

McKibben, Bill, *The End of Nature: Humanity, Climate Change and the Natural World*, 2nd edn, London; Bloomsbury, 2003.

McVeigh, Tracy, 'The party's over for Iceland, the island that tried to buy the world', *The Observer*, 5 October 2008, <http://www.guardian.co.uk/world/2008/oct/05/iceland.creditcrunch> (accessed 1 August 2009).

Mares, Isabel, 'Firms and the welfare state: when, why, and how does social policy matter to employers?', in Peter A. Hall and David Soskice, eds, *Varieties of Capitalism: The Institutional Foundations of Comparative Advantage*, Oxford: Oxford University Press, 2001, pp. 184–212.

Marx, Karl, *Capital*, I–III, trans. Ben Fowkes, Harmondsworth: Penguin, [1867, 1885, 1894] 1976, 1978, 1981.

Marx, Karl, *The Communist Manifesto*, ed. Frederic L. Bender, New York and London: W. W. Norton, [1848] 1988.

Marx, Karl, *Economic and Philosophic Manuscripts of 1844*, Moscow: Progress Publishers, 1974.

Mason, Paul, *Meltdown: The End of the Age of Greed*, London and New York: Verso, 2009.

Millbank, John, Catherine Pickstock and Graham Ward, eds, *Radical Orthodoxy: A New Theology*, London: Routledge, 1999.

Minsky, Hyman P., *Stabilizing an Unstable Economy*, 2nd edn, New York: McGraw Hill, 2008.

Monbiot, George, *Heat: How We Can Stop the Planet Burning*, 2nd edn, London: Penguin, 2007.

Mouffe, Chantal, *The Democratic Paradox*, London and New York: Verso, 2000.

Naish, John, *Enough: Breaking Free from the World of More*, London: Hodder & Stoughton, 2009.

New Economics Foundation, <http://www.neweconomics.org/gen/m1_i1_aboutushome.aspx> (accessed 5 June 2009).

Passerin d'Entrèves, Maurizio, and Seyla Benhabib, eds, *Habermas and the Unfinished Project of Modernity: Critical Essays on 'The Philosophical Discourse of Modernity'*, Cambridge and Oxford: Polity Press and Blackwell, 1996.

Pearce, Fred, *Confessions of an Eco-Sinner: Travels to Find Where My Stuff Comes From*, London: Eden Project, 2008.

Pearce, Fred, 'Ice on fire', *New Scientist*, 27 June 2009, pp. 30–3.

Pearce, Fred, *The Last Generation: How Nature Will Take Her Revenge For Climate Change*, London: Eden Project, 2006.

Pilkington, Ed, 'Climate target is guaranteed catastrophe', *The Guardian*, 7 April 2008, p. 1.

Pound, Ezra, *Make It New*, London: Faber and Faber, 1934.

Price, Andrew, *Slow-Tech: Manifesto for an Overwound World*, London: Atlantic, 2009.

Quinn, Tom, *Flu: A Social History of Influenza*, London: New Holland, 2008.

Rushkoff, Douglas, *Life Inc.: How the World Became a Corporation and How to Take It Back*, London: Bodley Head, 2009.

Sandel, Michael, 'BBC Reith Lectures, 2009', <http://www.bbc.co.uk/pro-grammes/b00729d9> (accessed 29 July 2009).

Sawday, Alastair, *Go Slow England*, Bristol: Alastair Sawday Publishing, 2008.

Schut, Michael, ed., *Simpler Living: Compassionate Life. A Christian Perspective*, Denver, CO: Church Publishing, 1999.

Schutz, Eric A., *Markets and Power: The 21st Century Command Economy*, Armonk, NY: M. E. Sharpe, 2001.

Segal, Jerome M., *Graceful Simplicity: Towards a Philosophy and Politics of Simple Living*, New York: Henry Holt, 1999.

Shiller, Robert J., *Irrational Exuberance*, 2nd edn, Princeton, NJ, and Oxford: Princeton University Press, 2005.

Silverman, Hugh J., ed., *Postmodernism – Philosophy and the Arts*, New York and London: Routledge, 1990.

Sim, Stuart, *The Carbon Footprint Wars: What Might Happen If We Retreat from Globalization?*, Edinburgh: Edinburgh University Press, 2009.

Sim, Stuart, *Empires of Belief: Why We Need More Scepticism and Doubt in the Twenty-First Century*, Edinburgh: Edinburgh University Press, 2006.

Sim, Stuart, *Fundamentalist World: The New Dark Age of Dogma*, Cambridge: Icon Press, 2004.

Sim, Stuart, *Irony and Crisis: A Critical History of Postmodern Culture*, Cambridge: Icon Press, 2002.

Bibliography

Sim, Stuart, *Post-Marxism: An Intellectual History*, London and New York: Routledge, 2000.

Sim, Stuart, ed., *The Routledge Companion to Postmodernism*, 2nd edn, London and New York: Routledge, 2005.

Singer, Peter, *The Life You Can Save: Acting Now to End World Poverty*, London: Picador, 2009.

Sloterdijk, Peter, *Critique of Cynical Reason*, trans. Michael Eldred, London: Verso, 1988.

Slow Food, 'Our philosophy', <http://www.slowfood.com/about_us/eng/philosophy.lasso> (accessed 30 June 2009).

Slow Food, 'The Slow Food manifesto', <http://www.slowfood.com/about_us/eng/manifesto.lasso> (accessed 30 June 2009).

Smith, Adam, *An Inquiry into the Nature and Causes of the Wealth of Nations*, I–II, eds R. H. Campbell, A. S. Skinner and W. B. Todd, Oxford: Clarendon Press, [1776] 1976.

Smith, Dan, and Janani Vivekananda, *A Climate of Conflict: The Links between Climate Change, Peace and War*, London: International Alert, 2007.

Soja, Edward W., *Postmodern Geographies: The Reassertion of Space in Critical Social Theory*, London: Verso, 1989.

Soros, George, *The Crash of 2008 and What It Means: The New Paradigm for Financial Markets*, New York: PublicAffairs, 2009.

Soros, George, *The New Paradigm for Financial Markets*, New York: PublicAffairs, 2008.

Stern, Nicholas, *The Economics of Climate Change: The Stern Review*, Cambridge: Cambridge University Press, 2007.

Stiglitz, Joseph, *Globalization and Its Discontents*, London: Penguin, 2002.

Tabb, William K., *Reconstructing Political Economy: The Great Divide in Economic Thought*, London and New York: Routledge, 1999.

Tainter, Joseph A., *The Collapse of Complex Societies*, Cambridge: Cambridge University Press, 1988.

Talbert, John, Clifford Cobb and Noah Slattery, 'The Genuine Progress Indicator 2006: a tool for sustainable development', *Redefining Progress*, <www.rprogress.org> (accessed 3 June 2009).

Tavakoli, Janet M., *Credit Derivatives and Synthetic Structures: A Guide to Instruments and Applications*, 2nd edn, New York: John Wiley and Sons, 2001.

Bibliography

Teather, David, 'Masters of the universe: shaken but not stirred', *The Guardian*, 1 July 2009, p. 23.

Tett, Gillian, *Fool's Gold: How Unrestrained Greed Corrupted a Dream, Shattered Global Markets and Unleashed a Catastrophe*, London: Little, Brown, 2009.

Therborn, Goran, *From Marxism to Post-Marxism*, London and New York: Verso, 2008.

Tilford Simon, 'Economic liberalism in retreat', *International Herald Tribune*, 17 July 2009, p. 6.

Tonder, Lars, and Lasse Thomassen, eds, *Radical Democracy: Politics between Abundance and Lack*, Manchester and New York: Manchester University Press, 2005.

Turner, Graham, *The Credit Crunch: Housing Bubbles, Globalisation and Worldwide Economic Crisis*, London: Pluto Press, 2008.

Unreported World: Children of the Inferno, Channel 4 (UK), 24 April 2009.

Venturi Robert, Denise Scott Brown, and Steven Izenour, *Learning from Las Vegas: The Forgotten Symbolism of Architectural Form*, 2nd edn, Cambridge, MA, and London: MIT Press, 1977.

Virilio, Paul, *Speed and Politics: An Essay on Dromology*, trans. Mark Polizzoti, New York: Semiotext(e), [1977] 1986.

Wheen, Francis, *Karl Marx*, London: Fourth Estate, 1999.

White, Adrian G., 'A global projection of Subjective Well-Being: a challenge to positive psychology', *Psychtalk*, 56 (2007), pp. 17–20.

'Why cocky pundits prosper, and why we love them', *New Scientist*, 6 June 2009, p. 15.

Wilkinson, Richard, and Kate Pickett, *The Spirit Level: Why More Equal Societies Almost Always Do Better*, London: Allen Lane, 2009.

Winterson, Jeanette, *The Stone Gods*, London: Penguin, 2008.

Wolf, Martin, *Fixing Global Finance: How to Curb Financial Crises in the 21st Century*, New Haven and London: Yale University Press, 2009.

Zakaria, Fareed, *The Post-American World*, London: Allen Lane, 2009.

Žižek, Slavoj, *The Sublime Object of Ideology*, London and New York: Verso, 1989.

Index

Index